NATIVES AGAINST NATIVISM

MUSLIM INTERNATIONAL
SOHAIL DAULATZAI AND JUNAID RANA, SERIES EDITORS

Natives against Nativism

Antiracism and Indigenous Critique in Postcolonial France

- - - - - - -

OLIVIA C. HARRISON

MUSLIM INTERNATIONAL

University of Minnesota Press
Minneapolis
London

The University of Minnesota Press gratefully acknowledges the financial assistance provided for the publication of this book by the Francophone Research and Resource Center and the Department of French and Italian at the University of Southern California.

Portions of the Introduction and chapter 3 are adapted from "Whither Anti-racism? Farida Belghoul, les Indigènes de la République, and the Contest for Indigeneity in France," *Diacritics* 46, no. 3 (2018): 54–77; copyright 2018 Cornell University; reprinted with permission by Johns Hopkins University Press. Portions of the Introduction and chapter 3 are adapted from "The White Minority: Natives and Nativism in Contemporary France," *boundary 2*, forthcoming; copyright 2023 Duke University Press, all rights reserved; reprinted by permission of the publisher, www.dukepress.edu. Portions of chapter 1 are adapted from "Decolonizing History: Algeria, Palestine, and the Movement for Migrant Rights in Postcolonial France," *Comparative Studies of South Asia, Africa, and the Middle East* 42, no. 2; copyright 2022 Duke University Press, all rights reserved; reprinted by permission of the publisher, www.dukepress.edu. Portions of chapter 1 are adapted from "Palestine as Rallying Cry: The Movement for Migrant Rights and the Question of Palestine in Postcolonial France," in *Palestine in the World: International Solidarity with the Palestinian Revolution*, ed. Sorcha Amy MacGregor Thomson and Pelle Valentìn Olsen (London: I. B. Tauris, 2023). Portions of chapters 2 and 5 were originally published as "Sounds of Palestine," in *Sounds Senses*, ed. yasser elhariry, 181–208 (Liverpool: Liverpool University Press, 2021). Portions of chapter 4 are adapted from "Minor Transpositions: Mohamed Rouabhi Stages the Colonial Cliché," in *Transpositions: Migration, Translation, Music*, ed. Alison Rice, 115–32 (Liverpool: Liverpool University Press, 2021). Portions of chapter 6 were originally published as "Palestine and the Migrant Question," in *Languages of Resistance, Transformation, and Futurity in Mediterranean Crisis-Scapes: From Crisis to Critique*, ed. Maria Boletsi, Janna Houwen, and Liesbeth Minnaard, 121–43 (London: Palgrave Macmillan, 2020); reprinted with permission of Palgrave Macmillan.

Published by the University of Minnesota Press
111 Third Avenue South, Suite 290
Minneapolis, MN 55401-2520
http://www.upress.umn.edu

ISBN 978-1-5179-1059-4 (hc)
ISBN 978-1-5179-1060-0 (pb)

A Cataloging-in-Publication record for this book is available from the Library of Congress.

Printed in the United States of America on acid-free paper

The University of Minnesota is an equal-opportunity educator and employer.

CONTENTS

PROLOGUE

A beautiful late morning in August 2019, Carpinteria State Beach, Santa Barbara County. Since my partner and I moved to Los Angeles in 2009, this has become one of our favorite spots, and we take our two daughters here often. We've barely set up our little camp when I hear a cheerful voice booming from the thicket of beach chairs and umbrellas ten feet to our left. "How do we know the Indians were here first? . . . They had a reservation." Thin laughs ring out, and a guffaw. The booming voice is that of a twenty-something-year-old, the laughs are those of his brothers or cousins, maybe also his dad, all from LA, it turns out—our kids befriended their clan. There is something unsettling about hearing this joke delivered on a state beach that explicitly acknowledges the displacement that makes possible our presence in Southern California. The interpretive playground located immediately behind the spot we've picked out is dedicated to the indigenous Americans who lived here when the Spaniards came, the Chumash. Perhaps unwittingly, the joke constitutes a tacit acknowledgment of the fact that Indians were, indeed, here first. We, however, didn't have a reservation.

How does one interpret this joke? Sitting uncomfortably in what was, moments before, "our" spot on the beach, I bristle at what I perceive to be its colonial arrogance, and also its recuperation of the figure of the "Indian" to articulate a nativist claim. To begin, the implication that we don't know if the Indians were here first (if we did, the joke would be superfluous). And then the play on the term *reservation*, voided of its terror and violence, equated with a mundane act that is somehow also elitist, and therefore worthy of mockery and scorn. "I was here first" is an expression associated with competition. The implication is clear: those who make reservations get first dibs, fairly or not. If the Indians were here first, we were here second. They had a reservation, we didn't. But that doesn't make us any less native, or nativist.

Primed by my training in colonial history and anticolonial theory, what I hear in this pun is the performance of settler-colonial legitimacy.

Fast-forward to an evening in October 2021. I've decided to write a prologue for my book, and I'm immersed in a worn first edition of Vine Deloria Jr.'s classic *Custer Died for Your Sins: An Indian Manifesto.* The chapter I'm reading is a particularly good one. Titled "Indian Humor," it offers a riotously funny and moving account of the importance of jokes, often self-disparaging ones, in the cohesion and survival of indigenous Americans in the United States. Suddenly, a jolt of recognition: "Popovi Da, the great Pueblo artist, was quizzed one day on why the Indians were the first ones on this continent. 'We had reservations,' was his reply."[1]

It turns out the joke about Indians, casually uttered on Chumash land, is an Indian joke, with a twist. In Deloria's telling, the pun on "reservations" was authored by an indigenous American in response to an apparently naive question (a "quiz") about prior occupancy—the very basis for indigenous claims to sovereignty in the United States. Popovi Da's whimsical retort manages to tease out the unspoken implications of the question ("Why were the Indians first?" is another way of saying "How do we know they were first?" or "Why should it matter if they were?") even as it satirizes the competition over nativeness that is staged in this disingenuous Q&A with a "native informant." The subtle critique of nativism that obtains in Da's joke, as it is relayed by Deloria, disappears in its contemporary retelling, which calls into question indigenous claims to prior occupancy, rather than colonial claims to nativism. At stake in the remediation of an Indian joke on occupied land is the continued contest for indigeneity in twenty-first-century America.

My discomfort upon hearing an "Indian joke" delivered in a familiar and beloved place was, in part, based on the sense of alienation that has regularly assailed me since the unleashing of discourses targeting "political correctness" and other liberal civilities during the presidential election of 2016. I should not have been surprised. The nativist arrogance that was displayed during that electoral season had an all-too-familiar ring. It was as if decades of French history had come crashing down onto the New World. What had been evident in France for the past half-century under the veneer of republican egalitarianism—an increasingly unapologetic affirmation of white, Christian, European identity against the "invasion" of foreign migrants—was suddenly creeping out from behind the pillars of American democracy. Working on grassroots antiracism in France, from the migrant rights movements of the 1970s to twenty-first-century collectives like the Indigènes de la république (Natives of the Republic), felt like writing a prehistory of our contemporary American moment. The shock of recognition I experienced hearing an Indian joke on Chumash land coincided with the realization that anti-immigrant nativism has something to do with anti-native racism.

Unlike the United States, France is not a settler colony. But it had a settler colony, and one that tried to secede from France, too: Algeria. Surveying the vast expanse of the Algerian plains, the French conquistadores of Africa compared themselves to New World pioneers—their contemporaries—and the *indigènes* to American Indians. For some, "extermination" was a noble precedent in the pursuit of racial supremacy.[2] Others sought to set France's civilizing mission apart from the United States' race wars. "I am not one to believe," writes Ferdinand Hugonnet, one of the most inspired apologists for colonization-as-civilization, "that we are fatally destined to push the inhabitants of Algeria into the desert, like the Yankees chase the Indians."[3] Fast-forward 250 years: the descendants of France's postcolonial migrants, from Algeria and the four corners of France's tricontinental empire, take on the identity *indigène* to claim nativeness in the land that colonized their ancestors. At stake in this reappropriation of a colonial identity is a contest for indigeneity that resembles, in tenor if not in tone, the competition for nativeness staged and satirized in Popovi Da's joke.

Natives against Nativism began as a study of the intersection of antiracist and pro-Palestinian activism in France, from 1970 to the present. Palestine remains a central interlocutor in the archive I mobilize in this book, for reasons I will detail below. In the course of my research, however, it became clear that I would need to contend with another figure of indigeneity in France, one that is often triangulated via the Palestinian question: the figure of the "Indian," disseminated, via Hollywood Westerns, to countless households in France, and remediated, as we will see, in anticolonial and antiracist literature from the 1980s to the present. Far from being occasional points of interest for antiracist activists, the twin figures of the Palestinian and the Indian have been instrumental, I argue, in developing a critique of colonial and postcolonial racism based on identification across imperial formations—in this case, France, the United States, and Israel.

The stakes and focus of the project have sharpened since I started researching the topic in 2011, partly in response to the rise of increasingly unapologetic anti-immigrant discourses across the political spectrum, and under pressure from a highly polarized cultural climate in which to speak critically of colonialism or race is now equated with "Islamo-leftism," an ill-defined amalgam of postcolonial and critical race theory, both purportedly imposed by the tyranny of U.S.-style political correctness. Against this blatant disavowal of decades of anticolonial and antiracist activism in France, the texts I analyze in this book—novels, memoirs, essays, militant newspapers, tracts, posters, manifestos, documentary films, unpublished plays, and film scripts by anonymous activists, little-known writers, and major public figures— are all invested to varying degrees in articulating what I will be calling *indigenous critique* throughout the pages of this book: a critical understanding of the colonial production of indigenous subjects (*indigènes,* "natives") and the afterlives of the history of subjectification in the postcolonial era. Mahmood Mamdani has persuasively argued that "the great crime of colonialism went beyond expropriating the native, the name it gave to the indigenous population. *The greater crime was to politicize indigeneity in the first place.*"[4] Mamdani's urgent critique of the politicization of indigeneity in the colony needs to be updated, I argue, in the context of the former colonial metropoles of Europe, where indigeneity in the sense of *nativeness* has become a rallying cry for the anti-immigrant right.

This book is about the political meanings of indigenous critique in a nation-state that presents itself as chronologically and ideologically postcolonial—although, as in the United States, Australia, and other settler colonies, a non-negligible number of French citizens consider themselves colonized today, from the outer reaches of the Pacific to the former metropole itself. As I will detail in the pages that follow, antiracist activists in France have, for decades, looked to indigenous struggles in other imperial contexts to think through their postcolonial condition. Stretching the borders of coloniality to include France's *poussières d'empire* (imperial dust), Tahitian writer Chantal Spitz reclaims the term *indigène* and its "politically correct" cousin *autochtone* from the colonial archive in order to reactivate anticolonialism in the purportedly postcolonial present.[5] More recently, antiracist activists in France have situated their struggles in continuation with indigenous resistance to colonialism since 1492—even though the demand for equal rights in postcolonial France and claims to territorial sovereignty in the Americas, the Pacific, and Palestine remain fundamentally different. As we will see, these claims to indigeneity are not always, or only, empirical. Rather than discount such forms of transindigenous identification as anachronistic, identitarian, and ideologically dangerous, as they habitually are in France, I take seriously their invitation to critique colonial modernity, writ large to include contemporary forms of nativist discourse in the postcolonial metropole. It turns out that *indigènes* have something to teach us about nativism.

ABBREVIATIONS

AGRIF Alliance générale contre le racisme et pour le respect de l'identité française et chrétienne (General Alliance against Racism and for Respect for French and Christian Identity)

BDS Boycott, Divestment, and Sanctions

CP Comités Palestine (Palestine Committees)

CRS Compagnies républicaines de sécurité (Republican Security Companies)

CSRP Comités de soutien à la révolution palestinienne (Committees in Support of the Palestinian Revolution)

FLN Front de libération nationale (National Liberation Front)

FN Front national (National Front)

GI Génération identitaire (Generation Identity)

GP Gauche prolétarienne (Proletarian Left)

IDF Israeli Defence Forces

JRE Journée de retrait de l'école (Day of Withdrawal from School)

MTA Mouvement des travailleurs arabes (Arab Workers' Movement)

OAS Organisation armée secrète (Secret Army Organization)

PIR Parti des indigènes de la république (Party of the Natives of the Republic)

PLO Palestine Liberation Organization

UEJF Union des étudiants juifs de France (Union of Jewish Students of France)

INTRODUCTION

- - - - - - - - - - - - - - -

Indigenous Critique

In January 2005, a collective of grassroots antiracist activists published an online petition calling for the constitution of a "postcolonial anticolonial" movement in France, "Nous sommes les indigènes de la république!" (We are the natives of the republic). The title of the petition is, in itself, a rebuke and a rallying cry. Coined by colonial administrators to refer to the inhabitants of the territories conquered by France, enshrined into law in the late nineteenth century with the Code de l'indigénat, the nomenclature *indigène* made official the distinction between citizens and subjects of France.[1] Although the Code de l'indigénat was abolished in 1946, for the signatories of the appeal it continues to structure the present:

> The treatment of populations hailing from the colonies [*issues de la colonisation*] extends colonial policies without being reduced to them. . . . The figure of the *indigène* continues to haunt political, administrative, and judiciary practices; it animates and grafts itself onto other logics of oppression, discrimination, and social exploitation.[2]

Breaking with the mainstream antiracist discourses that have dominated representations of racism in France since the founding of the Socialist Party–backed organization SOS racisme in 1984—discourses centered on universal, republican ideals of equality, tolerance, and secularism—the appeal insists on situating systemic racism in the *longue durée* history of the French empire and its aftermath, including the history of colonial and postcolonial migration.

"Nous sommes les indigènes de la république!" garnered more than a thousand signatures in two weeks and drew three thousand activists to its first event, launching a new antiracist collective, the Mouvement des indigènes de la république (renamed Parti des indigènes de la république, or PIR, in 2010). As scholars have noted, the context of emergence of the movement was a highly polarized one.[3] In addition to the divisive 2004 law prohibiting religious attire in schools—which, albeit couched in universal terms, clearly targeted Muslim women—debates on a proposed article of law mandating that schoolteachers "recognize the positive role of French presence overseas, in particular in North Africa," were raging at the time.[4] Ten months after the appeal was published, urban rebellions broke out across disenfranchised communities in France to protest the deaths of Zyed Benna and Bouna Traoré, two unarmed teenagers pursued by police officers, giving a renewed sense of urgency to the indictment of structural racism in the opening lines of the appeal:

> Discriminated against in hiring, housing, health, school, and leisure, persons hailing from the colonies [*issues des colonies*], former and current, and postcolonial immigrants are the first victims of social exclusion and precariousness. . . . The "banlieues" are said to be "lawless zones" that the Republic is called upon to "reconquer." Racial profiling, diverse provocations, persecutions of all kinds proliferate while police brutality, sometimes extreme, is only rarely sanctioned by a justice system that operates according to double standards.[5]

The government's recourse to a state of emergency law first put on the books during the Algerian War of Independence to quell the uprisings, and the racially coded language deployed by politicians and intellectuals alike, only confirmed the appeal's insistence on the links between colonial history and structural racism in postcolonial France.

Published simultaneously on the websites Oumma.com and TouTEsEgaux.net, and then on lmsi.net—websites known to be critical of the 2004 law banning religious attire in French schools—the petition quickly drew condemnations across the political spectrum, ranging from accusations of *communautarisme* (U.S.-style identity politics, perceived as a threat to the unity of the Republic) to a covert Islamist agenda and speculations about the alleged anti-Semitism of members of the collective.[6] But what irked commentators most about the appeal, I would argue, was the use of the term *indigène*. Inadmissible from an empirical perspective according to historians, anthropologists, and so-ciologists, the (mis)use of a colonial identity that no longer existed was proof of a pathological desire to compete for the status of victim, in par-ticular with the quintessential figure of the victim in France: the Jew.[7] In the words of the president of SOS racisme at the time, Dominique Sopo, the appeal is exemplary of an "exotico-victimary approach" to memory, where past colonial crimes are deployed to prove the perpetual victim-hood of the formerly colonized.[8] The right's reaction to grassroots an-tiracism has been even more caustic. In a now familiar spin on the be-lated turn to colonial history in the past several decades, the demand to historicize the present is cast as a call for "colonial repentance"—what, in a 1983 text that has become a classic of anti-immigrant discourses, Pascal Bruckner called "the tears of the white man."[9]

The almost consensual reading of the appeal as identitarian is par-ticularly ironic given the deliberately inclusive nature of the text, which begins by denouncing the indigenization of all inhabitants of the *ban-lieue,* and ends with an explicitly coalitionist call to found an anticolo-nial movement:

> Regardless of their origins, the populations of working-class neigh-borhoods [*les populations des "quartiers"*] are "indigenized," relegated to the margins of society....
>
> WE, descendants of African slaves and deportees, daughters and sons of colonized and immigrants, WE, French and non-French living in France, activists engaged in the struggle against the oppression and discrimination produced by the postcolonial Republic, launch an appeal to all those who have a stake in these struggles to gather in a Congress of anticolonialism.[10]

The emphatic use of the first-person plural in the petition's *envoi* articu-lates, it is true, a particular collective identity: we the descendants of enslaved and colonized populations, we who are French citizens and also immigrants, we the "inheritors" (*héritiers*) of the enslaved and colonized, as the appeal puts it elsewhere. And yet the final call "to all those who have a stake in these struggles" is left deliberately open. The charge of communitarianism—you are speaking only for, and to, the descendants of the colonized—only highlights the surreptitious forms of racialization at work in universalist critiques of particular claims for equality and justice. In this sense, the backlash against the appeal inadvertently gives credence to its indictment of racism: in France, immigrants and French citizens *issus de l'immigration* (of immigrant descent), as the expression has it—as if immigration were a hereditary condition—are seen as a "fifth column" mining France from within. Against the prevailing view of nonwhite French citizens as perpetual immigrants or foreigners, the appeal insists on the colonial genealogy of current forms of discrimination against "persons hailing from the colonies, former and current, and postcolonial immigrants." In so doing, it also sites migration and racialization in a centuries-long colonial history that begins not with decolonization and postcolonial migration, but with conquest, slavery, and settler colonialism. Against the dehistoricized view of immigrants as guests (predominant in the liberal discourse of hospitality) or invaders (ubiquitous in far-right discourse), the appeal anchors the antiracist struggle—what it calls "the decolonization of the Republic"—in the *longue durée* history of anticolonial resistance, from the African continent to France's overseas territories in the Antilles and the Indian and Pacific Oceans.[11]

Of course, the descendants of the colonized in France are not colonial subjects. Without subscribing to the reductive critique according to which such an appeal to indigeneity is either *communautariste* or anachronistic, it is important to acknowledge that the PIR's demands cannot be conflated with the claims of indigenous peoples in the settler colonies of the Americas and the Pacific Rim, claims that are centered round national sovereignty and land restitution. Indigeneity is still a metaphor for the racialized minority that wields it.[12] What is at stake, then, in claiming the term *native* to speak of French citizens of colonized descent and their antiracist allies? In an important sense, this term is a provocation, as evidenced by the instantaneous outcry against the PIR, which has only grown as the movement (and since 2010, the self-declared political party) has become more media savvy and more visible in the public arena. If historians are right that the status of the *indigène* under colonial law cannot be conflated with the history of racialization in postcolonial France, it is also true that, today, a significant number of French citizens and immigrants "hailing from the colonies" locate their experience of racialization squarely within the history of French empire. The use of the term *indigène* by the descendants of the colonized makes manifest what sociologist Abdellali Hajjat calls "le transfert colonial" (the colonial transfer) of discursive and legal forms of racism developed in the colonies.[13] Like the appropriation of the racial designations *arabe* (*beur, rebeu, rabza*) or *noir* (*renoi, black, kébla*) in the 1980s and 1990s, the use of the term *indigène* in the early 2000s both exposes and denounces the processes of racialization that produced these identities in the first place. But the term has a third, performative valence that is less frequently commented upon: by calling themselves *les indigènes de la république*, these decolonial militants are also claiming indigeneity—nativeness—in postcolonial France. The children and grandchildren of colonial subjects of France, relegated to the status of second-class citizens in the postcolonial metropole, are not, in fact, *immigrants* in the dehistoricized sense implied in media and political discourses across the political spectrum. To quote an antiracist slogan oft used by the PIR, "Nous sommes ici parce que vous étiez là-bas" (We are here, in France, because you were there, in the colonies).[14]

"Nous sommes les indigènes de la république!" is in this sense a performative, rather than empirical, declaration of identity, one that is wielded against the ahistorical view of postcolonial French citizens as perpetual outsiders. As PIR cofounder Houria Bouteldja continues to insist, *indigène* is first and foremost a political identity.[15] The catachrestic metaphor "We are the natives of the republic" simultaneously articulates subjection and subjecthood: as second-class citizens, we remain subjects of France (*indigènes*), and yet we are French subjects (natives of France). The double gerund offers an ironic reversal of white nativist claims to Frenchness, an antiracist appropriation of indigeneity (in the sense of nativeness) that is particularly hard to fathom for a small but vocal number of opponents of the PIR and, in particular, the movement's spokesperson, Bouteldja, whom they frequently invite to "go back to her country of origin" (she was born in France to Algerian parents).[16] The resistance to the articulation of indigeneity in this dual sense—denoting the endurance of colonial racial formations in the postcolonial present as well as the Frenchness of those colonized by France and their descendants—is itself symptomatic of pervasive forms of racism in postcolonial France.

At the same time, the activists of the PIR do not simply inscribe their struggle in the centuries-long history of the French empire. The term *indigène* also enables "transindigenous" identification across imperial formations, claiming indigeneity across the tricontinental expanse of more

than five centuries of European colonial rule.[17] If the main target of the
PIR's founding appeal is France and its empire, later texts published
by PIR members include European empire writ large in the purview of
critique. This expanded field of critique does not dilute the specificity
of the PIR's claims in France, I would argue. French imperial history is
part of the overlapping and intersecting trajectories of European empire, and it cannot be studied—or critiqued—independently from other
colonial formations. To take an example that is central in the archives
I mobilize in this book, the ongoing colonization of Palestinians is an
integral part of France's imperial legacies and afterlives. A major player
in the partition of Levant from the 1916 Sykes-Picot Agreement onward,
France played an outsized role in the production of the Palestinian
question, even though it never directly colonized Palestine. Palestine,
in turn, has been a key interlocutor for anticolonial movements in
France's colonies, particularly in the Maghreb and Mashriq and, today,
in postcolonial France. As we will see, Palestine has been central to the
emergence of distinctly postcolonial forms of antiracist militancy in
France.[18]

Forged in the pro-Palestinian solidarity movement—Bouteldja and
Youssef Boussoumah, two of the PIR's founding members, met in the
ranks of the Campagne civile internationale pour la protection du
peuple palestinien (International Civil Campaign for the Protection
of the Palestinian People)—the PIR has continued to mobilize around
a number of contemporary anticolonial struggles, including indigenous struggles in the Americas.[19] The internationalist orientation of
the movement constitutes a deliberate strategy to "provincialize" the
question of race in France, placing the history of racialization within
a transindigenous history that begins in 1492, with the conquest of the
Americas.[20] This is why in her recent, provocatively titled *Whites, Jews,
and Us,* Bouteldja urges her readers to "adopt the point of view of the
Native Americans," making 1492 the year zero of the decolonial struggle
she and her comrades are waging in France today.[21]

It is telling, in this respect, that the PIR translates *indigène* as "indigenous" rather than "native," a term that served a similar function in
the British empire, including, of course, the thirteen colonies that would
become the United States. Like *native* in English, *indigène* carries the
sting of racist colonial discourse, while *indigenous* has become a planetary rallying cry for the rights of First Peoples, and a juridical category

enshrined in international law. Translating *indigène* as "indigenous" establishes solidarity with indigenous struggles worldwide, writ large to include the Palestinian question. But it also reappropriates a colonial identity and transforms it into a term of critique. Inscribing contemporary forms of racism against postcolonial immigrants and French citizens in a centuries-long, multidirectional history of European imperialism, "Nous sommes les indigènes de la république!" offers a recent and particularly clear articulation of what I am calling *indigenous critique:* a critique of the colonial production of the legal, cultural, religious, and civilizational differences between colonizers and colonized (*indigènes, autochtones,* natives), differences that extend into the present day even as they are transformed in the new kinds of racism we term, ironically, nativist.[22]

Historicizing the Migrant Question

> No, we are not in their home, mom! [*Non, on est pas chez eux maman!*]
> We are not "guests"! Did you get an invitation card? I didn't! Enough,
> I've been told the same thing for thirty-five years! We are at home
> [*nous, on est chez nous*]! We were born here! And if we ended up here,
> it's not by sheer coincidence![23]

A moving portrait of two generations of Algerian migrants to France, Faïza Guène's 2020 novel *La discrétion* offers an updated version of the classic tale of intergenerational conflict that characterizes the novels and short stories written by the children of Maghrebi migrants to France starting in the early 1980s. To her "discreet" immigrant mother's plea to "accept" intolerance as the cost of French hospitality, her French-born daughter Hannah opposes indigenous critique: *jus soli* (the right of soil) and the weight of colonial history. And yet the history of migrant militancy in the 1970s belies the myth of the passive, apolitical migrant worker popularized in Beur and *banlieue* literature, from Mehdi Charef's *Le thé au harem d'Archi Ahmed* (1983; *Tea in the Harem,* 1989) to Guène's aptly titled *La discrétion* (2020). Symptomatic of what Saïd Bouamama calls "a veritable process of occultation of memory," Hannah's impatience with the discourse of "postcolonial hospitality" reactivates anticolonial critique in a present that has been sundered from its militant past.[24] In fact, Hannah's attempt to historicize, and critique, the figure of the migrant-as-guest inscribes itself in a decades-long history of antiracist activism that is rooted in anticolonial practice and theory, from Kateb Yacine's collective play "Mohamed prends ta valise" (1971; Mohamed pack your bags) to Nacer Kettane's critique of the notion of "jeunes immigrés" (immigrants youths) in the 1980s, which relegated the children of colonial subjects and postcolonial migrants to the status of perpetual foreigners.[25] One of the aims of this book is to tell the story of anticolonial antiracist activism from the 1970s to the present, from the first movement for migrant rights, which was, as we will see, firmly grounded in an understanding of colonial and postcolonial history, to the grassroots antiracist movements of the twenty-first century.

Guène's novel is symptomatic of the "occultation" of antiracist memory in France. But it also powerfully illustrates the enduring impact of what, in my previous work, I have called *transcolonial identification*, focusing on transversal processes of identification and comparison across the heterogeneous yet imbricated colonial contexts of North Africa and Palestine.[26] Given the importance of Maghrebi migration to France, it is not surprising that Palestine has played such a central role within migrant rights activism in France. Throughout the chapters of this book, I show that the Palestinian question has been an integral part of antiracist activism in postcolonial France, from the movement for migrant rights in the 1970s, which was inextricably linked to pro-Palestinian activism (chapters 1 and 2), to the antiracist movements of the 1980s, 1990s, and 2000s (chapters 3 and 4), and to the ongoing migrant rights movement (chapter 6). And yet another figure of transcolonial identification emerges from the archive of French antiracism: the figure of the "Indian" (*l'Indien.ne*), popularized by that colonial filmic genre par excellence, the Hollywood Western.[27]

The figure of the Indian as an incarnation of anticolonial resistance has a distinctly Maghrebi genealogy (it is also prevalent, as I will discuss in chapters 4 and 5, in Palestinian literature and thought). Beur and *banlieue* literature offers numerous, if usually fleeting, examples of transindigenous identification, from Azouz Begag's novel, *Le gone du Chaâba* (1986; *Shantytown Kid,* 2007), and Farida Belghoul's *Georgette!* (1986) to Mohamed Rouabhi's play "El menfi" (2000; The exile), Zahia Rahmani's memoir, *France, récit d'une enfance* (2006; *France, Story of a Childhood,* 2016), and Guène's *La discrétion,* where, in an obvious intertextual echo of *Georgette!,* the migrant patriarch devours Westerns on television. As I will show in my chapters on Belghoul (chapter 3), Rouabhi (chapter 4), and Jean-Luc Godard (chapter 5), the figure of the Indian has been central to reactivating anticolonial critique in postcolonial France, often twinned with that other quintessential figure of the colonized, the Palestinian.

As I discuss in individual readings of the figures of the Indian and the Palestinian, transindigenous identification can in many ways be complicit with colonial representations of indigenous subjects, and this despite the anticolonial and antiracist politics that motivate such representational practices.[28] As critics have argued for decades, the violence of reducing the great multiplicity of indigenous peoples in the American continent under the single nomenclature *Indian,* itself based on a geographical misunderstanding of tragicomic proportions, continues to play out more than five hundred years later. What of the violence of remediating the mythic figure of the Indian warrior caricatured by Hollywood, even when it is for anticolonial purposes (chapters 3, 4, and 5)? At stake here is the very terminology deployed in the antiracist corpus analyzed in this book, and also the nomenclatures I use as a critic. To the best of my abilities, I have sought to distinguish the language used in my sources (most often *Indien.ne,* but also *sauvage, Peau-Rouge* [Redskin], and *al-Hindi al-ahmar* [Red Indian]) from my own. I keep *Indian* to refer to the figure and opt for the adjective *indigenous* when speaking of formerly or still colonized subjects. Following Jodi A. Byrd's critique of the notion that indigenous Americans are a racial minority in need of assimilation to the settler-colonial nation-state—a notion that occludes ongoing practices of settler colonialism—I avoid using the term *Native American,* which, by analogy with the hyphenated expressions *Asian-American* and *African-American,* assimilates indigenous Americans to racialized minorities waiting for full citizenship, rather than colonized nations seeking sovereignty.[29] Without conflating the very different political, geographic, and temporal contexts that have produced the colonial identities *Indian, Native, Aborigine,* and *indigène,* among others, the adjective *indigenous* allows me to draw vectors of identification across heterogeneous colonial and national contexts while also insisting on the claim to indigeneity articulated by French

citizens "hailing from the colonies" against white nativist recuperations of indigeneity.

As my presentation of the PIR above suggests, the originality of the
movement's anticolonial antiracism lies in the claim it makes to indigeneity in postcolonial France, even if—and it is important to repeat
this—the situation of colonized indigenous Americans and the descendants of France's colonial subjects are not identical (sovereignty, for
example, is not one of the aims of the decolonial movement in France,
although political representation and increased autonomy are central
concerns). Against the republican ideals of assimilation and tolerance,
which obfuscate the colonial genealogy of the figure of the migrant,
antiracist activists insist upon the colonial history that makes them
French *indigènes,* in the dual sense of that term (native French, French
citizens from the colonies). The antiracist activists I discuss in this book
are not simply racial minorities making up a multicultural society that
"tolerates" them, more or less. They are part and parcel of the history of
French empire, a history that includes colonial settlement, forced displacement, migrant recruitment, family reunification, expulsion, and
detainment, among other forms of colonial and postcolonial population control.

One of the major political concerns of what I am calling *indigenous
critique* is to counter nativism, which has, ironically but not surpris-
ingly, managed to recuperate anticolonialism and antiracism to its own
ends. As I will show in chapter 3, the very history of antiracist activism
has been subjected to revisionist rewriting, turning decolonization itself into a call for "remigration": the expulsion of migrants from a finally
"decolonized" France. That the much-mediatized notion of the "right
to difference"—one of the slogans of the 1983 Marche pour l'égalité et
contre le racisme (March for Equality and against Racism)—has now
been co-opted by the nativist right to advocate for the deportation of
migrants shows the very real limits of discourses of inclusion, diversity,
and tolerance. To the injunction to assimilate into Frenchness (one nation, undivided), the anti-immigrant right opposes the right to separate: apartheid across national borders. In order to clarify the very real
stakes of indigenous critique in twenty-first-century France, I turn now
to nativist recuperations of the notion of indigeneity by a white majority
that represents itself as a "white minority."

The White Minority

Figures of a fantasy I am calling the *white minority,* the terms that surface in French nativist discourses—*anti-white racism, counter-colonization, white genocide, great replacement, reciprocal decoloniza-tion*—betray a persistent identification with the racialized, the colo-nized, the ethnically cleansed. Take, for example, the lawsuit brought by an association dubbed AGRIF (Alliance générale contre le racisme et pour le respect de l'identité française et chrétienne, or General Alli-ance against Racism and for Respect for French and Christian Identity) against Bouteldja for her use of a neologism, *souchien,* to refer to white people during a June 21, 2007, televised debate on Frédéric Taddeï's popular television program, *Ce soir (ou jamais!)* (Tonight—or never!).[30] It's worth quoting Bouteldja in full to capture the extent to which her comments were made to mean the opposite of what she is calling for here, epistemic decolonization:

> So what I don't like about the way we talk about things is that we al-ways focus on working-class neighborhoods [*les quartiers populaires*]. Working-class neighborhoods are lacking in knowledge, in political consciousness, we have to educate them etc., and we nev . . . and we completely ignore the rest of society and its privileges, the privileges of the rest of society, and what I want to say is that it's the rest of society that needs to be educated. It's to the rest of society that we have to explain, for example, on the simple question of history, it's it's it's the rest of Western society, well of s . . . [*de souche,* of roots], those we call *les souchiens,* because we have to call them something, white people [*c'est le reste de la société occidentale, enfin de s . . . , ceux qu'on appelle, nous, les souchiens, parce qu'il faut bien leur donner un nom, les Blancs*], that need to learn the history of slavery, of colonization.[31]

Grammatically, *souchien* is derived from *Français de souche euro-péenne* (French nationals of European "roots" or extraction), an expres-sion first used during the Algerian War of Independence. An awkward biological–botanical metaphor aimed at introducing a racial distinction not present in the legal definition of nationality (Muslim Algerians were French, too), the expression was meant to distinguish white French sol-diers in Algeria from troops previously known as *Français musulmans d'Algérie* (French Muslims from Algeria), redubbed *Français de souche nord-africaine* (French of North African extraction) for the occasion.[32] In truncated form, the expression *Français de souche* was popularized in the late 1970s by Jean-Marie Le Pen, veteran of the Algerian War, signatory to the 1960 pro–French Algeria Front national pour l'Algérie francaise and, in 1972, founder of the nativist Front national (FN) party, to demarcate French nationals of French, read *white,* extraction from those hailing from the former colonies, newly dubbed *immigrants.* If the mention of "European roots" has dropped out of the expression, its origins in colonial military jargon reveal that it has always conveyed a racialized understanding of Frenchness. The neologism that Bouteldja used on television is thus both ironic and critical: a *souchien* is a French national who claims to be a *Français de souche,* with all the fantasies of racial purity that expression belies. Most viewers, however, read the term *souchien* as a racial slur and felt authorized to return the favor. For Bouteldja's critics, *souchien* was an intentional pun on a homonymous expression, *sous-chien,* literally "under-dog," more accurately "less than a dog." (Unlike *underdog, sous-chien* is not an idiomatic expression in French.) YouTube user Le rider fou, whose thumbnail image, a Celtic cross, is a transparent affirmation of white identity, wonders: "If we are 'less than dogs' [*des "sous-chiens"*], what are they, less than shits [*des sous-merdes*]?? No to anti-white racism!!!"[33]

The *souchien* polemic reached its apex when AGRIF sued Bouteldja for "anti-white racism," using the very legal framework designed to pro-hibit hate speech—the 1972 loi Pleven—against an antiracist militant now accused of "racial injury" against whites.[34] It should not surprise us that AGRIF, a nativist organization formed in the battle to keep Al-geria French, has co-opted the legal measures awkwardly adopted by the French state to protect its minorities, many of whom hail from the former colonies. AGRIF's suit against Bouteldja, though unsuccessful in legal terms, is part of a much broader recuperation of anticolonial and antiracist discourses by anti-immigrant activists in France, from the think tanks of the Nouvelle droite (New Right), launched in the after-math of decolonization, to more recent associations and media outlets that might be grouped together under the label *droite identitaire* (nativ-ist right): Génération identitaire, Bloc identitaire, Fdesouche, *Le jour-nal des indigènes.* A cursory look at this non-exhaustive list of names is revelatory. The FN was founded by Le Pen, a hero of the war against the Front de libération nationale (FLN; National Liberation Front). *Les identitaires,* for their part, have recuperated a term associated with U.S.-style minority politics, branding white identity the repository of *l'identité nationale.* And *indigènes,* in far-right discourse, now means . . . *Français de souche.*[35] That the very names of nativist organizations mimic those of the colonized should not surprise us. The white minority was born at the colonial frontier.

Though the nomenclature *indigène* did not congeal into a legal category until the late nineteenth century—starting in 1881, the indigenous populations governed by France in Africa and Asia were subject to a separate penal code, known as le Code de l'indigénat—the nineteenth-century archive of military, administrative, and later literary texts concerning France's empire are rife with mention of *indigènes,* the "natives" that settlers and other colonists set out to displace. For advocates of both "extermination" and "pacification," the settler colonization of North America served as model and foil, giving historical fodder to claims of transindigenous identification in the twenty-first century. Writing at the height of the war of conquest in Algeria, the respected doctor Eugène Bodichon spoke in lofty terms of the "extermination" of the lesser races as "the role of the pioneers in America, the English in Oceania and Southern Africa, and [the French] in Northern Africa."[36] Alexis de Tocqueville, for his part, warned against following the American example in Algeria—what, in *Democracy in America,* he characterizes as the "destruction" of the Indians—even while advocating for extreme methods taken straight out of the U.S. playbook, including forced displacement, burning, looting, and *enfumades* (the indiscriminate practice of "smoking out" populations sheltered in caves).[37] "The fate reserved for American Indians and Australian Aborigines," writes historian Olivier Le Cour Grandmaison, "was a precedent that was frequently invoked [by those who proposed to] *exterminate* all or part of the 'Arabs.'"[38]

Equally interesting for my purposes here is the paradoxical identification of the colonial administrator, soldier, or settler with the figure of the *indigène,* a phenomenon Achille Mbembe dubs the "'indigenization' of the colonist."[39] A brief look at the colonial archive reveals that the appropriation of indigeneity is, from the outset, a central figure of colonial discourse. Take Tocqueville's 1847 "Report on Algeria," commissioned by the Assemblée nationale to support additional funding to finalize the conquest of Algeria. An erstwhile candidate for settlement, Tocqueville had made several trips to Algeria and was known as a fervent proponent of all-out war and "forced expropriation."[40] Alleging that the most fertile lands have gone to native subjects and not to European citizens, Tocqueville insists in the report on what, previewing anti-immigrant far-right discourses in France, we might call *préférence nationale* (the privileging of French nationals over foreigners) for settlers in the colonies. His plea for settler self-governance surreptitiously turns "la population indigène" (the native population) into "sujets étrangers" (foreign subjects).[41]

Notwithstanding Tocqueville's fantasy of "taking . . . the place of the vanquished," Europeans never formed a statistical majority in Algeria, nor indeed in any other French colony.[42] In Ranajit Guha's felicitous phrase, the settler is "not at home in empire."[43] Writing more than a century after Tocqueville, this is how anticolonial theorist Frantz Fanon described the figure we might call "the lonesome settler," by analogy with the lonesome cowboy of Hollywood Westerns:

> In the colonies the foreigner coming from elsewhere imposed
> himself using his cannons and his machines. Despite the success
> of pacification, in spite of his appropriation, the settler always re-
> mains a foreigner. . . . The ruling species is first and foremost the one
> from elsewhere, different from the autochthonous population, "the
> others."[44]

For Fanon, the domestication of the colony, based on the desire to take the place of the colonized, is futile, for the settler will never be a native. If the *autochtone* (Greek for *indigène*) wants to take the place of the foreigner (*allochtone*), it is because it was his place to begin with. In response to the usurpation of colonization, decolonization will undertake "the replacement of one 'species' of mankind by another."[45]

Fanon is speaking of the invention of a new man here, not racial warfare. And yet, his ironic appropriation of racial scientific discourse ("une 'espèce' d'homme") to speak of decolonization as a world-making enterprise would prove easily recuperable within nativist discourses. Fanon's poetic account of decolonization as a movement of "replacement" offers an unexpected preview of nativist discourses on migration in France. For the voice of the settler ventriloquized in Fanon's description of the colony—"'they want to take our place'"—eerily resembles the voice of the *Français de souche* in postcolonial France.[46]

I return briefly to the *souchien* affair to make visible the links between fantasies of replacement in the settler colony and postcolonial France. Camille9340, a YouTube user who posted an excerpt of Bouteldja's televised remarks on July 5, 2007, betrays an uncanny, albeit unintentional, understanding of the colonial genealogy of nativism in the brief introductory text posted beneath the video: "Imagine that in Morocco the french call the *marocains de souche 'des souchiens'* because we have to call them something, 'tanned people' [*les bronzés*]. I think they'll take the first plane for France and for good reason [*sic*]." The French expatriate community in Morocco—descendants of French settlers and postcolonial *coopérants* as well as today's business and diplomatic elites—become a "visible minority" in Camille9340's telling, which manages to slip in a racial term for Moroccans.[47] The calque expression *Marocains de souche*—why not say, simply, Moroccans?—also manages to naturalize a racialized understanding of national identity, projecting French fantasies of racial purity onto the object of France's racial paranoia, the region that is now purportedly "colonizing" France through migration. French racists are not welcome in Morocco, nor should "anti-white" racists be welcome in France. Hence, according to a YouTube user who goes by the transparently anagrammatic handle Faldo Itlehr, if Bouteldja doesn't like France, she can go back to her own country: "If French hospitality isn't to her liking, she's free to go back to her *bled* in Algeria."[48] Never mind that Bouteldja's "migrant" parents were already French before Algerian independence (France annexed Algeria in 1834, and its inhabitants became de jure French nationals). For Faldo Itlehr, citizenship is not commensurate with nationality.

That French imperial rule relied on a similar distinction between nationality and citizenship only underscores the colonial genealogy of these forms of nativism more clearly.[49] Moroccans, Algerians, Senegalese, and France's colonial subjects across Asia and Africa were all, legally speaking, *indigènes* (natives), French subjects bound by a separate penal code and deprived of the rights of citizenship. Camille9340's disingenuous invocation of *les Marocains de souche* reveals a displaced obsession with indigeneity: the nativeness of *Français de souche,* versus the foreignness of those Bouteldja and her fellow activists have dubbed the *natives of the Republic.*

What interests me here is the linguistic *détournement* that turns yesterday's natives and their descendants (*indigènes*) into immigrants (*immigrés*), and the emigrants of old (*colons,* settlers) into natives. The history of the use of these terms in the French language reveals that the story of the nativist right in France is, in part, the story of what Todd Shepard calls "the invention of decolonization" from a metropolitan point of view.[50] It is the story of how natives turned into immigrants, and immigrants into natives. In the words of a settler repatriated to France: "They threw us out of the country, they should stay there now."[51] What Nouvelle droite luminary Alain de Benoist calls "reciprocal decolonization" will, in his telling, complete the process initiated by the colonized in the middle of the twentieth century.

Like the expression *anti-white racism,* which co-opts antiracism for the benefit of the "white minority," *decolonization* has become a buzzword in the arsenal of the nativist right, redefined as the right to French self-determination. One of the principal theoreticians of the decolonization of France is Alain de Benoist, founder in 1968 of the unapologetically nativist Groupement de recherche et d'études pour la civilisation européenne (Research and Study Group for European Civilization). A modern-day crusader for the "right to difference," recast as a call for ethnic and religious homogeneity, Benoist started his career as coeditor of an underground pro–French Algeria journal in the waning years of French empire. His first essays, published after Algerian independence, continued to defend the actions of the Organisation armée secrète (the paramilitary Secret Armed Organization fighting to keep Algeria French), and later, apartheid and white minority rule in South Africa and Rhodesia.[52] What might explain the volte-face that makes Benoist a belated apologist for *"le droit des peuples à disposer d'eux-mêmes"* (the right to self-determination)?[53]

Benoist's recuperation of the terminology of anticolonialism is particularly agile, because it is couched in an apology for diversity, plurality, and self-determination. In a 1978 anthology of essays titled *Vu de droite,* Benoist clarifies the aims of the intellectual movement he helped launch in the aftermath of decolonization. The principal mission of the Nouvelle droite is "to frontally resist a pseudo-racism that negates differences and a threatening racism that is also the rejection of the Other—the rejection of diversity."[54] Benoist is clearly not taking aim at biological racism when he evokes a "threatening racism." The real menace, rather, is egalitarianism. In his review of a spate of recent publications on Arthur de Gobineau, author of *The Inequality of Human Races* (1855), Benoist suggests that the nineteenth-century racial scientist's magnum opus would have been more accurately titled "Essay on the Diversity of Human Races." "Gobineau distinguishes three great races," writes Benoist, "the white, the yellow, and the black, all three with qualities and defects proper to them, none superior in absolute terms, but which all risk to lose their personality by mixing." He concludes his patent misreading of the urtext of scientific racism by claiming that Gobineau is for "mutual respect and *reciprocal* decolonization."[55]

Benoist's disingenuous reading of France's most influential white supremacist—who was, as Tocqueville's personal secretary, also implicated in the pacification of Algeria—manages to turn biological racism into an apology for "le droit à la différence."[56] An expression coined by antiracist activists and institutionalized by the left-wing government in the 1980s, "the right to difference" was intended to allow for differences within the egalitarian, universalist framework of the French Republic. In the catchy phrase of the 1984 antiracist march Convergence, "la France c'est comme une mobylette, pour avancer il lui faut du mélange" (France is like a motorbike, in order to go forward it needs blend [oil]). Like his recuperation of decolonization, diversity, and self-determination, Benoist's antiphrastic use of "the right to difference" to mean separation (the very opposite of *mélange*) is another example of what, writing in the 1980s, Pierre-André Taguieff called "the strategy of 'retorsion' with respect the words and values of antiracism" by the Nouvelle droite.[57]

There is remarkable continuity in Benoist's instrumentalization of anticolonial and antiracist discourse, despite his recent efforts to distance himself from "ethnocentrism." Note the introduction, in the 2001 edition of *Vu de droite,* of the notion of "counter-colonization" (*contre-colonisation,* that is to say, the colonization of Europe by migrants), popularized in recent decades by advocates of "remigration" like Jean Raspail and Renaud Camus:[58]

While universalism tends to negate alterity by reducing the Other to the Same, ethnocentrism tends to reduce diversity by suppressing the Other, or by keeping the Other radically apart. In both cases, alterity is considered to be without interest, diversity without value. On the contrary, a positive conception of alterity consists in recognizing difference without using it to submit the existence of some to the desires, interests, or reason of others. Oppression not only negates the freedom of the oppressed, but also that of the oppressor. This is what Marx meant when he wrote that "a people that oppresses another cannot be free." We are familiar with the dialectic of the master and the slave: the two roles ineluctably change places. Those who have colonized ought not to be surprised when they are invaded in turn.[59]

In a typically selective use of the classic texts of the left, Benoist manages to turn Hegel and Marx into the harbingers of counter-colonization. The colonial dialectic will ultimately drive the former slaves not to emancipate, but to colonize their former masters. But Benoist's admonition that the master and slave will inevitably change places also clarifies the stakes of the metaphors he uses to speak, ultimately, of segregation: diversity, difference, alterity. Reciprocal decolonization will ensure that the races do not mix, to paraphrase Benoist's reading of Gobineau. The image of role reversal is, in fact, symptomatic of Benoist's identification with the colonized. If the colonized could legitimately consider themselves *chez eux* in their homeland, so too can *Français de souche* in theirs. Except that France is being "invaded," and *les souchiens* are rapidly becoming a minority.

This is a book about antiracism, told from the perspective of antiracist activists and writers. I have dwelled upon the recuperation of indigeneity by the anti-immigrant right in order to draw attention to the increasingly urgent stakes of what I am calling *indigenous critique*. Central to my investigation is the instrumentalization of anticolonial and antiracist discourses to nativist ends. How does one respond to accusations of racism wielded by white identity militants against racial minorities? Pointing the finger back at the "real" racists will not do. In an increasingly polarized era governed by ad hominem attacks delivered at electronic speed, we must take these questions seriously. Faced with the collapse of traditional notions of right and left, faced with new and pernicious forms of nativism across the political spectrum, it is imperative that we reclaim anticolonial antiracism from a white identity politics that has appropriated multiculturalism for its own ends. Exposing instrumentalist misreadings of anticolonial and antiracist texts by nativist activists is one step, but it is not sufficient. What is needed now, more than ever, is an effective strategy to read, analyze, and historicize the terms that are at stake: indigeneity, racism, decolonization, and minority, to name a few. In the chapters below, I attempt to parse out the field of struggle by "natives" against nativism.

Chapter Outline

Natives against Nativism centers round a notion that is of crucial importance to both antiracist activists and anti-immigrant militants in France: *indigeneity,* alternatively defined as a political identity born in the colonial contact zone, or as a naturalized expression of native belonging. As discussed above, these contrasting uses of indigeneity reveal that French nativism has deep roots in a centennial history of legal and aesthetic representations of colonial subjects. Contemporary antiracist discourse, in turn, is part of a decades-long history of resistance to colonial settlement and racial policy.

The chapters of this book are organized in loosely chronological fashion, from 1970 to the present. As we will see, the circulation of antiracist and anticolonial discourses within both antiracist and anti-immigrant circles sometimes defies the demands of chronology. The central question that drives the chapters of *Natives against Nativism* forward is the question I raised at the end of the prologue: What are the meanings, and stakes, of indigenous critique in postcolonial France? The multidirectional vectors that go from migrant to *indigène,* triangulated via Palestine and the United States, form the connective tissue of the book, even though the coordinates and idioms of postcolonial antiracist discourse vary widely across the historical, political, and textual registers I engage with. Each chapter traces a different battleground in the story of natives against nativism: the literature of the migrant rights movements of the 1970s and 2000s (chapters 1 and 6), Genet's Palestinian writings (chapter 2), transindigenous identification in Beur and *banlieue* literature (chapters 3 and 4), and the twin figures of the Palestinian and the "Indian" in Godard's films (chapter 5). There are other battlegrounds, of course. The story I tell here could be told otherwise. But the constellation of texts I mobilize in this book offers a particularly rich and complex picture of the colonial genealogies of nativism in postcolonial France.

Chapter 1 sets the stage for indigenous critique by historicizing the figure of the migrant as guest. I analyze fragments from the incomplete and scattered archive of the Comités de soutien à la révolution palestinienne (CSRP; Committees in Support of the Palestinian Revolution), the Mouvement des travailleurs arabes (MTA; Arab Workers' Movement), and the theater collective Al Assifa (The Tempest), to reconstitute the history of the struggle for migrant rights in postcolonial France. The Palestinian Revolution is a recurrent leitmotif in the movement's literature, which deploys a Maoist and Arab revolutionary lexicon to place the struggle for equal rights in France in a wider revolutionary struggle that includes decolonization in the Maghreb and Palestine. The tracts, ephemeral publications, photographs, militant films, video fragments, and transcribed skits I analyze in this chapter belie the myth of the apolitical migrant worker popularized by the media coverage of the 1983 Marche pour l'égalité et contre le racisme, better known under the ethnicized label Marche des Beurs. (I return to the erasure of this militant history in chapter 3, on Belghoul's novel *Georgette!*) If the CSRP's lionization of the Palestinian Revolution sounds outdated in the wake of Oslo and the dismantling of the Palestinian resistance that followed, the movement's insistence on the colonial genealogies of the migrant question is remarkably prescient. Chapter 1 ends with Bouchra Khalili's 2017 film *The Tempest Society,* which revisits the movement's theater collective in the context of the ongoing migrant crisis.

Largely forgotten today, the CSRP can be credited with launching both the pro-Palestinian and migrant rights movements in France, and it drew the active support of French luminaries like Michel Foucault and Jean Genet. Chapter 2 examines Genet's writings about migrants and Palestinians, focusing on his unrealized film script about a Moroccan migrant to France, "La nuit venue" (1976; Nightfall), and his two major texts on Palestine, "Quatre heures à Chatila" ("Four Hours in Shatila," 1983) and *Un captif amoureux* (1986; *Prisoner of Love,* 2003). While Genet's Palestinian writings have gained traction in recent years, his thoroughgoing critique of French nativism, refracted in unexpected ways through the prism of Palestine, has received considerably less attention. I argue that Genet's advocacy for the Palestinians, like his support for the Algerians and migrants before them, was rooted in a radical critique of the French empire in which he served after leaving the penal colony of Mettray. Genet's sustained critique of French colonialism, scattered across his late works, homes in on France's role in the partition of the Levant and implicates the writer in the production of the Palestinian question. Genet's solidarity with migrant workers and Palestinians—based on disidentification with the French state, rather than identification with the colonized other—allows me to set the stage for the complex forms of transindigenous identification I analyze in the chapters that follow.

Chapter 3 introduces the figure of the "Indian," cast as a hero of anticolonial struggle and source of inspiration for antiracist activists in postcolonial France. The recent appropriation of this figure by nativist activists in France requires a parallel reading of transindigenous identification in antiracist and nativist literature, as demonstrated by the 2013 republication of Belghoul's 1986 novel *Georgette!* by alt-right polemicist Alain Soral. What makes *Georgette!*, I wonder in this chapter, a parable of the dangers of immigration according to the nativist right? The first-person narrative of a seven-year-old girl who imagines herself to be an Indian princess, a "petite sauvage" (little savage) in her naive parroting of French racial hierarchies, *Georgette!* is a fierce portrait of French anti-Arab racism told from the rarely heard perspective of a child. Tellingly, the protagonist's identification with indigenous Americans springs from Western movies, which her father refuses to watch to the end because he wants the "Indians" to win. The most elaborate representation of transindigenous identification in Beur and *banlieue* literature that I know of—the figure of the Indian as anticolonial hero makes a regular, if somewhat cursory, appearance in this corpus—*Georgette!* articulates indigenous critique through identification with the first modern colonial subject: indigenous Americans. And yet *Georgette!* has become a weapon in the arsenal of France's nativist right, thanks in part to Belghoul's recent activism against "gender theory," her espousal of anti-Semitic conspiracy theories, and her consecration by alt-right entertainer Dieudonné M'bala M'bala. I speculate in this chapter on the dangers of indigeneity as an easily recuperable token of native identity for the French alt-right, which has managed to reframe antiracism as a competition for victimhood.

Symptomatic of the discursive free-for-all that characterizes the French alt-right, Soral's republication of *Georgette!* offers yet another example of the instrumentalized misreading of anticolonial and anti-racist texts by the nativist right. And yet as the Belghoul case shows, antiracist activists and writers who identify with the antiheroes of Westerns are not off the hook simply by virtue of their subject position. As Steven Salaita and others have argued, the matter of transindigenous identification is rather more complex. I turn in chapter 4 to the work of dramaturge Mohamed Rouabhi, author of several plays on Palestine, including one that stages an encounter between a Palestinian and an indigenous American. The result of theater workshops conducted in the West Bank and East Jerusalem shortly before the outbreak of the Second Intifada, "El menfi" (The exile) offers a multidirectional critique of French, American, and Israeli colonial and racial practices, through the remediation of colonial photography, in particular a photographic portrait of an Apsaroke (Crow) elder, taken by Edward Curtis in the early twentieth century. In this chapter I explore the possibilities of antiracist remediations of colonial iconography to counter racial stereotyping in postcolonial France. Against identitarian readings of Rouabhi's plays, I show that they resist unambiguous displays of solidarity, even as they triangulate the question of race in France through the prism of colonial and racial regimes in the United States. Rouabhi's collaborations with Palestinians also reveal that the figure of the Indian in French antiracist circles is, in part, a Palestinian figure.

In chapter 5, I delve further into the Palestinian genealogy of transindigenous identification in an examination of Godard's Palestinian films. Like Genet, Godard traveled to the Palestinian camps of Jordan in the early 1970s, and produced a substantial body of work that engages with Palestine, notably through a critique of representation in sound: *Ici et ailleurs* (*Here and Elsewhere,* 1974), the film he made with Anne-Marie Miéville, using rush footage shot in Jordan and Lebanon; *Notre musique* (*Our Music,* 2004), which stages an encounter between the Palestinian poet Mahmoud Darwish, author of the epic poem "The 'Red Indian's' Penultimate Speech to the White Man," and three indigenous American characters; and *Film socialisme* (2010). I analyze *Ici et ailleurs* and *Notre musique* alongside several of Godard's collectivist films ("One A.M.," 1968; *Vent d'est,* 1969) to piece together the appearance of the "Indian" in Godard's oeuvre, a figure that tracks, in sometimes surprising ways, with that of the Palestinian. I argue in my reading of sound layering in *Notre musique* that the encounter staged between Darwish and indigenous Americans does not constitute, pace critics like Jacques Rancière, an attempt to relativize the Jewish genocide, but rather a way to signal the stakes and dangers of indigeneity at the borders of Europe, specifically Sarajevo, where the film is set. I read the film as a warning against the instrumentalization of indigeneity in a Europe that defines itself as homogeneously white and Christian, at the site of a Muslim genocide that cannot but recall the ethnic cleansing of Palestinians. The Palestinian poet and indigenous Americans are not strangers or even exiles in the film. I argue, rather, that they signify the continued reactivation of indigeneity as a site of contest in postcolonial Europe.

The migrant question is one of the major through lines of the book, which culminates with a study of the resonances between the Palestinian question after 1948 and the current mass displacements from and across the Global South, expanding the frame of the book from postcolonial France to the former colonies of Europe—including Palestine—and France's current "overseas territories." Chapter 6 analyzes three recent texts about the so-called migrant crisis—Maki Berchache and Nathalie Nambot's film *Brûle la mer* (*Burn the Sea*, 2014), Nathacha Appanah's novel *Tropique de la violence* (*Tropic of Violence*, 2016), and Ai Weiwei's documentary *Human Flow* (2017)—to read the migrant question through the lens of Palestinian displacement. What does Palestine teach us about the current migrant crisis, and how, in turn, does the migrant question shed light on the question of Palestine? Zooming out from the French metropolitan context that forms the matrix for this book, this final chapter proposes to historicize the migrant question within a planetary frame, against the figure of the migrant as unexpected or unwelcome guest.

A final note on the politics of language, before I begin. Nowhere in this book do I make an empirical claim about who counts as indigenous. The point of indigenous critique is precisely to undercut any claim to nativism, whether in Palestine–Israel, France, or the United States. This is, of course, a highly marked usage for a term that has been used precisely to advocate for the rights of First Peoples, Aborigines, Pacific Islanders, Native Americans, Palestinians, Algerians, and other groups that have been, and in many cases continue to be, colonized. I hope the archive I mobilize in this book makes clear the political stakes of historicizing indigeneity as a colonial construct and political identification, rather than a verifiable, stable, or empirical identity. It is my hope that such a critical understanding of indigeneity serves, rather than impedes, the ongoing struggle for indigenous rights, sovereignty, and dignity across our wildly disparate but intimately connected decolonizing world.

CHAPTER 1

Palestine as Rallying Cry

Indigènes into Immigrants

I begin the story of natives against nativism with the first autonomous movements for migrant rights in postcolonial France: the Comités de soutien à la révolution palestinienne (CSRP; Committees in Support of the Palestinian Revolution, 1970–72), the Mouvement des travailleurs arabes (MTA; Arab Workers' Movement, 1972–76), and the MTA's performance collective, Al Assifa (The Tempest, 1973–76). Donated to the archives of La contemporaine at the Université Paris Nanterre by the late CSRP activist Saïd Bouziri, who single-handedly documented decades of migrant activism in France, the journals, tracts, minutes, photographs, and films that constitute the incomplete and fragmented archive of these movements attest to the emergence of distinctly trans-colonial forms of antiracist militancy in postcolonial France. In the 1970s, the figure that served as the rallying cry of the nascent migrant rights movement was Palestine.

One of the objectives of this chapter is to track the shifting vocabularies of antiracism in the aftermath of decolonization. This is, to a large extent, a lexicon that is no longer available to us. In the wake of Oslo and the progressive dismantling of what was once called the Palestinian Revolution, the CSRP's revolutionary fervor sounds both naive and outdated. And yet the CSRP's insistence on situating postcolonial migration within a broader transcolonial framework—from Algeria to Palestine and postcolonial France—has paved the way, I argue, for the antiracist battles that are fought in France today. Although the lexicon, methods, and battlefields of struggle have changed considerably over the past fifty years, 1970 marks the emergence of what I will be calling *indigenous critique* throughout the pages of this book: a sustained critique of the conditions that turned *indigènes* (natives) into immigrants in France.[1] Although the term *indigène* does not appear in the literature of these movements, the anticolonial antiracist discourse that emerges from this archive prefigures transindigenous identification with the figure of the "Indian" in Beur and *banlieue* cultural production in subsequent decades, as well as current critiques of the ongoing migrant "crisis."[2]

In contemporary France, the term *antiracism* conveys mammoth institutions such as the Mouvement contre le racisme et pour l'amitié entre les peuples (Movement against Racism and for Friendship between Peoples) and the Socialist Party–backed SOS racisme, not the clandestine forms of political organizing I discuss in this chapter. To specialists of postcolonial France, it might also convey the so-called Beur generation of the 1980s, long thought to be the first grassroots antiracist movement in the metropole. And yet the archive of antiracist activism among migrant workers and students shows ample evidence of a robust antiracist movement in postcolonial France, stretching back to the early 1970s, long before the emergence of the figure of the Beur activist. Ubiquitous since the much-mediatized Marche pour l'égalité et contre le racisme of 1983, the notion that the first generation of migrants from France's former colonies were apolitical is patently untrue. The appearance of SOS racisme on the scene the following year did much to perpetuate the stereotype of migrant workers who "hug the walls" (*rasent les murs*) rather than clamor for their rights. The institutionalization of what the French call *l'antiracisme* also robbed migrant workers of their agency, appropriating antiracist struggles within humanitarian discourses emphasizing tolerance, rather than equality.[3]

The central role of Palestine in the emergence of an autonomous movement for migrant rights in postcolonial France has been one of the casualties of this institutionalization of antiracism. More broadly, the erasure of grassroots migrant activism from the archive of what is commonly known as *antiracism* in France has severed contemporary forms of migrant activism from a rich history of political demands made from the aporetic position of the rightless. As I will argue in the final chapter of this book, the mass displacements of the 2010s are only the most recent manifestation in the history of migration from the Global South to the Global North, set into motion by European colonialism and its aftermath—a history that includes the forcible displacement of Palestinians. The movement for migrant rights in 1970s France is one of the coordinates in a decades-long history of migrant activism, culminating in the demands of displaced persons in the 2010s. In the face of this active forgetting of the anticolonial antiracist archive—what poet and migrant rights veteran Philippe Tancelin, in a recent interview, has called "strategies of erasure"—it is incumbent upon us to exhume the traces of this past, ephemeral and incomplete as they may be.[4]

Before analyzing the archives of the CSRP, MTA, and Al Assifa, I turn to a little-known militant film that has recently been made available online, but with an important omission: the eight-minute opening sequence on the Palestinian Revolution that framed the struggle of migrant workers in France as an anticolonial antiracist movement. Symptomatic of the elision of Palestine from the archives of antiracism in France, the distribution of this document nevertheless attests to a renewed interest in migrant movements in twenty-first-century France—including, paradoxically, the Palestinian question, which structures the struggle for migrant rights even in the redacted version of the film. As I will argue in my analysis of Bouchra Khalili's 2017 film *The Tempest Society* in the concluding section of this chapter, recent attempts to "reactivate" the partial archives of 1970s anticolonial antiracist movements in France have only taken on more urgency in light of the mass migrations of the 2010s, extending the transcolonial arc linking the migrant question to the Palestinian question into our purportedly postcolonial present.[5]

"We Are the Fedayeen of Palestine"

Halfway through the militant documentary *Compter sur ses propres forces* (1973; Self-reliance), we are introduced to a triad of activists. They are young—in their twenties perhaps—and speak French fluently, with just the slightest trace of a Maghrebi Arabic accent. Their attire is neat but casual: shirt and jacket or sweater, but no tie. The only conspicuous aspect of their appearance are the patterned bandannas tightly wrapped around their faces, leaving only their eyes and forehead visible under a shock of black curls. They are seated in pyramidal formation, shoulders slightly hunched, eyes cast downward as they discuss the struggles of migrant workers in subdued tones. In the background, a window is visible, with its ornate wrought-iron balustrade framed by floor-to-ceiling fabric curtains. The dishrag hanging from a laundry line thrown across a corner of the room, over what appears to be a small sink or table, contrasts with the elegant arabesques of the French window. This is not a bourgeois home. Still, though modest, the apartment looks too comfortable, too spacious to be workers' lodgings—the exiguous rooms rented out to migrant workers for an exorbitant price, which are featured prominently in the long sequence on the *mal logés* (poorly housed) that precedes this shot. These young men might be students, or workers. Perhaps they have borrowed the apartment of a French comrade for this scene.

Although these three young activists are not introduced as such, the film's credits suggest that they are members of the militant migrant rights group founded in Paris in September 1970, the CSRP. Comprised mainly of students and workers from France's former colonies in North Africa and the Middle East, the CSRP were closely allied with the Maoist Gauche prolétarienne (GP; Proletarian Left) and collaborated on antiracist campaigns with French activists, including, as we will see in the next chapter, prominent intellectuals and writers such as Michel Foucault and Jean Genet. But none of this context is explained in the film. All we see is a conversation between Arab militants in a Parisian apartment. As the camera pans out to take in a wider shot of the apartment, a large table or desk strewn with tracts and flyers emerges in the foreground, and a poster on the wall, initially illegible, reveals an iconic figure of revolution: a stylized black-and-white drawing of a Palestinian fedayee (freedom fighter), donning a *keffiyeh* and Kalashnikov (Figure 1).

Ubiquitous in the Third Worldist and leftist discourses in the 1960s, the figure of the fedayee played a unique role in the movement that was emerging within migrant circles in 1970s France: that of catalyst, ally, and exemplar in the struggle for migrant rights. The appearance of a fedayee in the background of a shot of migrant militants in Paris subtly reframes the image for the viewer as one of clandestine warfare. The bandannas worn by the three activists to disguise their features are a kind of military camouflage, akin to the Palestinians' combat gear. The poster of the fedayee accentuates the sense of danger already palpable in the activists' shrouded faces and subdued tones. Although they do not bear weapons, they run very real risks, including deportation, as well as retribution from employers and racist attacks by the armed militias that were patrolling migrant neighborhoods at the time.

Huddled together and at first oblivious to the camera filming them, the young militants become increasingly animated in their conversa-

FIGURE 1. *Militants of the CSRP discussing the struggle for migrant rights in a Parisian apartment. A stylized poster of a Palestinian fedayee is visible in the background. Screenshot from* Compter sur ses propres forces, *directed by Yannis Tritsibidas (1973). Courtesy of Yannis Tritsibidas.*

tion, speaking in urgent tones about the need for autonomy from traditional labor movements. The militant on the left is now holding his bandanna, which has come undone, to his mouth and nose, while the companion seated to his right recalls that Moroccan, Algerian, and Tunisian workers insisted—against the directives of the workers' union—on screening a pro-Palestinian film, *Palestine vaincra* (Palestine shall overcome), during the May 1971 occupation of the automobile factory Renault-Billancourt. Like the Palestinian poster on the wall, the centrality of Palestine in the migrant struggle is a given, and brooks no explanation. The activist looks up at the camera, at first hesitantly, then unflinchingly, as if he were including the film crew, and the film's eventual audience, into the militant cell so carefully staged in this scene. Its purpose is clear: to advocate for migrant workers' autonomy within the labor movements of postcolonial France, in the context of draconian immigration laws and increasingly virulent forms of racism targeting migrants. Palestine, in this scene, is what frames the struggle for migrant rights in France as an extension of the anticolonial struggle on metropolitan soil.

One of a few dozen militant documentaries about the plight of migrant workers in 1970s France, *Compter sur ses propres forces* attests to the centrality of the Palestinian question in the antiracist movement forged in the struggle for migrant rights in postcolonial France. It is, to my knowledge, the only film that explicitly frames this struggle in terms of solidarity with Palestine, although several pro-Palestinian documentary films—most notably *Palestine vaincra* and *Biladi* (My country)—were regularly screened at CSRP meetings and rallies to draw parallels between Palestinians and migrant workers.[6] As such, it offers a rare glimpse of the role of the Palestinian Revolution in the early days of antiracist militancy in France, and an audiovisual supplement to the incomplete and scattered archive of the CSRP.

In 2019, the film's director, Yannis Tritsibidas, digitized an abridged version of *Compter sur ses propres forces* and posted it on YouTube, with an important omission: the film's eight-minute introductory sequence, in Arabic and French, on the Palestinian Revolution. According to the synopsis posted on YouTube, the opening sequence, filmed in collaboration with the CSRP, was cut from the digitized version because "it no longer corresponds to the political reality."[7] In the twenty-first century, solidarity tourism in the occupied West Bank and homegrown Boycott, Divestment, and Sanctions campaigns have taken the place of the militant anticolonial support characteristic of pro-Palestinianism in 1970s France, from the first French delegation to the headquarters of Al-'Asifah (The Storm), Fatah's military wing, in Karameh, Jordan, to the ubiquitous use of "Palestine as rallying cry" in the migrant rights struggle.[8] And yet as we will see, the filmmaker's decision to truncate—or self-censor—the film fails to fully divorce the struggle for migrant rights from solidarity with Palestine.

Produced by the militant film collective Atelier pour un cinéma de lutte (Workshop for a cinema of struggle) in collaboration with the CSRP, the sixty-minute, 16 mm black-and-white film ends with a two-minute-long audiovisual montage that echoes the redacted introductory sequence, weaving together the struggles of the Arab masses, from Palestine and Morocco to France. Although the introductory sequence has been lost, the final montage clarifies the iconic role played by the

FIGURE 2. *Rally to protest racist crimes at an unspecified location in France. Protestors hold up giant portraits of slain migrant workers alongside Palestinian flags. Screenshot from* Compter sur ses propres forces, *directed by Yannis Tritsibidas (1973). Courtesy of Yannis Tritsibidas.*

Palestinian Revolution in the struggle for migrant rights in postcolonial France. First delivered in Arabic, and then in a slightly accented French voice-over, the rallying cry that overlays the closing shots of *Compter sur ses propres forces* articulates the unity of these struggles, even as the moving and still images scramble the coordinates of the map of anticolonialism and antiracism. A close-up shot of a photograph of the fifteen-year-old Djellali Ben Ali, gunned down by the companion of his concierge on his own doorstep, appears as the voice-over intones "We are the fedayeen of Palestine," while an aerial view of a rally to protest racist crimes reveals marchers bearing Palestinian flags next to giant portraits of the victims of racist violence (Figure 2). Nor is the Palestinian Revolution the banner of Arab workers alone. At the massive funeral for Pierre Overney, a Maoist activist killed by a security guard at the automobile factory Renault-Billancourt, it is the Palestinian flag that accompanies his portrait in the cortege. "Our strength is our unity," proclaims the narrator, mobilizing Maoist discourse against colonization and occupation in Palestine, state repression in Morocco, capitalist exploitation and racist crimes in France.[9]

Palestine does not figure in the film as a symbol of Arab unity, or at least not in the official idiom of pan-Arabism prevalent in state rhetoric at the time. The shot that follows the opening sequence on Palestine—the first shot in the abridged version available on YouTube—shows two CSRP activists, their faces shrouded in darkness against the bright light pouring in through the window behind them, speaking of the importance of September 1970 in rallying migrant workers in France. Known as Black September, the killing of thousands of fedayeen and civilians in the Palestinian bases and refugee camps of Amman by King Hussein's troops in September 1970 symbolized the betrayal of the Palestinian Revolution by Arab regimes—"la réaction arabe" (Arab reactionaries) as they are dubbed in the film—and triggered massive protests across the Arab world, including within migrant communities in postcolonial France. Ironically, the brutal excesses of a corrupt and authoritarian Arab regime can be credited with rallying postcolonial migrants against racism in France. Nor are nominally pro-Palestinian Arab regimes off the hook, as the CSRP's mobilizations against the abuses of the postcolonial Moroccan and Tunisian governments make clear. "September 1970 united the Arab masses in France," explains the CSRP activist. "The Arab worker knows that here in France he is continuing the struggle of his brothers in Morocco." In the film's audiovisual montage, these words are illustrated by still and moving images, including a photograph of protestors—their faces whited out to protect their identity from French and Moroccan police forces—bearing the banner "Let us save the condemned of Marrakesh" alongside giant Palestinian flags. Palestine is the cause that unites the Arab masses against their current oppressors, in the Arab world and in postcolonial exile.

In the following section I analyze the extant archives of the CSRP and MTA, movements that were animated by Arab workers and students alongside militants from the GP. In this reading, the CSRP is not a "footnote" in the history of French Maoism or, for that matter, the Palestine Liberation Organization (PLO) in France.[10] It is, on the contrary, an autonomous movement for migrant rights, forged in the Palestine solidarity movement. Unlike other pro-Palestinian groups in

France, like the GP's Comités Palestine, whose primary goal was to inform the public about the colonization of Palestine and rally its support, for the CSRP, solidarity with Palestine was a given. Its mission was to use Palestine as rallying cry, connecting the predicament of migrant workers in postcolonial France to the question of Palestine. Against the image of the migrant as an unexpected or unwelcome guest, the CSRP turned the North African migrant worker into a figure of resistance in the postcolonial metropole. As the CSRP put it in their December 1970 "Communiqué and appeal to all workers in France": "Brother workers, the Arab workers in France today all recognize themselves in the struggle of the Palestinian people."[11] It is this dynamic of recognition that I analyze in the following pages, looking first at the CSRP's and MTA's numerous publications—journals, tracts, flyers—and then at the theater troupe founded by CSRP and MTA militants, Al Assifa. The archives of the CSRP make it possible to sketch a portrait of the pro-Palestinian, antiracist movement that emerged in the wake of Black September, connecting the movement for migrant rights in postcolonial France to the most iconic anticolonial struggle of the time—the Palestinian Revolution.

The Palestinian of France

On February 11, 1971, the sixth issue of the bilingual publication *Fedaï: Journal de soutien à la Révolution Palestinienne* (Fedayee: Journal in support of the Palestinian Revolution) published an unsigned story titled, in French, "Dis-moi mon frère" (Tell me my brother), and in Arabic, "Hadith yadur fi maqha 'adi" (Conversation overheard in a neighborhood café). The story takes the form of a Socratic dialogue about the status of the Palestinian Revolution, five months after Black September. "Tell me my brother, the Zionists and other reactionaries . . . say that the Palestinian Resistance is over, that the Palestinian people are finished," queries one worker. Not so, responds his comrade: "Our fedayeen continue to fight, every day they attack the invaders, bearing their weapons. . . . Our people have become a people of combatants."

The story offers few surprises at the level of content and tone: Black September was the first major reversal of the fledgling Palestinian Revolution, which had "transformed a multitude of refugees into a people of combatants" with the Karameh victory of March 1968.[12] As in other parts of the world, pro-Palestinian activists in late 1960s France—a small but vocal minority composed of migrant workers, international students, and far-left militants—were fascinated by the figure of the fedayee, whose stylized profile adorned the posters, magazines, and ephemeral publications of these fringe movements, including *Fedaï*, the newsletter of the CSRP, and the logo of the MTA, which outlines a shrouded silhouette, left fist combatively raised in the air, in the shape of Palestine (see the cover of this book). "Dis-moi mon frère" is in this sense representative of the militant and militarized image of revolutionary Palestine that prevailed in radical left publications in post-'68 France, from the newsletters and communiqués of the many Palestine committees formed in the wake of the June 1967 Arab–Israeli war, to the GP's short-lived publication *Lutte palestinienne: Journal de soutien à la lutte du peuple palestinien* (Palestinian struggle: Journal in support of the struggle of the Palestinian people), which ran two issues in March and June 1969.[13]

What is remarkable about "Dis-moi mon frère," and what distinguishes the CSRP from other Palestine solidarity movements in France, is the dynamic of recognition it stages between migrant workers and Palestinians. In Frédéric Maatouk's poetic phrasing, the immigrant "is, in a way, the Palestinian of France."[14] Whether the dialogue between the two workers was overheard in a café and fictionalized or, more likely, invented, it betrays a slippage from solidarity ("our Palestinian brothers") to identification ("our people") that is more than simply rhetorical. That the two workers are not identified by nationality or even ethnicity—they are not named as Arab workers—only underscores the political, as opposed to identitarian, nature of this identification. If it is true that there is a Maghrebi genealogy to pro-Palestinianism in France—"Maghreb-Palestine, même combat" as the title of a September 1970 *Fedaï* story has it—"Tell me my brother" speaks to a singularly French articulation of *indigenous critique* in 1970s France: a critique, by the former *indigènes* (natives) of France's empire, of the legacies of colonialism and the persistence of racism in the postcolonial metropole.[15]

Abdellali Hajjat has convincingly argued that the militants of the CSRP were "the first 'political immigrants' . . . who considered France as a terrain of struggle for the 'immigrant cause.'" Whereas previously migrants to France mobilized around "the national cause" (Algerian independence during the war, miners' strikes in Hassan II's Morocco, state repression of dissident groups like Perspectives in Bourguiba's Tunisia), the CSRP forged a new type of political activism, one that has only gained in visibility since then: a grassroots antiracist movement pegging the struggle for equality in postcolonial France to anticolonial struggles worldwide, and most saliently, Palestine.[16] Founded in the wake of Black September by Moroccan, Algerian, Tunisian, Palestinian, Syrian, and Lebanese students and workers, many of them militants within the GP, the CSRP brought the vocabulary of decolonization to bear on the realities of racialization in postcolonial France.[17] The anticolonial idiom they disseminated in the form of tracts, communiqués, magazines, and popular theater has, I argue, deeply structured the grassroots antiracist movements that followed in their wake, from the MTA, founded by CSRP members in June 1972, to the 1983 Marche pour l'égalité et contre le racisme— witness the *keffiyehs* wrapped around the marchers' necks, ubiquitous in the iconography of the movement—and more recent collectives like the Parti des indigènes de la république (PIR).[18]

Little known in comparison with the more media-savvy movements that would follow, the CSRP nevertheless achieved a remarkable following among migrant workers in 1970s France. If some CSRP activists did not shy away from militant actions—sometimes at great personal cost—the organization's primary focus was grassroots organizing.[19] Demonstrations, strikes, walkouts, film screenings, magazines, flyers, cartoons, spray-painting, fund-raising, and blood donations were the main weapons of the CSRP. An undated tract published after a massive rally for Palestine in October 1970 places the quotidian tasks of antiracist activism within the "combat for liberty" of migrant workers: "In cafés we have conversations around photographs, we read the newspaper of the fedayeen. In the factories, on the streets, in buses, we post flyers under the nose of racist bosses [*sous le nez des chefs racistes*]."[20] The café conversation staged in "Dis-moi mon frère" offers a reconstituted archival trace of the micropolitics of activism: two workers in a café are already a militant cell. This local, ultrademocratic form of politics was of great importance to the CSRP, which drew relatively modest crowds to their rallies, ranging from several hundred to several thousand. And yet their presence was ubiquitous. The increasingly repressive measures taken by the police, who arrested and deported several CSRP activists and banned their principal publication, *Fedaï,* offer a paradoxical testament to the movement's visibility in postcolonial France. Beholden to "a strict political neutrality" by both French authorities and their countries of origin, migrant workers, particularly those invested in pro-Palestinian solidarity and migrant rights, could be subjected to arbitrary arrest, imprisonment, and deportation.[21] As Yoav Di-Capua has documented, Israel also had spies on the ground, keeping track of migrant activism with the tacit approval of the French police.[22] No wonder the prevailing image of the first generation of postcolonial migrant workers is that of an immigrant "hugging the walls." To manifest any sort of political opinion entailed very concrete risks. And yet, despite these risks, migrant workers continued to mobilize around the Palestinian question.

It is important to remember that in the 1960s and 1970s, pro-Palestinian sentiment in France was confined to radical left and migrant circles. The June 1967 and October 1973 Arab–Israeli wars elicited mass demonstrations in support of Israel, and an "unleashing of hatred" against Arabs.[23] In the context of the 1971–73 oil crisis and the 1972 attacks in Munich, there was scant room for solidarity with Palestine. And yet, attempts to contain or suppress CSRP activism cannot be explained by the predominance of pro-Israeli sympathies in France alone. The police repression that was exercised upon pro-Palestinian migrant workers had a distinctly French colonial genealogy, as a February 1971 CSRP tract makes clear:

> Fifteen days ago, *Minute* (a fascist journal that supported the assassins of the OAS) published a cover story titled: out with the Algerians! [*dehors les Algériens!*] The enemies of Palestine are the same as those who in France expel Arab workers from a *foyer* in Suresnes without housing them somewhere else. They want to stop us from supporting the struggle of our Palestinian brothers by all means: they arrest and condemn our comrade Hamza Bouziri to a six-month prison sentence, they want to scare people by parading their cops everywhere; they want to sabotage the demonstration in support of Palestine that was held at Barbès; they deport a comrade from the CSRP.[24]

The police repression of migrant activism—expulsions, arbitrary arrests, deportations—is implicitly connected here to an emerging racial discourse that is itself tributary to one of the most extreme forms of colonial racism, that of the *ultras* who fought to keep Algeria French. Even more remarkable is the politics of recognition that undergirds this critique. In a nearly paratactic juxtaposition—from the OAS and the far-right journal *Minute* to what, a few years later, militants from the Gauche révolutionnaire (Revolutionary Left) would characterize as "racist campaigns designed to facilitate the 'control of immigration'"— France becomes an "enemy of Palestine."[25] The anonymous author of this tract does not need to comment on France's role in the production of the Palestinian question, from the partition of the Levant to its ongoing military support for Israel, a context the CSRP's public was well aware of. Drawing a straight line from colonial-era racial terror to anti-immigrant discourses, and from the question of Palestine to the migrant question, the CSRP framed the struggle for migrant rights in explicitly anticolonial terms.

There is no small degree of irony to the fact that the pro-Palestinian activists of the first grassroots antiracist movement in France were perceived as foreign—why deport a pro-Palestinian migrant otherwise?— effectively buttressing the nativist right's argument that immigrants should go home ("dehors les Algériens!"). The invocation of Algeria in the tract has, I argue, the reverse effect: the Palestinian question concerns migrants because France colonized North Africa, and is now oppressing its former colonial subjects. In the words of Hamza Bouziri, the Palestinian question is an "integral part" of the struggle of migrants in France.

On December 29, 1970, CSRP activist Hamza Bouziri—brother of Saïd Bouziri, the archivist of the CSRP—was arrested while distributing tracts to protest the summary firing of a migrant worker who had put up pro-Palestinian flyers ("affichettes") at the Citroën factory in Nanterre, in the outskirts of Paris.[26] In a statement issued from prison, Bouziri explains his decision to go on hunger strike:

> I am in solidarity with the struggle of all other political prisoners in France who are struggling against the penitentiary system to obtain their political rights. But also, inspired by the glorious example given to us by our comrades from the FLN [National Liberation Front] who were detained during the Algerian war, going on hunger strike is

> for me a way to actively support the Palestinian Revolution. . . . The
> Palestinian Revolution is an integral part of the Revolution of all the
> peoples of the world who struggle for justice and liberty.[27]

It is striking that Bouziri does not call upon the notion of political sovereignty in his statement—the declared goal of both the Algerian and Palestinian revolutions—but rather the very republican notions of justice and liberty. Using a tactic, the hunger strike, associated with anticolonial struggles rather than the age of revolutions, Bouziri translates Enlightenment ideals into the idiom of anticolonialism. Invoking the example of Algerian revolutionaries imprisoned during the long war of independence—a war that ended only eight years prior to his action—Bouziri inscribes the struggle of migrant workers in France in a broader anticolonial struggle that includes the question of Palestine in its purview.

The stakes were already high when Bouziri initiated the first hunger strike in the history of the movement for migrant rights in France.[28] By 1972 the antiracist movement was on high alert. In the context of rising unemployment and a full-blown housing crisis, particularly for migrant workers confined to *foyers* and *bidonvilles* (shantytowns), the Marcellin-Fontanet circulars of January and February 1972 linking legal residency to employment and housing produced the first generation of *sans-papiers* (undocumented migrants) in France.[29] At the same time, a series of racist crimes, often unpunished or inadequately sanctioned, were terrorizing migrant communities.[30] The urgency of the moment called for a radicalization of the antiracist movement. The CSRP stepped up its activities: rallies, strikes, meetings, and mobilizations in support of the occupation of vacant buildings by *les mal-logés* (the poorly housed).[31] Without changing the militant logo or main title of its journal—*Fedaï*, framed by two drawings of a Kalashnikov—the CSRP shifted its center of gravity from pro-Palestinian activism to the migrant struggle. In the awkward formulation of the editorial insert on the front page of the first issue of *Fedaï nouvelle série* (Fedayee new series), published in July 15, 1972, "the journal *Fedaï* becomes the journal of Arab workers in France after having been the journal in support of the Palestinian Revolution for more than a year and a half, but it will continue to express support for the Palestinian Revolution."[32] Palestine did not disappear from the pages of the journal. On the contrary, the ways in which Palestine was mobilized within the antiracist struggle in France became even more explicit in the final issues of *Fedaï*.

On February 23, 1972—two days before it was banned—*Fedaï* published what was to be the last issue of its iteration as the *Journal de soutien à la Révolution Palestinienne*. Titled "Pour arrêter les crimes racistes descends dans la rue!"/"Linanzal ila al-shari'a hata nawqif al-jara'im al-'ansuriya" (Go down into the streets to stop racist crimes), the cover story offers an allegory of Palestine as rallying cry in the struggle against racism in France. Visually, what jumps out is not the text but an overexposed black-and-white photograph of Palestinians marching toward the camera in military fatigues, waving Palestinian flags above their heads.[33] A boy, perhaps ten years old, leads the march, his flag jutting out into "the street" of the French title, just below, and parallel to, the drawing of a Kalashnikov that strikes a diagonal line through the capital "I" of *Fedaï* (Figure 3). The fact that the journal is printed in gray scale makes it somewhat difficult to read the block letters superimposed on the black-and-white image:

Today there is a new wave of assassinations and a new campaign of racist intoxification. The circular of the Minister of Labor Fontanet says that one must not give work to immigrants. So the bosses are firing, like at Renault: Sadock Ben Mabrouk and José [Duarte].

The government maintains unemployment to keep salaries low and turn us into the bosses' slaves and the Minister of Labor wants to spread the idea that migrant workers [*les ouvriers immigrés*] are responsible for unemployment.

And so in Paris, the parallel police and the racist networks commit a series of attacks against migrant workers [*les travailleurs immigrés*]. It's a new offensive by the fascists to pit the French against migrants, to bring Arab workers down on their knees.

But we will not go down on our knees.

    Jellali Ben Ali in Barbès

    Aït Abdelmalek in Belleville

    Abdallah Zahmoul 16 years old found dead in the 19th
        [*arrondissement*]

  It has to stop

FIGURE 3. *Front page of the fifteenth issue of* Fedaï: Journal de soutien à la Révolution Palestinienne *(February 23, 1972). Visible beneath an editorial call to protest racist crimes in France is a black-and-white photograph of marching Palestinians bearing Palestinian flags. Courtesy of La contemporaine.*

Below the image, overlaid with this call to take to the streets, an appeal calling for the solidarity of French workers clearly links colonial and postcolonial subjection and calls for the right to political subjecthood in the postcolony: "Here we are far from our homeland, we came here to work because in our country we live in great hardship, and don't forget the remainders of colonialism that persist in our countries. We want to live like the other, like all the other, workers. We will fight for our rights until the end."[34] The image of the marching Palestinians, apparently unrelated to the content of the cover story, is a palimpsestic reminder of the conditions that brought Moroccans, Algerians, and Tunisians to France.[35] *Indigènes* in the colonies, migrant workers in France are "indigenized" once more through racially exclusive laws and racist crimes.[36] The rights they claim in France are analogous to the rights they were denied as colonial subjects: equal treatment under the law.

Published on July 15, 1972, the first issue of *Fedaï, nouvelle série: Journal des travailleurs arabes* documents the transcolonial understanding of the migrant question that was so central to the nascent antiracist movement. Here the counterpoint is lexical as well as visual, embedded in the colonial terminology used, unselfconsciously in this case, to speak of racism in France. According to the cover story on the killing of Rezki Arezki, gunned down in Lyon by a neighbor on June 6, 1972, among the twenty-five hundred demonstrators assembled at the rally on June 17, many raised "FLN [Algerian] and Palestinian flags" alongside portraits of the victim. When a French person takes the mic to denounce racist crimes, "an old immigrant interrupts him to say: 'I want to say that we are not against all *pieds-noirs*. . . . The majority of French people, the majority of *pieds-noirs*, are not racist. They are with us.'" An Algerian worker leaving the demonstration agrees: "We demonstrated calmly to show that we are not racist against the *pieds-noirs*, nor against the French. We are against the racists, against the bosses who take us for slaves."[37]

It is telling that both migrants use a term designating European settlers in Algeria (*pieds-noirs*, literally "black-feet") to speak of white people in France.[38] Although they use it in positive rather than negative terms—not all "settlers" are racist, many are our allies—their appropriation of a term forged in the colony speaks volumes to the distinctly colonial genealogy within which racist acts such as the murder of Arezki are placed. It also serves as a reminder of the reasons for the presence of North Africans in France: yesterday's *indigènes* are today's migrant workers. The fact that protestors waved Algerian and Palestinian flags at the rally further serves to visually anchor antiracism within a broader anticolonial struggle that connects the revolutionary past (Algeria) to the revolutionary present (Palestine and France).

The CSRP journal's subtitular shift from "Journal in support of the Palestinian Revolution" to "Journal of Arab workers" foregrounds the organization's main arena of activism, migrant rights. But as the palimpsestic cover of the last issue of *Fedaï: Journal de soutien à la Révolution Palestinienne* makes clear, it also signals the naturalization of the equation between anticolonial solidarity and the struggle for migrant rights in France. As early as 1971, CSRP militants were urging that the movement be broadened from its activist base—a handful of "agitators" known to the police forces—to the larger community of migrant workers. Palestine was to be the "banner of dignity" for migrant workers in France, and the catalyst for the CSRP's dissolution into the masses. "We must turn the Fedayee into the image of the liberation of the masses and the image around which we will unite the French."[39] Inspired by the Palestinian Revolution, the founding of the MTA in spring 1972 represents a shift in tone rather than substance.[40] The MTA's publications continued to foreground the struggle for migrant rights in France alongside the Palestinian Revolution and pro-democracy movements in the Maghreb, taking for granted the homology between these disparate but interconnected sites of struggle. The result was a particularly trenchant diagnosis of the historical links between past and present forms of oppression.

In a supplement to the first issue of the MTA's new publication, *Al Assifa: La voix des travailleurs arabes* (Al Assifa: The voice of Arab workers), the editorial board summarized its postcolonial diagnosis of the plight of migrant workers: "Oppressed Arab workers have been living in France for years. Formerly colonized peoples, they were torn from their homelands to thin out [*dégrossir*] the ranks of the unemployed in Morocco, Algeria, and Tunisia, and to work in inhumane conditions and in this way increase the profits of the bosses in France."[41] Confirming the analyses of the CSRP in its publications, the founding editorial of the journal of the MTA articulates a double critique of the North African postcolonial regimes and French immigration policies that make possible the exploitation of migrant labor in France. Like its predecessor *Fedaï*, the title of the MTA's publication also clarifies the iconic role of the Palestinian Revolution for postcolonial migrants in France. Named after the military wing of the anticolonial Palestinian movement Fatah, *Al Assifa* is as militant a term as *Fedaï*, one that would have carried the same appeal among migrant circles while having the advantage of being less immediately legible to the French authorities. In the slippage from *Fedaï* to *Al Assifa,* then, we can read a strategy of legibility, differently positioned with respect to the MTA's diverse audiences: migrant workers versus the institutions that oppress them. Theater, too, was to be a formidable weapon in the MTA's arsenal, aimed at both migrant workers and the forces lined up against them.

One of the MTA's principal arenas of activism in its founding years was performance: amateur theater, improvisation, music, and song. The MTA's performance collective, also named Al Assifa, would turn migrant workers into militants (activists) in the streets, cafés, and factories of postcolonial France. In the final sections of this chapter I analyze the archival traces of the performances staged by Al Assifa and reflect on the conditions for animating this incomplete archive in a time of renewed attention to migrant rights.

Activists Acting

In 1973, Maoist activists Geneviève Clancy and Philippe Tancelin, trained in the "theatrical interventions" of May '68, and CSRP/MTA militant Mohamed "Mokhtar" Bachiri formed a militant performance collective, Al Assifa.[42] Refusing the labels associated with theatrical conventions—theater, troupe, stage, actors, even "street theater"[43]—Al Assifa described itself as "a collective made up of migrant workers and French workers that participates directly in the movements and struggles of migrant workers in France."[44] The members of the collective are not actors; they are "activists acting [*de[s] militant[s] faisant la comédie*]."[45] Their stage? The factory, the *foyer,* the *cités HLM* (*habitations à loyer modéré,* or low-income housing developments), the café, the street. Al Assifa's first play, "Ça travaille, ça travaille et ça ferme sa gueule" (They work, they work, and they shut up), was a series of sketches staged at the Lip watch factory in Besançon during a strike in August 1973, while police officers were shooting tear gas canisters to disperse the thousands of workers occupying the factory.[46] This context is not fortuitous: migrant workers-turned-amateur actors were literally putting their bodies on the line by performing. In the words of Olivier Neveux, "the fact that these are 'Arab bodies' is not anecdotal. . . . It is scandalous to see Arabs onstage; to see Arabs assemble; to see Arabs conversing in a country where violent racist acts create a climate of fear and clandestineness."[47] Theatrical representation is, in this context, a performance of political subjecthood against political subjection.[48]

Al Assifa would tour throughout migrant communities in France, Belgium, and Switzerland from 1973 to 1976, performing "Ça travaille" as well as "C'est la vie de château, pourvu que ça dure" (That's the life, let's hope it lasts) and, after a reshuffling of the collective in April 1976, "Ali au pays des merveilles" (Ali in wonderland), "Couscous au poulet" (Chicken couscous), and "Le labyrinthe."[49] Inspired by Maghrebi popular theater traditions, in particular the storytelling practice of *al-halqa* (literally, the "chain" or circle assembled round a storyteller), as well as Maghrebi musical traditions, Al Assifa's performances changed according to current events, actor improvisation, and the participation of the public. In an undated flyer, the collective explains: "History and current events form the backdrop [of our plays], which leads us to constantly transform and add elements. We perform in Arabic and in French, according to the characters and the public." Labor strikes, hunger strikes, building occupations, and racist murders were the urgent political context of a theatrical practice cast as a "weapon" in the migrant struggle.[50] Here is how Clancy and Tancelin recall one of the first productions of "Ça travaille" for the striking autoworkers of Chausson:

> A circle drawn in the courtyard of the occupied factory, in which we act. One after the other, the scenes: the ministers, the cardboard boxes [*l'emballage*], the television. The Chausson workers get up, they start acting immediately [*ils rentrent dans le jeu directement*]. They push the minister of African labor affairs, take his place, continue the dialogue with the French minister, tell anecdotes about recruitment operations they witnessed or experienced.
>
> When we start packing up they grab hold of the cardboard boxes and continue the scene. Infusing it with their own experience. They also show how to resist it. As soon as the television begins to spew

lies, the comments ring out. "Aren't you ashamed of yourself, you're lying, it's not true!"

And when we come to the scene of Fatna Diab's witness account [of her brother Mohamed's death in a police station], we hear a silence heavy with all that is known, all that is feared. At the end of the play there is a spontaneous concert of darboukas and bendirs. A concert they will maintain throughout the following days when, fighting against the CRS, they will fight also with their songs, their music linked to their cries, their demands.[51]

As demonstrated in this vignette, Al Assifa's plays do not simply represent the plight of migrant workers. They move those represented, who are also the actors onstage, into collective action. "We refuse realism," in the words of one of the members of the collective. "When we take to the stage, that is to say a place, a space in which . . . we are going to reconstitute time through a series of images, we necessarily make a choice. For us, this choice is the struggle."[52] An extension of the factory, the neighborhood, the café, the space of performance becomes a springboard for migrant rights activism.

Though there are no extant manuscripts of Al Assifa's plays, fragments published in Clancy and Tancelin's 1977 memoir *Les tiers idées* make it possible to piece together the scene in which the Chausson workers intervened, a scene designed to historicize, and critique, the importation of migrant labor.[53] As Clancy and Tancelin explain, "Ça travaille" was the fruit of an encounter between antiracist militants and French workers on strike at Lip who, when they were told about the plight of migrant workers in France, asked "why they didn't go back home." After "a longer and more detailed confrontation [about] the magnitude and complexity of our [migrants'] situation," Lip workers challenged Al Assifa to put on a play that would make their situation legible to French workers.[54] The result was "Ça travaille," a series of sketches that denounced the trade in bodies obtained through negotiations between France and the postcolonial regimes of its former colonies, as demonstrated in the following conversation between the African minister of labor and the French secretary of state:

-Hello?
-Hello!

-Am I speaking with the French minister of foreign affairs?

-Mister D . . . secretary of state on the line.

-This is the African minister of labor.

-Delighted, how are you?

-Not good.

-Not good?

-Imagine, I've received complaints from your government about the shipment of tomatoes that I sent you.

-I heard about that, but rest assured, it was a diplomatic error, I hope that's not why you're calling me?

-No, I have an offer for you: they're strong, they're strapping, they work, they work, and they shut up.

-You mean your workers, I see, well send me, let's say. . . .[55]

As the initial case of mistaken identity makes clear, immigration is not a foreign affair, but a domestic matter. Decolonization has transformed the colonies from overseas possessions—under the purview of the ministry of foreign affairs—to a reservoir for surplus labor in the metropole. That the African minister represents African labor writ large clearly implicates all postcolonial regimes in the export of cheap labor to the metropole, not simply Algeria, France's prized settler colony. The minister's use of the impersonal third person—*ça*, literally "that," in French slang, a mark of disrespect—further objectifies the bodies that are shipped to France. In the words of the final chorus:

We have become merchandise.
We are the foreigners [*les étrangers*], the immigrants.
We are the workers.
We are the men, the slaves of modern times.[56]

The metaphor of slavery transforms Africa into the site of a new deportation, designed to satisfy the needs of the French *patronat* and the bellies of Africa's corrupt leaders.

Surveying his new recruits, who now have cardboard boxes marked with names of automobile factories on their heads (Citroën, Renault, Chausson . . .), the African minister of labor puts them in their place: "Who cares what you look like [*qu'importe votre tête*], you're not here to think but to shut up [*vous la fermer*]. . . . When you're not at home, you

shut up . . . no politics."[57] The measures taken to "control immigration"—
both in the sense of limiting and surveilling migrant workers—in the
early to mid-1970s, while not constituting a separate body of law per
se, nevertheless attest to the double standards applied to immigrants
from France's former colonies. Ironically, the police's frequent attempts
to interrupt or disperse Al Assifa's plays—the ubiquitous "dispersez-
vous!"—offer a literal interpretation of the play's title, which might more
idiomatically be translated with the imperative: "Work, work, and shut
up."[58] Against this interdiction of speech, Al Assifa's plays transformed
migrant workers into "activists acting."

I have argued that the insistence by CSRP, MTA, and Al Assifa activists on the colonial genealogy of immigration to France is part of
a decades-long reactivation of anticolonial critique in the purportedly postcolonial present. If the routes and vectors of migration have
changed in the intervening years, the migrant question in France has
not been resolved. Then, as now, the migrant question calls up the question of Palestine, as I will argue in the final chapter of this book. For
now, and by way of conclusion, I turn to a recent work that revisits the
extant archives of Al Assifa in our present moment, bringing migrant
workers' struggles in France to bear on the refugee crisis of the 2010s.

Reactivating the Archive

Shot with a digital camera in an abandoned factory-turned-theater in
Athens in November 2016, Franco-Moroccan artist Bouchra Khalili's
film *The Tempest Society* premiered at the fourteenth installment of the
major contemporary art exhibition documenta, held in Kassel, Germany, and Athens in spring 2017. A multimedia artist working across
film, photography, sound, and text, Khalili had already produced several well-recognized artworks about the migrant experience and the
legacies of anticolonialism when she set to work on a new film.[59] *The
Tempest Society* brings these two histories together, situating the archive of the first migrant rights movement in France in relation to the
ongoing migrant question in order to apprehend a "continuum of resistance" across the Mediterranean and into the present.[60] The fruit of
Khalili's independent research on Al Assifa and the workshops she held
with three young Athenians—Isavella Alopoudi, Elias Kiama Tzogonas,
and Giannis Sotiriou—the film is, in Khalili's words, "a hypothesis":

Three Athenians from different backgrounds form a group in
Athens to examine the current state of Greece, Europe, and the
Mediterranean. To do so, they gather together on a theater stage, approached as a civic space. They name themselves *The Tempest Society*
to pay homage to *Al Assifa* ("The Tempest" in Arabic), a theater group
active in Paris in the 70s composed of North African workers and
French students. . . . Forty years after, the forgotten legacy of Al Assifa
finds a site for reactivation in Greece.[61]

Like Al Assifa's plays, *The Tempest Society* is a collaborative project,
based on weeks of conversations between Khalili, Alopoudi, Tzogonas,
Sotiriou, and the other characters that appear in the film: a Kabyle
student-turned-activist for migrant rights, a Nigerian woman who was
born and raised in Athens yet remains undocumented, and a Syrian
refugee who started a theater troupe in Athens. The opening sequence
of the film, titled "The Story," documents their discovery of the scattered
archives of Al Assifa. As Khalili puts it in an interview published in the
catalog for the video installation, "My task . . . starts from the awareness
that the whole story cannot be reconstituted. It is lost. That is a matter
of fact. The question becomes: what can we do with what remains?"[62]
Photographs, a short Super 8 film, and the ephemeral publications of Al
Assifa are the media that allow the members of *The Tempest Society* to
tell this story.[63]

In the vast, empty space of a factory-turned-theater in the postindus-
trial outskirts of Athens, images of a performance of Al Assifa in the
occupied Chausson factory flicker silently on a small television monitor
set up next to a long wooden table and four chairs on what appears to
be a stage, framed by imposing concrete steps—the putative bleachers
of this deserted theater. As if in answer to the voice-over that follows—
"How does one inherit this story while the traces have disappeared?"—
the camera offers a montage of archival images, alternatively narrated,
in voice-over, by Sotiriou, Tzogonas, and Alopoudi: photographic portraits of Mohamed "Mokhtar" Bachiri, Geneviève Clancy, and Philippe
Tancelin, the three founders of Al Assifa; photographs of Al Assifa activists playing music or confronting police officers in the streets of Paris; a
worn first edition of *Les tiers idées,* Clancy and Tancelin's 1977 memoir; a close-up shot of scenes from the Super 8 film playing on the television monitor, where we can see Bachiri and Tancelin dancing, to the

delight and merriment of the workers assembled in the courtyard of the factory.

Overlaid onto the silent sound track of the final frames of the Super 8 film, we hear footsteps echoing as someone slowly approaches the table where Sotiriou, Tzogonas, and Alopoudi are now seated. From stage left enters Tancelin, visibly aged and yet undeniably present. The contrast between the youthful image we have just seen and the much older body that appears is less stark than the realization that this body is still alive, almost larger than life now that we have heard his story. As Tancelin sits down, the Athenians take a photographic portrait of a member of Al Assifa and place it, like a mask, in front of their faces. Tancelin begins to read from *Les tiers idées* as the montage of archival images resumes, culminating in a final shot of the quartet: Tancelin stage left, the Athenians donning their photographic masks in the center, and stage right, a new scene from the Chausson performance on the television monitor: the migrant labor recruitment scene from "Ça travaille," featuring workers donning cardboard boxes bearing the name of the factories they will be shipped to (Figure 4).

In an interview published in the 2019 catalog for *The Tempest Society,* Tancelin revisits this scene, and the archival footage that he discovered, for the first time, on the stage set by Khalili. Although some of the details are different in Tancelin's retelling—the African minister of labor is Moroccan, the French minister is the minister of labor, not the secretary of state—he is referring here to the production of "Ça travaille" during the May 1975 occupation of the automobile factory Chausson. The scene Tancelin is speaking about here is the one I analyzed above, on the basis of Clancy and Tancelin's retelling in *Les tiers idées.* Here, again, Tancelin insists on the spontaneous, improvisational, and collaborative dimensions of the production—on what was not visible in the frame of the television monitor in Athens in 2016:

> In the excerpt we see only a tiny part of the play. For example, we do not see the scene between the two Ministers, the Moroccan Minister of Labor and the French Minister of Labor, discussing the quota of immigrant workers to send to France. In the following scene, we perform the workers arriving in France, wearing cardboard boxes on our heads. But that day, suddenly we were interrupted by one of the viewers. He started shouting, "It did not happen like that." He joined

FIGURE 4. *Veteran migrant rights activist Philippe Tancelin reads from his book* Les tiers idées *while three Athenians hold up photographs of members of the theater troupe Al Assifa (*left to right, *Tancelin, Geneviève Clancy, and Mohamed "Mokhtar" Bachiri). Stage right, a television set plays footage of a performance of Al Assifa's first play, "Ça travaille, ça travaille et ça ferme sa gueule," during the 1975 strike at the auto factory Chausson. Screenshot from* The Tempest Society, *directed by Bouchra Khalili (2017). Courtesy of Bouchra Khalili.*

us and showed us how it is to land in France as an immigrant worker. He did not speak. He mimed the scene. And of course, we watched him doing it. . . . A spectator, concerned in the first place with the story we are telling, objects to our version of the story and shows us how to perform that situation and how to stage it.[64]

Something is undeniably lost in the remediation of Al Assifa's performances in Khalili's film: it is the process of "activists acting." The camera shows members of the collective acting in the midst of, and for, migrant workers. In Khalili's words, "We see you, in an occupied factory, performing in front of dozens of North African workers on strike."[65] But it does not capture the "interruption" of the migrant worker in the scene, the physical act of taking the place of the actor onstage. As Tancelin suggests, the performance of "Ça travaille" cannot be reconstituted.

And yet, something happens in the remediation of the archives of Al Assifa in *The Tempest Society*. By "reactivating" the archive of Al Assifa—however incomplete or irretrievable it may be—in the present, Khalili's film links the migrant rights struggles in 1970s France to migrant activism in Greece in the 2010s. "As one of the last surviving members of Al Assifa," Tancelin explains, the experience of appearing in a film documenting this past summons the past on set, in the company of a new collective of "activists acting": three Greek citizens, a Kabyle migrant, an undocumented Athenian, a Syrian refugee, and all those they represent.[66] Like a modern-day chorus, these characters are the voice of the demos, albeit a demos without rights. In the words of Elias, a Greek citizen born in Kenya: "We will speak for ourselves, and for those who cannot speak."

"The Story" culminates in a palimpsestic collage of photographs spanning more than forty years—in Alopoudi's cryptic words, "Paris, 1972–1978. Athens, 2016. . . . The struggle here and elsewhere, yesterday and today." Black-and-white photographs and photographic contact sheets of members of Al Assifa, outdoor productions and scenes staged in a theater, musical performances in the street, and altercations with the police begin to fill the surface of the table at which Tancelin was seated a few moments before, as the Athenians carefully place these images and overlay them with photographs, some in black and white but most in color, of the 1973 student uprising in Greece, anti-austerity protests in Syntagma Square, protesting North African migrant workers, their fists raised in the air—they were the first migrants to go on hunger strike in Greece, in 2011—or Syrian refugees holding a banner stating: "We escaped from death in Syria to the vagrancy in Greece." In the center of the collage is a photograph of Tancelin, in the role of the French minister of labor, placing cardboard boxes bearing the names of French automobile factories on the heads of North African workers (Figure 5).

The attentive viewer will recognize this image as the recruitment skit in "Ça travaille," caught on tape in the flickering monitor in the preceding scene, as Tancelin closes *Les tiers idées* and leaves the stage. The image of the automobile workers playing their own role remains visible as the more recent images of demonstrations overlay the edges of the collage. At the heart of the decades-long panorama of protest that fills

FIGURE 5. *Collage of photographs from the archive of the militant theater collective Al Assifa (1972–76). At the center of the table is a photograph of the recruitment scene in "Ça travaille, ça travaille et ça ferme sa gueule," in which migrant workers don cardboard boxes bearing the names of the French factories they will be shipped to. Screenshot from* The Tempest Society, *directed by Bouchra Khalili (2017). Courtesy of Bouchra Khalili.*

the table after Tancelin's departure, this image is the starting point in a "continuum of resistance" that culminates, in the film, with the Syrian refugees' protests in Syntagma Square in 2014. Like the CSRP militants of the 1970s and the North African migrants of 2011, they, too, are on hunger strike, using the idiom of anticolonial revolution to articulate a demand for migrant rights in the present.

In an interview published in the catalog of Khalili's video installation, Tancelin assesses the interplay between past and present he experienced on the set of *The Tempest Society:*

> I then quickly had the feeling that the missing ones, the absentees, were coming back, and that they had come to bear witness at the very moment that I was representing them. . . . They were there. I could feel it very strongly. But again, that was also to do with the atmosphere:

this beautiful light and the immensity of the space, the great concentration of the visual apparatus: one table, four characters and a
few photos. The extreme simplicity was overwhelming. And in this
the sense of their presence impressed me a lot. I saw these young
Athenians holding pictures of us on their faces. It was like a reverse
shot. The absentees were suddenly there, but the photos also formed
an image of the past like a screen projecting onto the present.[67]

The present becomes a screen on which images of the past form a pa-
limpsest of migrant rights activism, in France but also in Europe at
large, connecting the plight of migrants to Europe in 2017 to the migrant movements in 1970s France and, implicitly, the ongoing Palestinian question.

The Palestinians do not figure in Khalili's film, barring a passing
mention of Bachiri's activism in the pro-Palestinian movement, and the
tribute to Fatah in Al Assifa's name. And yet by a stroke of translational
luck, the expression Tancelin uses to speak of his lost comrades, *les absents,* is rendered as "the absentees" in English, drawing a fortuitous
parallel between the activists of Al Assifa and dispossessed Palestinians
from within the 1948 borders of Israel—"present absentees" in the paradoxical formulation of Israeli jurisdiction. Writing in the twenty-first
century, Tancelin fortuitously reminds us that the Palestinians continue to be colonized.[68] The Palestinian echoes in this formulation also
invite us to recover the international solidarities of the movement for
migrant rights in France. In reading the present through the lens of the
past, the "reverse shot" offered by the photographic palimpsests in the
opening sequence of the film invites a transcolonial reading of the migrant question.

After excavating the traces of Al Assifa for *The Tempest Society,*
Khalili turned her attention to a writer who was deeply involved in
the nascent migrant rights movement in 1970s France: Jean Genet.[69]
Khalili's film *Twenty-Two Hours* takes Genet's brief visit with the Black
Panther Party in the spring of 1970 as its focal point, reconstituting his
embassy through the archival and editorial work of two Black American
women, addressing the camera in 2018. The audiovisual traces of this
"radical ally" of the Black Panthers is also a testament to the centrality
of the Palestinian cause in France, as evidenced in the photographs that
flash up on the screen, showing Genet alongside Black Panther activists

and Palestinian fedayeen.[70] As I will argue in the next chapter, Genet's militancy for the Palestinians is inseparable from his engagement in the antiracist struggle in France. As an outsider who nevertheless benefited from the intersectional privileges of Frenchness, whiteness, and fame, Genet transformed anticolonial solidarity into the staging ground for a complex critique of nativism in the metropole.

CHAPTER 2

Jean Genet and the Politics of Betrayal

The Palestinians

One of a handful of writers and intellectuals who rallied round the CSRP in the early 1970s, the iconoclastic writer Jean Genet offers a particularly rich case study in the battle of natives against nativism in postcolonial France. A tireless advocate for the Black Panther Party and the Palestinian resistance in the 1970s and 1980s, Genet also wrote fierce condemnations of French colonialism and anti-immigrant racism, from his 1961 play *Les paravents* (*The Screens*), published at the height of the Algerian Revolution, to his late writings on Palestine, "Quatre heures à Chatila" ("Four Hours in Shatila," 1983) and *Un captif amoureux* (1986; *Prisoner of Love,* 2003), which denounce France's role in the partition of the Levant and its long-standing support for Israel. Unlike the activists of the CSRP, however, who "recognize themselves in the struggle of the Palestinian people," Genet's trenchant critiques of racism and colonialism in these works are based on a more complicated relation to the Palestinians.[1] What Genet called his "privilege"— his positionality as a white Frenchman—made outright identification impossible, even when, at the height of his militancy for the Palestinian cause, he claimed to "become Palestinian."[2] In fact, Genet's support for the Palestinians was never unconditional. "The day the Palestinians become a nation like other nations," he declared in 1983, "that's where I'm going to betray them."[3]

Against the critical grain, which tends to read Genet's turn to Palestine as a cipher that rearticulates the major themes of his early work—imposture, love, betrayal—I propose to take seriously the politics of betrayal in Genet's Palestinian writings.[4] An *enfant trouvé* (foundling) and foster child who spent his adolescence in a penitentiary colony and the war years behind bars, Genet famously reveled in the capitulation of France to the Nazis—just deserts, according to him, for the nation-state that had imprisoned its ward.[5] But how do the politics of betrayal, easily legible with respect to France, apply in the context of Palestine? Although Genet was a vocal critic of the state of Israel, he never explicitly advocated for the foundation of a sovereign Palestinian nation-state. Palestine is less a rallying cry in his writings than it is an admonishment against the perils of identity—perils that are nowhere more salient than in the anti-immigrant, nativist discourses that were gaining ground in France when Genet was writing his late works. Against white nativism and what he calls "the 'settled' nations," Genet's writings sketch a complex critique of discourses of indigeneity in France and Palestine.[6]

Before examining the politics of betrayal in Genet's Palestinian writings more closely, it's worth exploring how, historically, Genet's stance on Palestine is inseparable from his mobilizations against anti-Arab racism and his critique of nativism in postcolonial France. Critics have tended, for good reason, to focus on the links between Genet's advocacy for the Black Panther Party and the Palestinians. What is less known and, I argue, equally important is how closely Genet's pro-Palestinian activism tracks to his antiracist militancy in France.

In 1969, Genet was introduced to Mahmoud Hamchari, the representative of the PLO in Paris, who invited him to visit the Palestinian camps and military bases in Jordan.[7] The following year, Genet met with two representatives of the Black Panther Party in Paris. In the spring of 1970 he traveled clandestinely to the United States—he was unable to secure a visa due to his status as an ex-convict—before embarking for Jordan, where he resided from October 1970 to April 1971, and then from September to November 1971.[8] Upon returning to France, Genet demonstrated, signed petitions, and raised funds on behalf of the co-mité Djellali, named after Djellali Ben Ali, a fifteen-year-old Algerian boy killed by a white Frenchman on October 27, 1971.[9] No stranger to the French police, Genet had already been beaten up during a sit-in to protest the inhumane living conditions that led to the death of five African workers in Aubervilliers in January 1970, and he continued to participate in antiracist demonstrations throughout the 1970s.[10] It is very likely that Genet, who had just returned from his second tour in the Palestinian bases when he joined the comité Djellali, was aware of the CSRP's activism for Palestine and that he attended some of their rallies and meetings for Palestine. What is certain is that his antiracist activism in the metropole is closely linked to his militancy on behalf of the Black Panthers and Palestinians.[11]

That Genet situated the Palestinian question within a transnational imperial history is evident from the very first text he wrote about the Palestinians. Commissioned by Bruno Barbey, a photographer he met in a Palestinian camp in Jordan, "Les Palestiniens" appeared in the fourth issue of Magnum's magazine *Zoom* in August 1971, alongside Barbey's photographs of fedayeen and refugees. In a series of ten short photo-essays, Genet delivers his first explicit indictment of colonialism since the end of the French empire a decade earlier, reactivating the question of political relationality in terms of his—and thus his readers'—complicity in the colonization of Palestine. Genet begins not by commenting on the images but by contextualizing them. Zooming out from the clichés captured in the photographs—fedayeen at rest, little girls bearing weapons, bodies strewn on the ground, an endless sea of refugee tents—Genet situates them in a narrative that implicates his readers, no matter how remote they may feel these images to be. No surprise, he comments sarcastically, that Europeans should fail to be "moved" by Israel's repression of the Palestinians. Not only are they responsible for the creation of the Jewish state—after "two thousand years of humiliation," from the pogroms to extermination, in Genet's succinct phrase—they are complicit in the colonial violence this state now wields:

> The Jews terrorize and kill the Arabs. What European would be moved by this [*quel Européen pourrait s'en émouvoir*]: France terrorizes and kills the Arabs of North Africa, the Malagasies, the Indo-Chinese, the Black Africans. England does the same elsewhere. Belgium too. As does Holland in Indonesia, Germany in Togo, Italy in Ethiopia and Tripolitania, Spain in Morocco, Portugal we know where. The Zionists are guilty, and all of Europe bears the guilt of Zionism.[12]

Genet's use of the historical present, nine years after France's withdrawal from Algeria ("France terrorizes and kills the Arabs"), is not only idiomatic in this passage. A major player in the production of the Palestinian question—France brokered the infamous Sykes-Picot Agreement with England in 1916, splitting up what was left of the Ottoman Empire and paving the way for the foundation of a Jewish state in the Levant—France is directly implicated in the colonization of Palestine. The parallelism between "the Jews" (Israelis) and "France" in Genet's prose implicates French colonialism in the continued colonization of Palestinians.

I do not want to gloss over the slippage from "Jews" to "Zionists" (and, implicitly, Israelis) in the opening sentence of this passage, which sets up a reductive parallelism between "the Jews" (taken to mean *Israelis*) and "France." There is, by now, a sizable corpus of critical texts that accuse Genet of anti-Semitism. Given the decades-old tendency to conflate anti-Zionism with anti-Semitism, in France and elsewhere, it is hardly surprising that Genet's virulent critiques of Israel have been chalked up to an atavistic anti-Jewish sentiment.[13] Although Edmund White is categorical—"not a single anti-Semitic word exists in Genet's published works"—other critics offer a more nuanced approach, analyzing, for example, Genet's writings about the Nazi occupation of France as a critique of patriotism that nevertheless implicates Genet in the violent convulsions of European history.[14] But Genet's language also reflects a conflation between Jewishness and Israeliness that is foundational to Zionist discourse, and subtends his concatenated use of the terms *Jews* and *Zionists* in this passage. That Genet naturalizes the Zionist equation between Israeli and Jew should not distract us from the purpose of the French–Israeli parallelism that obtains: to expose the responsibility of Europe, and singularly France, in the production of the Palestinian question.

Indeed, Genet's indictment of colonialism in "Les Palestiniens" gives way, in the text, to a critique of the nativist discourses that were gaining traction in 1970s France. The French are implicated in the terrorizing and killing of Palestinians by virtue of their anti-Semitic and colonial past. And they continue to be implicated in the present by what Genet terms their anti-Arab racism: "An anti-Arab racism, almost a sickness, is so deeply entrenched in every European that one might well wonder whether the Palestinians can count on our help, however slim it might be." The fact that Genet cites the recent celebration of the Crusades ("in France we just celebrated the seven hundredth anniversary of the death of Louis IX, called Saint Louis") in his indictment of racism is telling. The Crusades were being mobilized by far-right parties like Ordre nouveau at the time to anchor French identity in august anti-Muslim histories dating from before the era of French colonialism. Genet's la-

conic evocation of European empire fills in the historical void enter-
tained by anti-immigrant movements to erase the messy postcolonial
linkages between France and its former colonies, an erasure that Genet
dates back to France's conquest of Algeria:

> First Roland, then Saint Bernard, Godefroy de Bouillon, Guy de
> Lusignan, Richard the Lion-Hearted, Louis IX, and whoever else, with
> all their Crusades against the Muslims, were so magnified during the
> period when the Europeans were crushing the Arab peoples—I mean
> between 1830 and 1962—that one might wonder, but very innocently,
> whether History—that of France, among others—was not written in
> the nineteenth century for the purpose of forming men who, in all
> good and bad faith, would have contempt for the colonized.
>
> The justification of an atheist and bourgeois History that will have
> used the Catholic Crusades for the miserable ends of an enduring
> colonialism [*aux misérables fins d'un colonialisme qui dure encore*].[15]

From France's colonial expeditions to the anti-immigrant movements
of the early 1970s, the chronicles of the Crusades have served to justify
anti-Arab racism and delegitimate Arab resistance to colonial racism,
whether in Algeria, Palestine, or contemporary France.

As a nineteen-year-old corporal in the engineer corps of the Levan-
tine troops stationed in Damascus in 1930 and then, from 1931 to 1933,
in the Seventh Regiment of Moroccan Riflemen in Meknes, Genet was
well positioned to understand "the contempt for the colonized" he describes in this passage.[16] Writing some ten years after the end of French
empire, Genet also had good reason to speak of colonialism in the present tense. Though he does not provide any contemporary examples of
French anti-Arab racism in "Les Palestiniens," migrant workers were
the targets of a deadly wave of racist crimes when Genet was writing his
photo-essay. The migrant rights movement in which he was involved at
the time of writing forms a crucial context for his indictment of European racism in "Les Palestiniens." It also informs, as I will show, Genet's
approach to the Palestinian question in his witness account of the massacres of Sabra and Shatila, and in his posthumous book on the Palestinians, *Un captif amoureux.*

"The immigrant workers have never asked me for anything," Genet
claimed in a 1970 interview, in response to a question about why he

had chosen to help the Black Panthers rather than migrant workers in France.[17] And yet his texts on the colonial and migrant questions—his play about the Algerian Revolution, *Les paravents*, several circumstantial texts, and the little-known film script I analyze in the next section, "La nuit venue" (Nightfall)—attest to the fact that he was deeply committed to the antiracist cause in France.[18] As we have seen, the Palestinian question was one of the central preoccupations of the migrant rights movements in which Genet was involved. Unsurprisingly, "La nuit venue" thematizes Palestine as rallying cry in the nascent antiracist movement in France. But it also announces the critique of nativist articulations of identity that subtend Genet's Palestinian writings. As I will argue in the following sections, the figure of the migrant worker remains central in Genet's Palestinian corpus, revealing a sustained and multidirectional attention to the permutations of racism, from Palestine–Israel to postcolonial France.

The Migrant Worker

Genet worked on the scenario for "La nuit venue" from 1975 to 1977, following an intense period of antiracist and pro-Palestinian activism.[19] Unrealized and never published, it nevertheless forms a crucial intertext for his writings on Palestine. Set during a single day and night, October 8–9, 1974, "La nuit venue" depicts the trials and tribulations of A. (in some versions, Abdel Aziz), a freshly recruited Moroccan worker who is shipped to France, only to discover the many faces of racism. In a series of scenes set in rural Morocco and the working-class neighborhoods of northern Paris, the script inventories the plight of migrant workers in 1970s France. A train conductor, a hard glint in the "blue of the eye"—"Le bleu de l'oeil" was Genet's original title for the film—throws A. out of first class, hurling a racial slur at him; a policeman patrolling an unauthorized market in la Goutte d'Or knocks over a crate of oranges; migrant workers argue with their landlady over the latest rent increase; far-right demonstrators put up posters saying "No to immigration"; an undocumented Algerian is deported, while the recruitment of cheap labor in A.'s native Morocco continues unabated, in a scene that echoes Al Assifa's parodic representation of labor recruitment in Africa. But instead of donning cardboard boxes marked with the name of the factory they will be shipped to, the migrant workers in "La nuit venue" have their hands stamped by a French foreman in a Moroccan cemetery. The glance that A. shares with an Arab worker toiling in a construction site as his train pulls into Paris serves as a foreshadowing of the fate that awaits the aspiring immigrant, who quits after only twenty-four hours in the metropole. In the most dramatic version of the script, A. returns to Morocco, accompanied by the coffins of deceased migrant workers whose bodies are being repatriated for burial in the homeland, and is arrested upon arrival by Moroccan police forces.[20]

Based on an "original idea" by Genet's Moroccan protégé, Mohamed El Katrani, and funded to the tune of 4.5 million old francs, "La nuit venue" was set to begin filming in Paris and Tunisia when Genet abruptly called the project off.[21] Although the extant manuscript and typescript scenarios give little indication of the cinematography Genet envisioned- he was to codirect the film with the painter Ghislain Uhry—the last, bound copy of the script includes notes in the margins of a scene that depicts, in "stylized" fashion, the antiracist, pro-Palestinian movement that Genet had been involved with since the early 1970s.[22] As they wander through the streets of Paris, A. and an Algerian comrade see African workers putting up posters of the iconic Congolese leader Patrice Lumumba on palisades erected near the Sacré-Coeur Basilica—the only notable landmark of the working-class, migrant communities of northern Paris that are the setting for the Parisian sequences in the film—followed by Arab workers putting up "posters in Arabic."[23] The CRS descend upon the scene, and the African and Arab workers flee. The script cuts to a scene in which a sex worker is giving orders to an Arab customer, signifying both what has been dubbed "the sexual misery" of the migrant worker and the pervasiveness of racial hierarchies in the underworld, before returning to the palisades scene in more detail.[24]

The allegorical quality of the palisades scene in "La nuit venue" recalls the highly stylized *mise-en-scène* of Genet's earlier satire of colonialism, *Les paravents,* in which the martyred matriarch Kadidja orders the Algerian rebels to sketch their victories on huge screens that move across the stage, producing a series of colorful, "monstrously enlarged" drawings of severed body parts and war booty.[25] Genet's notes in the margins of the script for "La nuit venue" make it clear that he was writing a sequel of sorts to *Les paravents*, with scenes depicting the figures of the financier, the judge, and the priest—representing, according to Genet, the three domains of colonial rule—the "hideous" monuments honoring French soldiers who died in Algeria, and Vietnamese migrants accusing the French of crimes in Indochina. The script also recalls the infamous "bataille des *Paravents*" (battle of the *Screens*), which violently pitted pro–French Algeria militants—including Jean-Marie Le Pen, future chairman of the far-right, anti-immigrant party Front national—against Genet and his troupe when the play premiered in Paris in 1966. Genet's confrontation with the white nativist movement born out of French Algeria was undoubtedly a source of inspiration for a scene in "La nuit venue" that we might dub the *battle of the palisades*.

In this scene, wooden barriers—the kind that are erected around construction sites—become a screen for competing claims to the space of representation. Here, the African and Arab workers are in competition with their Jewish, French, and leftist counterparts, whose posters symbolize the causes they are expected to support: anticolonialism, pro-Palestinianism, Zionism, white supremacy, and communism. In the margins of the page, Genet specifies the content of the Arabic-language posters put up by Arab workers: "Palestine vaincra" (Palestine shall overcome), a rallying cry, as we have seen, of the pro-Palestinian and antiracist movements in France:

> Here, in my opinion, is where the poster scene [*cette scène des colleurs d'affiche*] that started earlier should continue.
>
> Remember: first Blacks put up a poster about Lumumba. Then Arabs—some for a nightclub, others for "Palestine shall overcome."
>
> This is when the posters start going up on the palisades again, in this order:
>> Arabs, in Arabic characters,
>> Jews, in Hebrew characters,
>> French people, Celtic cross,
>> Leftists, hammer and sickle.
>
> Such that the palisade is covered with posters that overlap, put up by activists wielding a pot of glue and brushes, without any team encountering another.
>
> Or rather, occasionally a tardy activist finds himself in the midst of an opposing team and runs away in fear.[26]

One of the most easily visualized scenes in the scenario of "La nuit venue," the battle of the palisades recalls the absurdist tableaux of *Les paravents,* in which the costume is the character: outsized settlers, police officers, and soldiers standing on stilts, shoulders, belly, and buttocks beefed up with padding, versus diminutive Arabs wearing colorful rags. In this scene, it is the icon, the symbol, in some cases the language, that stands in for the identity of the *colleur d'affiche:* Lumumba, Palestine, the Arabic language, Hebrew, the Celtic cross, the hammer and sickle. It is important to note that these symbols represent different things entirely. To place posters of anticolonial heroes next to markers of white identity is, in itself, absurd. The very fact that a poster of a Celtic cross, a regional sign appropriated by the ascendant far-right party Ordre nouveau, precursor of the Front national, as a symbol of white, Christian identity, might "overlap" with a poster of Lumumba or Palestine, icons of anticolonialism and antiracism in France, allegorically stages the concrete struggle that antiracist activists were waging at the time. That the Celtic cross represents "French people" (*des Français*) in the script, rather than nativist activists, betrays Genet's deep-seated suspicion toward French identity, coeval, in this instance, with a racial supremacy founded in a mythical religious-ethnic identity.

What do we make of the fact that Genet places anticolonial and antiracist activism alongside, and against, leftist militancy and white identity politics? The "battle of the palisades" is not a simple affirmation of antiracist and anticolonial solidarity. I'd like to suggest that the palimpsestic overlaying of anticolonial, pro-Palestinian, Zionist, white supremacist, and communist iconography, and the panic of the activist accidentally stranded in the enemy camp, offers a gently satirical allegory of the battle between *indigènes* and nativists in 1970s France, without leaving any doubt as to where Genet's sympathies reside. This scene stands out because it offers an example of Genet's critique of identity as it is deployed in racist discourse (the Celtic cross) but also, paradoxically, in antiracist discourse. The gentle rebuke of Palestine as rallying cry is not a disavowal of the struggle that Genet was deeply involved in at the time. The object of satire, rather, is the naturalized equivalence between symbol and cause, between Arab workers and pro-Palestinianism. What remains—beyond the affirmation of solidarity-as-identity—is what, in his Palestinian writings, Genet called *revolution:* here, the antiracist struggle itself, not its iconographic and performative trappings.

One of Genet's earliest Palestinian texts, a transcription of a conversation that can be read as a very early draft of *Un captif amoureux,* helps to clarify the parody of identity politics in "La nuit venue." In his recollections of a conversation with "seven young Palestinians one evening in Paris" in September 1972, shortly after his last trip to the Palestinian bases in Jordan, Genet clarifies what the Palestinian Revolution means to him:

> What happened to me in these bases was the following: while the Palestinian revolution remained to some extent abstract and strange to me, I realized that it had not only changed the Palestinians but also changed me. Let me explain. In Europe, out of innate indolence, I used to consider the function, and not the man. The waiter was necessary to put the plate and the glass on the table and to fill the glass, but if he fell ill the plate and the glass would still be put in front of me—another waiter would have taken his place. This happened at all levels and with all functions: every man was exchangeable within the framework of his function and, except in rare cases, we only noticed the function. In the Palestinian bases the opposite happened: I changed in the sense that my relations changed, because all relations were different. No man was exchangeable as a man; we noticed the man only in regards of the function, and the function was not a service to maintain a system, but a fight to smash the system.
>
> A revolution which does not aim at changing me by changing the relations between people does not interest me; what is more, I doubt whether a revolution which does not affect me enough to transform me is really a revolution at all. The Palestinian revolution has established new kinds of relations which have changed me, and in this sense the Palestinian revolution is my revolution.[27]

That Genet romanticizes the Palestinian Revolution in this passage, as in his other Palestinian writings, is not in question. Genet himself would spill a considerable amount of ink pondering the attraction he felt for the Palestinians.[28] More interesting, however, is Genet's critique of his alleged "innate indolence"—a characterization that smacks, paradoxically, and perhaps intentionally, of reverse Orientalism or self-

Orientalization. The vignette he offers here is much more quotidian, and in that sense, too, more subtle, than the parodic tableaux in *Les paravents*—Europeans towering over Arabs on stilts—or the battle of the palisades in "La nuit venue." Hiding behind the apparently innocuous example of the restaurant server is a sophisticated and often counterintuitive critique of a particular kind of essentialism that reduces man to function: racism.[29] Substitute "migrant worker" for "waiter" in the above passage, and the antiracism of Genet's account of "his revolution" becomes clear. Against the fungibility of the migrant worker, endlessly substitutable in the economy of migrant labor, Genet looks for the political subject of revolution.

What is at stake, then, in the battle of the palisades analyzed above, is the risk of confusing the man with the symbol. In the script, this is the kind of identification that leads to various instances of racial interpellation, and in the last version, to the expulsion of A.'s Algerian friend. The fact that A. and his comrade stumble upon a scene of pro-Palestinian activism before their arrest and expulsion is all the more poignant when we remember that CSRP activists were jailed and deported for their pro-Palestinian activism in France. Migrant workers were being identified, by the French state, because of their support for Palestine. Genet's satire of identity politics in this scene is also aimed at the French state's identification of its postcolonial subjects. Indigenous critique cuts both ways: white nativism and racial identification are the twin targets of "La nuit venue."

As discussed in the introduction, policing was a central aim of colonial law, as exemplified in the penal code reserved for France's colonial subjects, the Code de l'indigénat. In other texts, Genet explicitly mobilizes colonial history in his critiques of anti-Arab racism, including the code's legacies in France. In a short essay titled "No matricule 1155" ("Registration No. 1155"), written for the catalog of a 1982 exhibition about immigration, Genet singles out the term *indigène* in his indictment of the exploitation of colonial labor in the metropole. "No matricule 1155" is the identification number of Salah Ahmed Salah, a thirty-year-old Moroccan migrant worker who arrived in France in 1940, when Morocco was still a French protectorate. Drawn up by the ministry of labor for a member of the "personnel indigène" (native personnel) of France, the ID card—"of the same pink as the one that used to color the map of the globe, indicating the French Colonial Empire"—is evidence, for Genet, of the colonial genealogy of the migrant question. "Qui nous avons été, Français, qui nous sommes encore c'est probable, des archives trop bien tenues et conservées nous le crachent en pleine gueule" (What we have been, we French, what we probably still are— these archives, too well maintained and preserved, spit it all back in our faces). Reading Salah's ID card, Genet finds "a vocabulary that does not concern us: *shashiyya, tarboush, serwal, duwar, kundura,* native [*indigène*] . . ." If Genet is not interested in local color, he has already noted that *les bureaux indigènes* (the bureaus in charge of colonial subjects) are responsible for coming up with two types of "natives": soldiers and workers ("soldat Marocain et travailleur Marocain").[30] From the intricate machinery of the colonial bureaucracy, Genet salvages a singular example of the figure that, by 1982, had been painstakingly severed from France's rose-colored colonial past: the migrant worker. The protagonist of "La nuit venue," this figure remains present in more subtle ways in Genet's Palestinian writings, connecting the Palestinian question to anticolonialism and antiracism in France in a complex critique of nativist identity.

Becoming Palestinian

Although Genet wrote several occasional texts about the Palestinians after his sojourns in the bases and camps of Jordan in the early 1970s, the Israeli invasion of Beirut in summer 1982 was the catalyst for his major Palestinian writings, "Quatre heures à Chatila" (1983) and *Un captif amoureux* (1986). It is in the texts he wrote during this period that Genet articulates most forcefully the "affinities" that tie him to the Palestinians, as well as the notion of betrayal as a revolutionary political sentiment.[31] What Genet offers in these texts is a radical critique of identity, whether colonial, national, or nativist, not only in Palestine– Israel but also in postcolonial France. Indeed, the figure of the migrant worker—hardly one that immediately comes to mind when thinking of Palestine—serves to anchor Genet's critique in a colonial map that extends across the rose-colored empire of Genet's native France.

At the height of the Israeli war in Southern Lebanon, Leila Shahid, president of the General Union of Palestinian Students in France, asked Genet to write a text about Palestine for the *Revue d'études palestiniennes*. Unwilling, at this stage, to publish a text based on his memories alone, Genet accompanied Shahid to Beirut on September 12, 1982. After a two-month siege (June 6–August 12), the PLO had agreed to move its headquarters to Tunis. The Palestinians who remained in the refugee camps of West Beirut were under the protection of the French, Italian, and American troops of the multinational force stationed in Beirut. One day after his arrival, Genet witnessed the sudden departure of the U.S. Marines, which precipitated the withdrawal of the French and Italian troops. On September 14, the newly elected president of Lebanon, Bachir Gemayel, head of the Christian Kataeb (Phalange) militias, was assassinated. Defying international agreements, the Israeli Defense Forces (IDF) entered Beirut and set up checkpoints at the entrances of the Palestinian camps in West Beirut. On September 17, a nurse from the Akka Hospital facing the camp of Shatila rushed to the apartment of Leila Shahid's mother to alert Shahid and Genet that something terrible was happening in the camps. Two days later, they were finally able to enter Shatila and the adjoining camp of Sabra, accompanied by two American photographers. From September 16 to 18, an untold number of Palestinian refugees, men, women, and children—estimates range from hundreds to several thousand—had been slaughtered by Kataeb militias, assisted by flares shot from the IDF command post two hundred meters from one of the entrances to the Shatila refugee camp. The first European to witness the aftermath of the massacre, Genet would compose, upon his return to Paris a few days later, a chilling account of what he saw, "Quatre heures à Chatila."[32]

Alternating between painfully detailed descriptions of the maimed and disfigured bodies piled up in the narrow alleys of the Sabra and Shatila refugee camps and vibrant images of the youthful fedayeen encountered in the Palestinian bases of Jordan ten years earlier, "Quatre heures à Chatila" begins to explain the "spell" (*sortilège*) that the Palestinians exerted on Genet, refugees and fedayeen both.[33] It also clarifies the political stakes of pro-Palestinianness for an anticolonial, antiracist French writer who, when Shahid approached him to write an article for the *Revue d'études palestiniennes,* was drafting a short text on a Moroccan migrant in France ("No matricule 1155") and working on *Le langage de la muraille* (The language of the wall), a film script about Mettray, the penal colony where he spent his adolescence, and a reservoir, according to Genet, for settlers in French Algeria.[34] As Edward Said compellingly argues in a short but moving text about Genet, "What tied him to Palestine . . . after revolution was forgotten in Algeria was that it continued in the Palestinian struggle." Though Said locates this realization in the final pages of *Un captif amoureux*—in a passage I will return to below, on the "erasure" of France by Palestine—the evidence of what Said calls the "survival" of Algeria in Genet's Palestinian writings is also to be found in "Quatre heures à Chatila."[35] So, too—and this Said does not note—is the figure of the migrant worker.

Genet's *ekphrasis* of the massacre concludes, paradoxically, with a comparison between the beauty of the Palestinian fedayeen and the beauty of the Algerians in the waning hours of French empire. Here is how Genet characterizes the beauty of the colonized transformed by the process of liberation in the closing pages of "Quatre heures à Chatila":

> In France, before the Algerian war, the Arabs weren't beautiful, their gait was awkward, shuffling, they had ugly mugs, and almost suddenly victory made them beautiful; but a little before victory was assured, while more than half a million French soldiers were straining and dying in the Aures and throughout Algeria, a curious thing happened to the faces and bodies of the Arab workers: something like the intimation, the hint of a still fragile beauty which was going to blind us when the scales finally fell from their skin and our eyes. . . . Is a revolution a revolution when it has not removed from faces and bodies the dead skin that made them ugly? I am not speaking about academic beauty, but about the intangible—unnamable—joy of bodies, faces, cries, words which are no longer cheerless, I mean a sensual joy so strong that it chases away all eroticism.[36]

The contrast between the abjection of the rotting bodies in the camps and the glory of the warring fedayeen should not only be read as a romanticization of the guerrilla fighter, even if the pages of Genet's Palestinian writings are filled with self-conscious paeans to the beauty of the fedayeen. The beauty Genet speaks of here is that of the migrant worker, not the FLN operative. The Algerian worker in France before Algerian independence—the *indigène* in the metropole—serves as a reminder of the figure that Genet had been writing about in his abandoned film project, "La nuit venue": the postcolonial migrant on whose face the beauty of revolution has faded. If Genet was invested in the

Palestinian Revolution, it was also because this revolution was "carried over" in the antiracist movement in France.[37]

Genet's invocation of Algerian workers in the colonial metropole serves to ground his critique of Israeli colonialism in an expanded imperial map. In *Un captif amoureux,* Genet would explicitly blame the French forces for abandoning the Palestinian refugees, condemning "France's betrayal of the civilian population when its soldiers slipped away and eclipsed themselves."[38] In "Quatre heures à Chatila," Genet witnesses the departure of *les paras*—the moniker given to the special forces deployed in Algeria during the infamous "battle of Algiers" in 1957—along with the American and Italian multinational forces, implicating France and its Western allies in the killing of Palestinians.[39] Already manifest in the parallelism between France and Israel in "Les Palestiniens," Genet's disidentification with France is consummated before the spectacle of the "terroriz[ing] and kill[ing]" of Palestinian refugees.[40] Cut off from the rose-colored empire he once served, Genet feels himself "become Palestinian": "Since the roads had been cut off and the telephone was silent, deprived of contact with the rest of the world, for the first time in my life, I felt myself become Palestinian and hate Israel."[41] The complex web of responsibility Genet sketches in earlier passages—Phalangist, Israeli, European, and American—gives way in this passage to a metonym for colonialism in the present: Israel.

And yet Genet's "choice" of the Palestinians is inextricably linked to his critique of French colonialism and racism, which continues to haunt the distant shores of France's former empire. "The proximity of death, still hovering over the earth [*encore à fleur de terre*]" is what allows him to feel the justice, the rightness (*justice, justesse*) of the Palestinian cause:[42]

> The choice one makes of a privileged community outside of one's birth, given that one's belonging to a people is native, this choice is based on an irrational membership, which is not to say that justice has no role, but this justice and the entire defense of this community take place because of a sentimental, perhaps even sensitive, sensual, attraction; I am French, but I defend the Palestinians wholeheartedly and without judgment. They are in the right because I love them. But would I love them if injustice had not turned them into a vagabond people?[43]

Echoing the trope of the wandering Jew, the expression "vagabond people" points to the historical irony that turned a diasporic people into a settler state, and the native inhabitants of Palestine into a nation of refugees.[44] Given how often the term *vagabond* has been used to describe the itinerant writer, it also surreptitiously highlights Genet's "sentimental" attraction to the Palestinians. But what is remarkable about Genet's choice of the Palestinians in "Quatre heures à Chatila" is the break with the native community that precedes it. Genet is "juridically" French.[45] Politically, he chooses to "become Palestinian."

As Said puts it succinctly in his essay on Genet, "imperialism is the export of identity."[46] What Genet is after is the identitarian logic of imperialism. And yet the rhetorical flourish in Genet's account of his "choice" of Palestine—he loves the Palestinians because they are in the right, and they are in the right because they are oppressed—betrays a suspicion of "native belonging to a people" *tout court:* not only Genet's native Frenchness, but also any claim to nativeness, be it French, Algerian, or Palestinian.[47] Paradoxically, Genet manages to articulate a critique of nativeness through his attachment to the Palestinians, even though what they claim is, precisely, indigeneity to Palestine, their ancestral home. He is interested in the process of claiming one's rights, not in what he calls the "institutionalization" of hard-won rights. Here is the full version of Genet's statement on betraying Palestine, given in an interview a year after Shatila, in the company of Leila Shahid: "Listen, the day the Palestinians become an institution, I will no longer be on their side. The day the Palestinians become a nation like other nations, I won't be there anymore. . . . I think that's where I'm going to betray them. They don't know it." Pressed to explain, Genet concludes: "If I were alive I don't know if I could adhere to a Palestine that has been made into an institution and has become territorially satisfied."[48]

Although one should take Genet's public statements with a grain of salt—Genet was the first to admit that he was performing a certain image of himself before interviewers—the notion of betrayal he alludes to here is consistent with the more complex critiques of nativism found in his Palestinian writings, none more so than *Un captif amoureux.* The passage that Said alludes to when he speaks of the "survival" of Algeria in Genet's Palestinian writings is a case in point. I'm not sure Said seized the subtleties of Genet's invocation of Algeria here, which serves as an admonition for the Palestinians, lest they too "forget" revolution:

When a drawing has too many defects in it the artist rubs it out and two or three rubs with the eraser leave the paper perfectly blank again. With France and Europe rubbed out I was faced with a blank space where France and Europe used to be, a space of liberty in which Palestine as I experienced it would be inscribed, but with alterations that worried me. Like Algeria, like other countries, it was forgetting revolution in the Arab world, it thought only of the territory out of which a twenty-second state might be born, bringing with it what was expected of a newcomer: Law and Order. But did this revolt, that had been outlawed for so long, really aspire to be a law that would have Europe as Horizon [*aspirait-elle à devenir loi dont le Ciel serait l'Europe*]? I've tried to say what it became; but having become *terra incognita* for me, Europe was erased.[49]

Palestine erases Europe and France and forms the blank page on which Genet can project his revolution. But once institutionalized as a state, Palestine, like Algeria before it, risks to join the ranks of "'settled' nations."[50]

Without minimizing the risks of "settlement," the portrait Genet paints in *Un captif amoureux* offers a "fantasy" of what Palestine might become.[51] It captures the beauty of a people on the cusp of revolution—a "blinding" beauty that allows Genet finally to break free from his native country and choose a community to his liking. "I started to write the book around October 1983," Genet writes toward the end of *Un captif amoureux*, "and I became a stranger, a foreigner to France [*et je devins étranger à la France*]."[52] Finally rid of his *francité* (in spite of what he mocks as his "Celtic physique"), Genet is free to adopt the cause of the migrant worker, the Black Panther, the Palestinian, all figures of the stranger/foreigner in a France that continues to "have contempt for the colonized."[53] An ode to the Palestinians he loved and lost, *Un captif amoureux* is Genet's vision of Palestine as utopia, to borrow Said's felicitous formulation: "In a very literal way the Palestinian predicament since 1948 is that to be a Palestinian at all has been to live in a utopia, a *nonplace,* of some sort."[54] The erasure of a "defective" France is what allows Genet to sketch this portrait of a future revolution that will become "[his] revolution."[55] And yet, as we will see, France remains implicated in the very concrete erasure of Palestine. Genet's posthumous tribute to the Palestinians offers a multidirectional critique of colonialism, racism, and nativism, from the United States to Palestine–Israel and France.

Banlieue Palestine

Scattered throughout the pages of *Un captif amoureux* are intimations that Genet encountered Palestine from the margins of France's rose-colored empire, in a pidgin language at the intersection of Darija (Maghrebi Arabic) and *parigot* (Parisian vernacular): Maghrebi youth met on a train from Souss to Sfax in 1968 while they were traveling clandestinely to enlist in the Palestinian Liberation Army via Tunisia, Libya, and Egypt; Arabic poems dedicated to the Palestinian Revolution, first discovered in a library in Sfax and then at the Palestinian stand that made a brief appearance at the Sorbonne in May '68; and, in the Palestinian bases of Jordan, in the Parisian slang of one of Genet's most vividly painted characters, Mubarak, a Sudanese volunteer in Fatah's army.[56] "Tout c'qui s'passe ici c't'encore à cause de vous. V'z'êtes responsable du gouvern'ment d'Pompidou" (Everything that happens here is because of you.... You're responsible for the Pompidou government), charges Mubarak, "not only in French but in slang [*en argot*], with a working-class accent [*l'accent faubourien*] and a Maurice Chevalier vocabulary."[57]

Genet's delight at finding the popular tongue of his down-and-out Paris years in the Palestinian bases of Jordan is matched only by the prolixity of his new friend, who claims that the language he speaks is, in fact, the product of French colonialism. "You needed a common language to conquer us," he patiently explains. "The Basque soldiers who spoke Basque, the Corsicans Corsican; soldiers from Alsace, Brittany, Nice, Picardy, the Morvan and the Artois all poured into Madagascar, Indochina and the Sudan and were forced to learn Parisian French, the language of their officers, trained at Saint-Cyr." Recalling that Jules Ferry served as minister of education before becoming minister of the colonies—Ferry's school reforms are largely credited with making Île-de-France French the de facto language of the Republic—Genet speculates on the colonial origins of the language he wields: "The light, sensitive French that gradually spread all over France may have been born of the terrified trembling bequeathed to mainland France by little soldiers from Brittany, Corsica and the Basque country, conquering and dying in the colonies."[58] Mubarak becomes for Genet "an obvious heir to the hooligans of the old Parisian *banlieue*" and "the guardian of . . . the working-class accent I'd been looking for for so long that I'd come to think it had vanished, perhaps died. As languages can."[59] The only places where Genet still hears *parigot*—and *verlan,* the prison slang popularized in the working-class neighborhoods of Paris in the mid-twentieth century—are the light rail trains radiating ever farther out from Paris *intramuros,* now packed with "half-Senegalese, quarter-Arabs and complete Guadeloupians."[60] Genet's fractal list constitutes an ironic acknowledgment of the not-quite-Frenchness of those newly arrived from the four corners of France's empire. Despite their foreignness, a Sudanese fedayee in Jordan and France's migrant workers have become the vehicles of the disappearing language of the French working class.

I begin my reading of *Un captif amoureux* with Genet's discovery of Parisian slang in the Palestinian bases of Jordan not because it is particularly central to his narrative—it is not—but because if offers a counterintuitive entry point into Genet's posthumous memoir, one that allows me, in closing, to reveal the stakes of Genet's critique of nativism. *Un captif amoureux* is not a linear narrative of Genet's time with the Palestinians, but rather a "book in waves. Ten times, twenty times, the same scenes, the same characters come crashing down to cast new memorial wrecks."[61] If the majority of these scenes reconstitute his memories of the Palestinian camps and bases of Jordan and Lebanon, others evoke his discovery of Parisian slang in the Palestinian bases, his service in the French colonial army, and, in a passage that harkens back to the battle of the palisades in "La nuit venue," pro-Palestinian activism in Paris.

One of these recurring scenes, also the earliest in chronological terms, takes us to Damascus circa 1930, shortly after an anticolonial revolt quashed by the French. "If the city was devastated it was because of the French army, which didn't surprise me because this army to which I had belonged for several weeks controlled, encircled the city . . . for the first time in my life I saw a city imprisoned by young soldiers." Fresh out of the penal colony of Mettray, Genet's first assignment was to build a fort. With zero experience of masonry, Genet was nevertheless assigned a squad of "tirailleurs tunisiens" (Tunisian infantrymen)

who obeyed not him but *"a certain idea of France."*[62] "Although not a settler in Damascus, I was, perhaps unwittingly, a janissary of the settler,"
writes Genet, playing on his former identity as a *colon* (also the word for
settler or colonist) in Mettray. The fort falls to pieces as soon as a can-
non is fired from it to "honor . . . the work of the young French engineer
and these brave natives [*indigènes*]," in the words of his commanding officer. Humiliated, Genet falls ill and is sent home for a month of conva-
lescence. But the damage is done. A direct result of the 1916 Skyes-Picot
Agreement, which carved out the Levant between French and British
mandates, France's iron-fisted rule over Syria becomes the fertile terrain, in Genet's proleptic narrative, for the birth of the Palestinian
Revolution he would come to love. "That tiny, grotesque but monumental disaster prepared me to become a friend of the Palestinians."[63] A
conscript of one colonial occupation, Genet will become the witness of
another.[64]

Un captif amoureux also clarifies the stakes of betrayal in Genet's
oeuvre, grounding his disidentification with France in a critique of
French colonialism and racism that culminates in his "becoming
Palestinian." For in between mandate Syria and occupied Palestine,
in Genet's retrospective telling, lies France's defeat by the Germans in
June 1940. Cast, in other texts, as a form of revenge against the France
that had imprisoned him—as a former convict, Genet was stripped
of his civic rights in perpetuity—the "jubilation" he feels before the
defeat of his homeland is tantamount in the following passage to the
Schadenfreude of the colonized.[65] Note the echoes of the French occupants of Syria encircling Damascus, or of the IDF cordoning off West
Beirut, with Genet oscillating between the position of the colonizer and
the colonized:

> France where, between the ages of six and eight, I felt like a stranger,
> like a foreigner [*je me sentis étranger*]. . . . France lived all around me.
> She thought she contained me when I was in France even far away from
> her [*en France même loin d'elle*]. All around me she circled, just as her
> empire, pink painted on the map, circled the globe; an overseas empire
> in which I could have gone all around the world without a passport,
> though only steerage. That foolishly proud empire, never troubled
> before except by the empire of India, was invaded, almost without op-
> position, by a few battalions of handsome fair-haired warriors.[66]

The mobility of the French national who, no matter how destitute, is able to travel throughout France's empire without a passport—a right that has been taken away from the Palestinians, as Genet reminds us on several occasions—is suddenly suspended.[67] "The proud French, so proud of their colonies, became their own migrant workers." The conflation between French nationals and migrant workers is not innocuous: under German occupation, the French have become foreigners/strangers in their own country. The intrusion of an apparently unrelated memory—the Nazi occupation of France—surreptitiously reveals the colonial genealogy of the figure of the migrant worker, the native (*indigène*) turned foreigner. From between the cracks of Genet's fissured tower in mandate Syria, which he imagines overcome by weeds, emerges the image of the Palestinian people: "Moss, lichen, a few dog roses capable of pushing up through the red granite were an image of the Palestinian people breaking out everywhere through the cracks."[68]

Genet's account of France's role in colonizing the Levant in *Un captif amoureux* helps clarify his outrage at European indifference in "Les Palestiniens," Genet's first text on the Palestinian question. "What European would be moved by this: France terrorizes and kills the Arabs of North Africa, the Malagasies, the Indo-Chinese, the Black Africans."[69] That the French fail to be "moved" by the killing of Palestinians is not simply due to a lack of interest, as Mubarak will suggest. It is tantamount to a willful act of forgetting, or what, in another colonial context, Ann Laura Stoler names *disregard*.[70] *Interest* is nevertheless the word Genet uses ironically to transcribe Mubarak's prediction about *Un captif amoureux*. "You'll write a book," confirms Mubarak, "but you'll have trouble getting it published. The French aren't interested in the Arabs."[71] Instead, Mubarak suggests that Genet write a script for a film that he would direct. The moving image might make up for the lack of "interest" the French have in the Arabs. It might force them to see the Palestinians.

Had Genet written a scenario for a film about his time with the Palestinians, which scenes would he have selected for inclusion? Edmund White's description of the cinematic qualities of Genet's writing applies especially well to *Un captif amoureux,* which is structured through juxtaposition, not narrative: "Through flashbacks, flash-forwards, broken sequences, Möbius-strip replays of scenes, fade-outs, jump-cuts and montage, Genet applies the full vocabulary of cinematic techniques."[72] The medium of film would lend itself particularly well, I suspect, to the cuts between Palestine and the different coordinates of the French empire, from mandate Syria to postcolonial Tunisia and Genet's native Paris.

One of the first scenes in *Un captif amoureux* seems to come out of the pages of a film script, enabling, in visual terms, the camera to follow two narrative threads unfolding at the same time: "The king [of Jordan] was in Paris when the Bedouin troops dug up the bodies of the fedayeen killed between Ajloun and the Syrian frontier, to kill them again." While "the butcher of Amman" shops for a new Lamborghini in the city of lights, the women of Baqa camp negotiate with the Jordanian army to smuggle a French priest serving as a courier between the fedayeen and French leftists out of the camp, claiming that they are going to . . . Palestine. "Elles osèrent un scénario, elles le jouèrent" (The women wrote a script and proceeded to perform it), writes Genet. During this performance (Genet writes "représentation théâtrale"), King Hussein is on his way to the Elysée Palace, where the president of the French Republic, Georges Pompidou, offers him friendly advice: "Don't shoot." Here is what, Genet speculates, Hussein sees from the window of his car:

> When the women of Baqa left the camp claiming that they were going home to Palestine, King Hussein was going up part of the avenue de l'Opéra on his way to lunch at the Elysée Palace. I've been told the grey-green dome was the first and perhaps the only thing he saw: it had "PALESTINE SHALL OVERCOME" [*PALESTINE VAINCRA*] painted on it in huge white letters. . . . Nowhere in the world seemed safe from the terrorists: the Paris Opéra, haunted by both Fantomas and, in its cellars, by the Phantom, was now haunted in its attics by the fedayeen. The brief warning lasted a long while despite rain and sun, and despite orders from Pompidou. He must have laughed.
>
> But twenty times or more on the grey walls of Paris, near the Opéra and elsewhere, I saw Israel's answer to PALESTINE SHALL OVERCOME. Sprayed on hastily, unobtrusively, almost shyly, it read: "Israel shall live" [*Israël vivra*].[73]

Narrated some one hundred pages into the book, this scene is recalled in the midst of Genet's account of the demolition of his ill-fated fort in

Damascus, in the closing pages of *Un captif amoureux*. Without warning, Genet's account of mandate Syria "cuts" to the graffiti battle evoked above: "The distance between 'PALESTINE SHALL OVERCOME' and 'Israel shall live' is that between a sword blow and a bud." The French janissaries and the Israelis wield the scepter that cuts down the grass of Palestine, but this grass only grows stronger, penetrating into the fissures of the fort until "the prison [is] ruined."[74]

Although Genet does not mention this in his memoir, one of the boldest actions of the CSRP took place the day of King Hussein's visit to the Elysée Palace, on July 23, 1971—the same state visit narrated in the opening pages of *Un captif amoureux*. Outraged by the "Butcher of Amman's" renewed assault on the fedayeen less than a year after the massacres of Black September, a core group of CSRP activists and Maoist militants headed to the Jordanian embassy in the swank neighborhood of Neuilly-sur-Seine and threw Molotov cocktails at the building, setting it ablaze. As they fled the scene, they took the time to hang a Palestinian flag on the gates of the embassy, and then quickly dispersed. Christian Riss, a Maoist activist, was shot in the chest by a police officer. Others were detained and interrogated in the days following the incident. Although the attack on the Jordanian embassy was not, according to militants, a success—some even credit it with the eventual dissolution of the CSRP—it marks, in spectacular fashion, the symbolic role of the Palestinian Revolution in the French antiracist movement.

As we have seen in chapter 1, Palestinians and Israelis were not writing on the domes, walls, and palisades of Paris; pro-Palestinian and pro-Israeli activists were. Genet, for his part, wrote on a page from which Europe had been erased. That a monument of the capital of imperial France should be "haunted" by the fedayeen in the final pages of Genet's posthumous memoir serves as a striking reminder of the persistence of the Palestinian question in postcolonial France. Like the battle of the palisades in "La nuit venue," the Opéra scene in *Un captif amoureux* stages Palestine as rallying cry for the antiracist movement that was emerging from within the ranks of migrant workers in postcolonial France. If "La nuit venue" poked fun at the facile symbolism of political identities—Lumumba and Palestine for migrant workers, hammer and sickle or Celtic cross for French militants—Genet's admonition against the dangers of identity have proved prescient in ways even he could not have foretold. In the discursive free-for-all that is contemporary French politics, anti-immigrant activists have become the unlikely heroes of the "decolonization" of France.

While Genet was writing his memoir, a new generation was mobilizing around the battles fought by migrant workers in the 1970s. The "quarter-Arab" train passengers speaking *verlan* in Genet's ode to the language of his down-and-out Paris years would, in the 1980s, take up the question of Palestine, as well as the figure of the "Indian," within the emerging antiracist movement founded by the children of Maghrebi migrants to France. In many ways a continuation of the movement for migrant rights launched in the 1970s, the movement that crystallized around the 1983 Marche pour l'égalité et contre le racisme marked the entry of *antiracism* into the lexicon of French republicanism, with both salutary effects and unexpectedly troublesome outcomes. Indeed, if the CSRP was met with a combination of indifference and outright hostility when it was founded, the so-called Beur movement has been subjected to subtle forms of political recuperation from the outset, and not only by the well-meaning liberals who repackaged antiracism as a plea for tolerance. As we will see in the next chapter, which begins with the 2013 republication of an antiracist novel by the alt-right, indigeneity has become an explicit arena of struggle in the battle of "natives" against nativists.

CHAPTER 3

The Contest for Indigeneity in Postcolonial France

On the Republication of *Farida Belghoul's* Georgette!

Whither Antiracism?

For decades a commonplace of liberal *bien-pensance,* antiracism has taken on an acute sense of purpose and urgency in twenty-first-century France. Grassroots initiatives like the Parti des indigènes de la république (PIR) and, more recently, the Comité vérité et justice pour Adama (Truth and Justice for Adama Committee) have grown in visibility in the wake of spectacular acts of police violence against "populations hailing from the colonies," in particular young Black and Arab men.[1] These movements have restored to the term *antiracism* the radical edge it acquired during the popular protests against racist violence organized by the CSRP and other militant migrant rights movements in the 1970s and 1980s. Indeed, one of the salutary effects of twenty-first-century activism is that it helps reactivate a decades-long archive of antiracist militancy in France. The work of migrant rights activists in the fields of radio (Radio Assifa, Radio Soleil, Radio Beur), journalism and audiovisual media (Agence IM'média), music (Carte de séjour, Ministère des affaires populaires, Rocé), and theater (Al Assifa, La Kahina) are finally receiving the attention they deserve, thanks in part to the archival efforts of artists and activists like Mogniss Abdallah, Hajer Ben Boubaker, and Bouchra Khalili. As I suggested at the close of chapter 1, the mass migrations of the 2010s have accelerated a belated interest in the history of antiracist activism.

At the same time, the refusal to contend with the violent histories that have produced the racially stratified society that is contemporary France—slavery, colonial rule, forcible displacement, and the opening and closing of borders according to the whims of the labor market—continues unabated. If anything, French civil society is more polarized today than it was in the aftermath of the Algerian War of Independence, when the far-right *ultras* were a strident minority, albeit one that helped launch a powerful nativist movement in postcolonial France. If the 1980s witnessed the institutionalization of antiracism, relegated to the abstract humanist notion of tolerance enshrined in the slogan of the Socialist Party–backed SOS racisme, "Touche pas à mon pote" (Hands off my pal), antiracist activists are now accused of importing U.S.-style identity politics, when it is not "islamo-gauchisme" (Islamo-leftism) or "anti-white racism." The thirty-year anniversary of the 1983 Marche pour l'égalité et contre le racisme—rebranded Marche des Beurs in the press—became the occasion to mark both the consecration of tolerance as a fundamental value of the French Republic and the paradoxical recuperation of the rhetoric of anticolonialism and antiracism from the most unlikely quarters: the nativist right.[2]

One of the remarkable features of the new anti-immigrant discourse that emerged in the 1970s, and has only grown stronger since, is the recuperation of *indigeneity* it relies on. If, as we have seen, the legal category of the *indigène* (native) was forged at the colonial frontier, the notion of indigeneity paradoxically returned to the metropole in the guise of *nativism:* the claim that only those with ancestral roots in France can be French. Decolonization, I argue, is the pivot that enabled this appropriation of indigeneity-as-nativism. With the demise of the French empire in 1962, French settlers, many of them born in the colonies, made their definitive return to France. According to a belated nativist logic, colonial migrants—freshly minted nationals of a sovereign nation-state—were no longer welcome in the metropole. Or, to paraphrase anti-immigrant discourse from the Nouvelle droite (New Right) that emerged in the late 1960s to the *identitaires* of the 2010s: we left Algeria, now you leave France. The refusal to acknowledge the colonial roots/routes of migration—that is, the refusal to historicize the migrant question—is one of the principal tactics of the nativist right, including the media enterprises of the French alt-right, to which I turn in the following section.[3]

In this chapter, I track the paradoxical recuperation of antiracist discourse in anti-immigrant circles through a particularly telling case study: the republication, in 2013, of a Beur novel by one of France's most influential alt-right ideologues, Alain Soral. Published in 1986 by

Farida Belghoul, a figurehead of the antiracist movement launched by the French-born children of North African immigrants, *Georgette!* has garnered an improbable and belated following within nativist circles in twenty-first-century France. Ironically, one of the most vocal critics of the recuperation of the Marche pour l'égalité et contre le racisme briefly turned into the *Arabe de service* (token Arab) of the nativist right, in an unwitting demonstration of the contest for indigeneity in postcolonial France. An eloquent example of the blurring of the left-right paradigm that until recently governed our political lives, the Belghoul case offers a dire warning about the risks inherent in the co-optation of indigeneity as an articulation of origin (we were here first) rather than critique (we are here because you were there). As we will see, the recent recuperation of Belghoul's novel is based on a tendentious misreading of indigenous critique as *nativism.*

Recuperating Antiracism

In 1986, Farida Belghoul published *Georgette!,* one of the first novels by a French writer of Maghrebi origins.[4] The author of two experimental documentary films and a founding member of Radio Beur, Belghoul was already known, at the time of publication, as an antiracist activist. In 1984 she helped launch Convergence 84, a mass mobilization to mark the one-year anniversary of the Marche pour l'égalité et contre le racisme, the event that put an entire generation of Maghrebi French youth on the political map, and the question of postcolonial racism on the national agenda. The rousing speech Belghoul delivered at the demonstration's final rally in Paris turned her, briefly, into an icon of the grassroots antiracist movement of the 1980s. It also coincided with the rise of the Socialist Party–backed association SOS racisme, which introduced its famous yellow hand and the slogan "Touche pas à mon pote" at Convergence 84. While Belghoul and her comrades continued to organize in the fields of culture and community associations, SOS racisme began its rapid ascent in left-leaning media circles, subtly replacing the protestors' intransigent demands for equal rights with "le droit à la différence" (the right to difference), a plea for diversity that has cruelly backfired with regard to both French universalism and the new forms of culturalist racism the *marcheurs* were combating in the first place. As a figurehead of the grassroots antiracist movements of

the 1980s, Belghoul's short-lived fame thus coincides with the beginning of a decades-long recuperation of antiracism by center-left parties
and associations in France. Paradoxically, her work has also been recuperated in recent years by the nativist right, which has managed to
market *Georgette!* as a warning against the perils of immigration.

Georgette! was largely forgotten until its recent rediscovery by *la
fachosphère,* the blogosphere of the French alt-right.[5] In 2013, the conspiracy theory-driven polemicist Alain Soral published a new edition
of *Georgette!* under the label of his evocatively alliterative press Kontre
Kulture, presenting the novel as a cautionary tale about "the human
and psychological drama of immigration," which, he explains, "is always an uprooting, a violence"—for migrants, of course, but also for
those who "welcome" them. Remarkably, Soral manages to turn what,
attending to the psychic dimensions of migration, Abdelmalek Sayad
called the "suffering of the immigrant" into a pseudo-humanitarian argument for closing the doors of France.[6] Soral's intentions are clear from
the video presentation of the novel, which splices in footage of Olivier
Besancenot of the Nouveau parti anticapitaliste (New Anticapitalist
Party) speaking to undocumented African migrants at a *sans-papiers*
strike: immigration may "turn on [*faire bander*] globalists [*les mondia-
listes*] and the far left," but it is good neither for immigrants nor for their
hosts.[7]

Equally if not more puzzling is Belghoul's apparent endorsement of
Kontre Kulture. After countless hours scouring Belghoul's and Soral's
websites and social media accounts, I have yet to find a statement by
Belghoul condemning her appropriation by the alt-right. On the contrary, it is still possible to find evidence of her complicity in this operation, although many of the videos in which she appears have been taken
down. I will say more, below, about Belghoul's unexpected *virage à droite*
(rightward turn). For now, let me just mention Soral's video presentation of the novel, which includes a decontextualized clip of Belghoul explaining, in a recent video I will return to later, that the title "Georgette"
was, for her, a way to say "j'rejette" ("I reject," a near homophone of
Georgette in colloquial speech)—an ambiguous statement that Soral exploits to suggest, through montage, that immigrants are incapable of
assimilating. Superimposed on the video of Soral presenting the novel
from the comfort of his signature red couch is a photograph of Soral
giving a radiant Belghoul a thumbs-up on the occasion of her Quenelle

FIGURE 6. *"Alain Soral presents:* Georgette!, *by Farida Belghoul." Soral discusses Belghoul's novel on his signature red couch, a Quenelle d'Or trophy visible behind him. Screenshot of video posted on Kontre Kulture's YouTube channel. September 12, 2018.*

d'Or, an alt-right prize given to her by someone who has been cropped from the photograph: Dieudonné M'bala M'bala, a hugely popular co-median who has built his career on controversy, most notably in a series of provocative skits on Israel and frankly anti-Semitic skits on Jews, and in his intentionally equivocal statements on terrorism.[8] A parody of the Oscar trophy, arms rearranged to make Dieudonné's signature *quenelle* gesture, the gilded figurine Belghoul holds in her hands—also visible in the video behind Soral, who has earned multiple Quenelles d'Or—is awarded annually to a person whose anti-establishment profile is wor-thy of Dieudonné's attention (Figure 6). If the most obvious, crass mean-ing of the *quenelle* can loosely be translated as "up yours," critics—and some admirers—have also seen in it a not-so-subtle inversion of the Hitler salute, an interpretation Dieudonné has not worked very hard to refute. How did the tragic tale of a second-generation French-Algerian child become a weapon in the arsenal of the French alt-right?

This chapter tackles the recuperation of grassroots antiracism in France, paying particular attention to the ways in which anti-immigrant groups have succeeded in co-opting anticolonial and anti-racist discourses to their own ends. Particularly worrisome are the ways in which the nativist right has weaponized diversity and racial difference against immigration and multiculturalism, launching campaigns against "counter-colonization" and, more recently, "anti-white racism." Equally troubling is its instrumentalization of pro-Palestinianism, which has become synonymous in France—perhaps even more so, as I write, than in the United States—with anti-Semitism, and which is indeed reduced to an overtly anti-Semitic "competition of victimhood" in Dieudonné's skits, as I will discuss below. At the antipodes of the CSRP, the *marcheurs,* and the antiracist activists that are the object of this book—all of whom are very intentional in distinguishing pro-Palestinianism from anti-Semitism—Dieudonné, Soral, and the later Belghoul exemplify the co-optation of pro-Palestinianism to anti-Semitic ends in twenty-first-century France. Before reading *Georgette!,* against Soral, through the lens of indigenous critique, I briefly sketch out the trajectory that turned Belghoul into a darling of the French alt-right.

From Convergence 84 to Route de la Fidélité

As a figure of both antiracism and archconservative activism, Belghoul defies the categories that too neatly carve out the social and political field in France: right versus left, racist and antiracist, progressive and reactionary. Hailed in the 1980s as the face of Convergence 84, Belghoul is best known today as an outspoken critic of the implementation of "gender theory" in French schools: an ongoing state-led effort to promote gender equality and combat sexism and homophobia from preschool to high school.[9] It is not a coincidence that Belhgoul emerged as a heroine of social conservatism in 2013, the year that marked the thirty-year anniversary of la Marche pour l'égalité et contre le racisme. Invited to speak about her experience organizing Convergence 84, Belghoul used this new public arena to mobilize, not against racism, but against "l'éducation à la sexualité" ("sexual" rather than "sex" education) in the French school system. As I detail below, Belghoul's trajectory from antiracist activism to a conspiracy-theory-inflected social conservatism is what made possible the paradoxical recuperation of *Georgette!* by the nativist right.

After publishing *Georgette!,* Belghoul retired from public life and began teaching French and history in a technical high school in the *banlieue* of Paris. She made her return to the public stage in 2008, when she took her three children out of school and established a short-lived homeschooling organization, Remédiation éducative individualisée à domicile (Individualized Educational Remediation at Home) to combat illiteracy in *les quartiers populaires* (working-class neighborhoods).[10] Initially pitched as a grassroots effort to palliate the insufficiencies of national education in the *banlieue,* Belghoul's organization now bills itself as a socially conservative alternative to a school system portrayed as dangerous to children. In 2013, in the context of massive resistance to gay marriage—signed into law in May 2013—Belghoul launched the Journée de retrait de l'école (JRE; Day of Withdrawal from School), a campaign to boycott schools to protest the implementation of a curriculum promoting "equality between girls and boys."[11] The JRE quickly propelled Belghoul to internet stardom. In October 2013, Soral released a forty-minute televised interview on the website of his organization, Égalité & réconciliation (Equality & Reconciliation, hereafter E&R), in which Belghoul warns viewers that their children are being "turned LGBT" under the pressure of a powerful lobby that has replaced the mission of the national school system, "liberté, égalité, fraternité," with a new anthem, "athée, illettré, LGBT" (atheist, illiterate, LGBT).[12] Belghoul has continued to denounce the "LGBT lobby" and its nefarious effect on French families of diverse origins, most recently as part of her Route de la fidélité (Road of Fidelity) pilgrimage to the crypt of the Seven Sleepers, a Christian–Muslim pilgrimage first undertaken by the Orientalist Louis Massignon in the 1950s.[13]

From Convergence 84 to Route de la fidélité, from antiracist films and novels to ultraconservative advocacy: Belghoul is in no way exemplary of the grassroots antiracist movements I am documenting in this book. Yet her idiosyncratic itinerary is symptomatic of the ways in which antiracist discourse has been co-opted and distorted by social forces that are not only archconservative but often openly racist. Her trajectory from antiracism to social conservatism and her rapprochement with the French alt-right have, if anything, made it easier for the likes of Soral to delegitimize antiracism entirely. Soral's promotional video for *Georgette!* offers a master class in this particular form of recuperation, starting with the unattributed interview in which Belghoul claims that "Georgette is also a way for me to say 'I reject.' And what did I reject at that time? I rejected the France . . . that had turned us into children of immigrants, children robbed of their own history, and represented . . . as marionettes that could be manipulated."

Notwithstanding the incipient paranoia in the final clause, viewers versed in the history of the migrant rights movement will understand that Belghoul is taking aim here at French republican universalism and the assimilationist imperatives imposed upon France's former colonial subjects. Those invested in a dehistorized, culturalist understanding of immigration will glean a different message from Soral's video. The tracking shots of striking African *sans-papiers* spliced with interviews with center-left and far-left politicians vaunting the merits of French hospitality make it clear that Soral is not using Belghoul's statements to incriminate the unacknowledged racism of the French state, but rather to warn against the perils of immigration for the host society.

In addition to decontextualizing Belghoul's indictment of republican France through montage, Soral's video fails to provide the context in which she made these comments, a context that further explains how an antiracist novel made it in *la fachosphère:* Belghoul's crusade against "gender theory." Although Belghoul's video on the "sexual education" of children in French schools, also published on Soral's website, does not include the "j'rejette" excerpt, Belghoul's attire, the background of the video, the camera angle, and the image quality clearly show that the "j'rejette" segment is from the same video interview. Halfway through her disquisition on the perils of sex education and gender theory, Belghoul speaks proudly of her father, "a formerly colonized, illiterate Kabyle immigrant" who told her every morning before she set out for school that she should listen to the teachers ("écoute-les"), but not believe them ("ne les crois pas"). Readers of Belghoul will recognize this vignette from *Georgette!,* in which this scene serves to underscore the limits of the discourse of assimilation—disseminated, in large part, via a purportedly egalitarian educational system—rather than question the merits of the protagonist's education. Georgette's father wants her to succeed in school, without losing her culture or her religion. Georgette, for her part, just wants to fit in. The failure of the French national school system to promote genuine equality for all French pupils, regardless of their origin, is what drives Georgette to her untimely death, not the incompatibility of her home culture with republican values.[14] In a remarkably selective rereading, Belghoul cites her own novel to convey her deep-seated mistrust of French national education—this time, on the grounds of its corrupting influence. Soral, for his part, surreptitiously frames Belghoul's statement as proof of migrants' reluctance to assimilate. To different ends, Belghoul and Soral redeploy *Georgette!* for their own purposes: in the first, a scene dramatized in the novel is resignified to denounce the degeneracy of the French school system; in the second, a decontextualized statement by Belghoul serves to warn Soral's viewers against the perils of welcoming unassimilated immigrants who "reject" national education.[15] Without conflating Belghoul's current agenda with Soral's, it is undeniable that her espousal of conservative causes has made her palatable in alt-right circles in ways that are simply unimaginable for her former comrades in the antiracist struggle.

Belghoul has also helped cement the notion that advocacy for Palestine is synonymous with anti-Semitism, most visibly after her association with Dieudonné, best known for inviting Holocaust denier Robert Faurisson to share the stage with him on multiple occasions. On June 21, 2013, Dieudonné bestowed a Quenelle d'Or on Belghoul (the one she is holding in that photograph) for another video interview with E&R, in which she blames not only SOS racisme, the Socialist Party–affiliated organization founded in 1984, but also the Union des étudiants juifs de France (UEJF; Union of Jewish Students of France) for the co-optation of the Beur movement.[16] Though Belghoul has since distanced herself from both Dieudonné and Soral, her numerous video appearances present ample evidence of her dubious political positions.[17] Proud of her Kabyle ancestry and Muslim roots, allied to some of the most conservative Catholic groups and far-right actors in France, Belghoul frequently denounces the "Zionist lobby" in France in terms that amalgamate anticolonial anti-Zionism and a centuries-long tradition of anti-Semitic conspiracy theories.[18]

Belghoul's case is fascinating in part because she does not correspond to the "good Muslim" figure Mahmood Mamdani and others have analyzed as being essential to the clash of civilizations discourse that has structured representations of Islam in the West for the past thirty years.[19] Unlike prizewinning Algerian novelists Boualem Sansal and Kamal Daoud, Belghoul is not a champion of anticlerical secularism against an Islam viewed as antithetical to the principles of Western democracy: the separation of church and state, freedom of expression, and gender equality.[20] On the contrary, Belghoul places her religious identity front and center and claims to speak for Muslims and Catholics

alike. Her immigrant origins have helped establish her street credibil-
ity in the alt-right milieus she frequents, validating the positions she
now holds as representative of a number of French Muslims. The paradoxical result of this strange alliance is that one of the most prominent
activists of the 1980s, who fought against the climate of racism fueled
by the Front national, an overtly ethnonationalist party born out of the
bloody battle to preserve French Algeria, has become a darling of nativist groups nostalgic for *la plus grande France,* and in particular, France's
prized colony, her father's native Algeria.

Contrasting Soral's recuperative politics with the anticolonial antiracist movements that emerged in the wake of decolonization and continue to mobilize around racial discrimination, police brutality, and
structural inequality, I argue that what is at stake in the recuperation of
antiracism by the nativist right is a contest over *indigeneity* in postcolonial France. Where Soral strategically co-opts a Beur novel to demonstrate the perils of migration and multiculturalism, antiracist activists
redefine indigeneity to signify not who was here first—and attendant
appeals to collective memory and identity—but who has a right to be
here, and why. In the section that follows, I read *Georgette!* through the
lens of indigenous critique, against nativist recuperations of the novel.

"Inzians" Don't Live in France . . .

Belghoul is not simply a YouTube polemicist. She is also a writer, one
whose work resists the uses to which it has been put. The tragicomic
tale of a seven-year-old girl who is ridiculed for "walking like an Arab"
and imagines herself instead as "une indienne [*sic*]," an American Indian
woman at war with her (post)colonial oppressors, *Georgette!* is one of
the first literary case studies in what we might call *transindigenous
identification* in Beur literature.[21] The figure of the Indian is not inci-
dental to the deconstruction of racial discourse in *Georgette!* On the
contrary, the critique of racism delivered in the novel hinges on identification with indigenous Americans.

Reading between the lines of the child narrator's perspective, what
emerges is a complex and often bitingly funny critique of ordinary
racism. The novel unfolds over the course of a single school day, interrupted by the narrator's thought associations and memories of episodes
in her family life. The central conflict that propels the narrative to its

tragic end occurs in the classroom, when the teacher chastises her pupil for failing to complete her work, because she opens her notebook "the wrong way" (29). Through a series of flashbacks, we learn that the narrator's father modeled a sentence for her to copy in her notebook, from the Qur'an, that is, from right to left. This scene is the first in a series of misunderstandings between the narrator and her teacher—over the ink-blot on her hands, the state of her backpack, her reluctance to answer when spoken to—that lead the little girl to run away from school. After an encounter with a kindly elderly woman who asks her if she would write letters on behalf of her absent sons, Pierre, Paul, and Jean (which the narrator imagines signing with the equally French name Georgette), she runs off again and is hit by a car. "J'étouffe au fond d'un encrier" (I am suffocating at the bottom of an inkwell) are her last words, marking her death with the stamp of writing (163).[22]

Given that Belghoul's post-Convergence activism has centered on what she considers to be a failing, degenerate school system, the fact that the primary arena of her first and only novel is an elementary school bears some discussion. There are, in fact, a number of clues that tie this early Beur novel to what has become the author's principal focus, including the notions of decency and shame surrounding the bodies of children. The narrator is proud not to be a "pisseuse" (pisser), unlike "Bernadette [qui] tient son zizi dans une main. Elle a pas honte cette fille de se toucher devant la classe!" (Bernadette [who] is holding her privates in her hand. Shame on her for touching herself in front of the class! [54]). And yet it is important to insist that *Georgette!* is a novel, one that is narrated not by an adult crusading against "sexual education" at school, but by a seven-year-old girl who is highly aware of the ways in which her body is made legible to the world. Whereas the narrator describes herself as "une fille la plus propre" (a most cleanest girl) as opposed to her "disgusting friends" who "pee and poo in their pants" (55), she shares with them other physical disorders, albeit metaphorically. One of her classmates was born with cleft hands ("I squeeze my neighbor's rotten fingers in my hand" [12]), while Mireille, her closest friend, has a lisp ("a maggot in her mouth" [37]). When, to her horror, the narrator realizes that she has dipped her fingers in the inkwell, she stuffs her hands in her pockets, and is unable to take them out when the teacher tells her to retrieve her backpack: "I'm handicapped and she's helping me!" (28). Mortified about the notebook incident ("je suis déshonorée à vie" [I'm dishonored for life]), she regrets that she hails from "a family of blindmen!" (58). Unable to follow the lesson, incapable of explaining the misunderstanding about the notebook, she describes herself as "deaf" and "dumb" (64, 68).

Bodily excrements and physical handicaps are metonymically linked, in the novel, to the narrator's experience of racialization. Mireille, the little girl with a lisp, is the one who tells the narrator that she "walks like an Arab." The narrator is outraged (clearly, she understands *Arab* to be an insult): she is proud of her demeanor, but considers that she walks "comme un vieux" (like an old man). Her disappointment is especially cruel because she had given her friend a secret trick to get rid of her lisp: spit on the ground three times and then squish the maggot that fell out of your mouth with your feet. In the scene I will focus on in my reading below, Mireille calls the narrator "peau rouge" (69, redskin). Later, Mireille confesses that she "knows" her friend is "une inzienne" (an inzian) because her mother asked her who taught her to act like a "petite çauvaze" (a little zavage). When Mireille asks what a savage is, her mother is unable to come up with a satisfactory definition: "a savage is a savage." To which Mireille replies: "An inzian, for example? . . . I know one!" Her mother accuses her of lying, and Mireille explains to her incredulous friend: "Soi disant que les inziennes vivent pas en France! Ze le sais bien, moi que tu vis ici!" (As if inzians didn't live in France! But I know you live here! [78–79]). Mireille already "knows" that Indians are savages. She also "knows" how Arabs walk: the first-generation migrant is hunched over his work or hugging the walls (*raser les murs* also means staying out of sight), as the narrator does, circling the play yard until recess is over.

This dialogue between Mireille and the narrator follows the second example of racial interpellation in the novel. In this scene, the teacher asks the class whose turn it is to go to the blackboard. The narrator knows she is up, but she cannot find the little red pot that was placed on her desk to designate her. Mireille gets up to retrieve it from under her desk, and cracks a joke: "C'est rigolo, z'donne le pot rouze à une peau rouze!" (That's funny, I'm giving the red pot to a redzkin!). The teacher calls the class to order, asks Mireille to save her little secrets for later ("elle a pas entendu, soi disant!" [as if she hadn't heard!]), and tells the narrator to sit down: "I fall into my seat. I missed my turn! The pot is in my hand. It's not a red pot any more. I'll never call it that again. It's a yoghurt pot disguised as a terrible insult" (69–70).

Whereas the narrator rejected the racial nomenclature *Arabe,* she adopts the colonial identity *Indienne* as if it were her own. At recess, she circles the yard in the cold: "I drag myself around like a redskin. I'm walking like an indian! . . . I'm barefoot. Buck-naked [*à poil*] like the savages!" (71–72). Later, when the bell rings and the teacher asks the children to line up "en file indienne" (in single file), she imagines that is she is climbing a mountain, barefoot, to retrieve her horse, her long braid and colorful dress floating in the breeze: "I'm a savage. And I have to keep this secret forever" (116). The humiliation she feels when Mireille cracks the *pot/peau rouge* joke is due as much to her exposure, her forced coming out as Indian, as to her understanding of the racial slur itself: "How do you know I'm an indian [*une indienne*]? I never told you I don't like cowboys and that I like indians better! So how do you know?" In the confrontation that ensues, the notion of recognition, the epistemic violence of naming her *sauvage, indienne,* of outing her ("I know one!"), is what is at stake, more than the validity of the claim. Not surprising, then, that the narrator describes her "red skin" as "a mask" (77–78).

Few critics and commentators have given identification with indigenous Americans in *Georgette!* the central role that it deserves, despite the fact that the excerpt of the book given on the back cover of the first edition is taken from this extended scene of racial interpellation—a notable choice for a publication that would have been marketed as a Beur novel:

> I'm a little wild cat that doesn't see itself. I hide behind a mask on my face. Every morning I make myself look pretty and cute, I stick a red skin on my face. I walk to school, my red face is beautiful. It shines like a golden jewel. People are jealous of my beauty. They don't know it's a ruse. Behind it, I'm hiding a little beast [*un petit affreux*] with bloody claws, like the teacher's nails. I come up to the first kid who gets in my way, he thinks I'm beautiful, and then I take off the mask. He's so afraid he falls down. First I rip up his skin, then I kill him for good . . . I'm not drunk, I'm not telling a fake story. I have a mask of beauty on my face and it's a ruse of war. (77)

If the narrator is at war, it is because she is under attack: by her teacher, by her best friend and her best friend's mother, by her father's employer who tells him to "go home" if he's not happy (34), by passersby who throw trash in his face because "we pay you enough," by drivers who speed through puddles to spray him with dirty water (32–33), by neighbors who complain that the kids make too much noise at night (49), not to mention by the weight of a colonial past that continues to bear on her father, an indigent, illiterate recruit for the French economy (160).

What, then, makes this novel a prime candidate for Kontre Kulture? Soral's edition of *Georgette!*—subtitled "or the little girl without a name"—gives an altogether different snapshot of the novel on the back cover:

> Georgette! No one will answer this call, for Georgette is no one's name, not even the name of a little girl torn between two cultures and two traditions, between what she learns from her French schoolteacher and what she learns from her parents, uprooted immigrants who hold onto a plot of land in their home country [*au pays*] so they can be sure to find eternal peace when their time has come. Like her brand-new notebook, which changes directions—from Arabic to French—when she leaves home to go to school, this nameless little girl does not know who she is, caught between love and shame for some, admiration and hatred for the other. She is from neither here nor there, and so she seeks refuge between dream life and reality, in a world all to herself, a world she can master, where she can saddle a galloping horse at will, remove maggots, be a barefoot indian or a tiger in a little cat's body . . . Until reality catches up with her.

Torn between cultures, languages, and, it is implied, values ("what she learns from her parents"), unnamed and apparently without origins, full of love and shame for her own and hatred and admiration for the other—note the singular, abstract "other" that is the object of her animosity—the narrator is not an indigenous American warrior in this summary, but a lost child who seeks refuge in dream life and winds up dead ("reality catches up with her").

Ironically, the summary presented on the back cover of the Kontre Kulture edition of the book is in keeping with liberal readings of the novel, which present it as an allegory of postcolonial schizophrenia. As

Gil Hochberg has recently suggested, postcolonial readings of *Georgette!* as the tragedy of the immigrant caught between two cultures have paved the way for Soral's reductive recuperation of the novel.[23] But the Kontre Kulture edition goes further than this, subtly suggesting that migrants should go home by evoking the plot of land the narrator's father has kept in Algeria, and failing to mention that his son wants him to sell it. In the novel, the father's attachment to the homeland is foreign to his children, who are French even though they are the objects of a racializing, and often racist, gaze. If the narrator runs away from school, it is not because she "rejects France," as Soral's promotional video suggests, but because she is made to understand that she is a savage, an Arab, an Indian. The double portrait of a first generation nursing a hope for return and a second generation growing up French—"living here," like Mireille's imaginary Indians—is entirely lost on potential buyers browsing the list of Kontre Kulture titles, as is, of course, the central importance of indigeneity, not as the deluded fantasy of a nameless, uprooted child but as a political identity that continues to have resonance within antiracist movements in France.

To my knowledge, only two critics have dwelled upon the meaning of indigeneity in *Georgette!* In her nuanced reading of the visual metaphors of race in the novel, Laura Reeck analyzes the "mask of the red skin" as a mark of invisibility (covering over her Arabness) that nevertheless "[announces the narrator's] irrefutable and provocative presence in the visual field," and briefly speculates on the rhetorical links between Belghoul's novel and the PIR.[24] In an early study of Belghoul's novel, Mireille Rosello discusses a scene in the racial interpellation sequence (immediately following the confrontation with Mireille) in which the entire family is assembled in front of the television to watch a Western movie, hoping against hope the Indians will win (the narrator's father leaves the room before the end of the film, since he knows how it will end). Against the facile interpretation of the novel as an allegory for the identitarian *déchirement* of "second-generation" Maghrebi immigrants to France—the reading Soral will offer of *Georgette!* in 2013—Rosello argues that the narrator plays with ("declines," in Rosello's felicitous phrase) the stereotype of the bloodthirsty Indian in a complex deconstruction of stereotypes of Arabs.[25]

Building on Reeck's insight that the figure of the Indian is a proxy for race in the novel, and Rosello's reading of disidentification with the white heroes of Westerns, I propose that we read *Georgette!* as an early articulation of *indigenous critique* in postcolonial France: a multilayered, sophisticated, and increasingly controversial critique of pervasive forms of racism in France, including white nativism. By taking on the identity of an indigenous American, the narrator is claiming indigeneity in France. Or, to paraphrase Mireille when the narrator asks her how she "knows" she's an Indian: my mother says there are no natives in France, but you're a native, and you're here.

The Contest for Indigeneity

There is an important distinction to be made between the kinds of transindigenous identification that interest me in this book and the instrumentalization of indigeneity by someone like Dieudonné, who has recently come under fire by antiracist militants for stoking a "competition of victims" that has pitted the children of postcolonial migrants against Jews—many of them of colonial descent—in France.[26] One of the stakes of reading *Georgette!* against the novel's co-optation by the nativist right lies precisely in distinguishing between anticolonial and antiracist practices of identification and instrumentalist uses of "the suffering of the immigrant" or, in the case I discuss below, indigenous American struggles, to identitarian ends.

Given the widespread appropriation of indigenous American symbols for all kinds of political purposes, including advancing an anti-immigrant agenda, we ought to be particularly suspicious of Dieudonné's adoption of the feathered headdress—indelibly associated with "Indians" since the heyday of ethnographic photography and Western films—to advertise his 2018 stand-up comedy show *L'émancipation*, which delivers Dieudonné's usual cocktail of anti-establishment and anti-Semitic jokes[27] (Figure 7). Dieudonné has frequently pitted the figure of the Indian against other racialized figures, in particular Jews. In a skit titled "Le championnat de la victimization" (The championship of victimization), Dieudonné stages a four-way contest between Amerindians, Australian Aborigines, the African diaspora, and Israel (with Dieudonné playing all roles). After asking Elie Wiesel, spokesman for Israel in the skit, why he is also representing the Aborigine team—after a *différend* between Africans and West Indians, Wiesel will recuperate the cause of "black suffering" as well—the host invites the

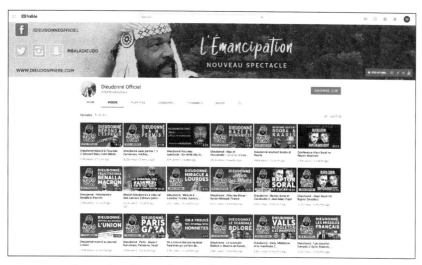

FIGURE 7. *Promotional image for Dieudonné's 2018 show* L'émancipation, *depicting the comedian in feathered headdress. Screenshot of Dieudonné's YouTube channel, Dieudonné Officiel. September 12, 2018.*

representative of the Amerindians to the stage. A charismatic leader who goes by the name of Morales, the Amerindian leader is disqualified after he veers off script to denounce the co-optation of the contest by Israel, shouting "Viva la Palestina!" to the thunderous applause of Dieudonné's audience.[28]

A representative example of the conspiracy-theory driven anti-Semitism of Dieudonné's shows, "Le championnat de la victimization" is a parody of the competitive memory field described by Michael Rothberg, as well as a performance of it.[29] Indeed, memory is partly what Dieudonné is after. In a more recent sketch titled "Le devoir de mémoire" (The duty to remember, a phrase associated with Holocaust remembrance), Dieudonné tells his young interviewer, who is "preparing a thesis [*un mémoire*]" in journalism: "Je veux rien à voir avec cette histoire, d'accord? . . . Chacun sa mémoire. Je me démerde avec ma mémoire, tu te démerdes avec ta mémoire" (I don't want anything to do with this, OK? . . . To each his own memory. I'll take care of my memory, you deal with your own shit).[30] Ostensibly a send-up of Dieudonné's demonization in the press—the skit is part of his 2016 show *Les médias*

(The media)—this quid pro quo about the "duty to remember" (as opposed to the "thesis assignment" the young journalism student is preparing) perfectly captures the zero-sum approach to competitive memory: you take care of your memory, I'll take care of mine. Faced with the duty to remember the Holocaust, Dieudonné protests: "I wasn't even here for this whole memory business. We were in Africa!"

The irony here is that Dieudonné did "take care" of someone else's memory, by inviting Holocaust denier Faurisson for a surprise guest appearance in his 2008 show *J'ai fait l'con* (I screwed up). The 2016 skit in fact revolves around Dieudonné's controversial exercise of the freedom of expression (the topic his interviewer is writing her *mémoire* about), including, most glaringly, his Holocaust denial, which he manages to reiterate within the sketch by turning the tables on his interviewer ("What's the question, exactly?—The gas chambers.—So, what about them?—Well, did they, did they exist?—Oh, because you are having doubts, young lady?") and refusing to answer the question (he ad-libs a musical jingle instead, spelling it out for his ingénue interviewer: "didou didou dîîîîîîîîîî"). But Dieudonné's identitarian spin on memory (my memory versus your memory) also papers over his own instrumentalization of memories that are, in fact, not his own: the Palestinian cause, indigenous American history, and French antiracism, repackaged as rhetorical fodder for the alt-right entertainment business.

Benjamin Stora was one of the first public intellectuals to use the expression *guerre des mémoires* (memory wars) to speak of the conflicts between social groups who ostensibly share a past, yet claim competing versions of it.[31] A historian of the Algerian War who was born in Constantine and raised in France, Stora is frequently invited to share his thoughts on the "demand for memory," in the double sense of "need" and "claim," that emerged among second-generation postcolonial immigrants in the 1980s, a demand that has only made itself more pressing since. In his scholarship and public statements, Stora has focused on competing memories of the Algerian War of Independence, which has produced distinct and often mutually exclusive memories: those propounded by the Algerian or French state or, in France, by veterans, *pieds noirs* (repatriated settlers), Algerian immigrants, Algerian Jews, and most recently, *harkis,* Algerians who fought for France and were subsequently interned in camps in the French provinces. These conflicts over memory extend the colonial *différend* into the postcolonial era, re-litigating "un passé qui ne passe pas" (a past that refuses to pass), a past that continues to structure the present, from racial profiling to naturalization laws.[32]

I am tempted to situate Soral's racially tendentious co-optation of a Beur novel as a contemporary iteration of what Stora calls *memory wars,* or better yet as a war against memory, and in particular against the memory of the antiracist struggle in which Belghoul herself was deeply involved. At the same time, there is a risk—one that might best be described as tactical—in using a memory studies framework to speak of racism in these new, troubling configurations. For in the "devoir de mémoire" skit, Dieudonné is able to downplay and ridicule major historical events (slavery and genocide) through memory relativism (you have your memories, I have mine). This is also what has happened, on a smaller scale, with the recent history of antiracism. In his promotional video for the Kontre Kulture edition of *Georgette!,* Soral uses Belghoul to present antiracism itself as a memory, not an ongoing struggle, as a past subject to refutation rather than interpretation. Why should the French tolerate unassimilated, ungrateful immigrants who say "j'rejette" to the France that "welcomes" them? Belghoul's memory of antiracism is not only reframed to say the opposite of what she meant ("I reject the France that rejected me"), it is also written off as irrelevant, or at least secondary to present battles: against "gender theory," for example, or immigration. This is what enables Soral to speak in the same breath of the plight of the immigrant (Belghoul's painful memories) and the perils of African *sans-papiers* (the present threat to France), or to present a little girl's identification with the first modern colonial subject as a fantasy that will be her demise in a society that has forgotten why she was there in the first place.

So how do we convey the urgency of antiracist discourse for a public too quick to forget the colonial past and the ways in which it structures the present? How do we redeploy this discourse against its instrumentalization by the likes of Dieudonné and Soral? I have argued that, notwithstanding Belghoul's recent trajectory, *Georgette!* undermines the uses to which it has been recently put, exposing the colonial production of immigration (the export of cheap labor to the metropole) that is conveniently "forgotten" in the Kontre Kulture clip—which naturalizes the metaphor of French hospitality it ridicules in the video—as well as forms of racism that are structurally and rhetorically linked to the racial hierarchies of the civilizing mission. The narrator's identification with the figure of the Indian is the linchpin for the deconstruction of racist discourse in the novel. If her friend Mireille finally admits that "les z'inziens comme toi, ze les aime beaucoup" (inzians like you, I really like them), the narrator prefers her Indians savage—with their masks on and their claws out—because, in fact, the war is not over (89). To the injunction "chacun sa mémoire," she might retort: my memory is also your memory; I am here because you were there.

The literary and cultural output of the new generation of postcolonial citizens in 1980s and 1990s France, problematically ethnicized under the label *Beur literature,* similarly attests to a political claim to indigeneity in France. Where the narrator of *Georgette!* identifies with a heroine of anticolonial resistance to articulate a critique of postcolonial racism, other writers "hailing from the colonies" invoke Palestine to make sense of their experience as postcolonial subjects. Mohamed Rouabhi, the playwright I turn to next, does both, staging an encounter between an indigenous American and a Palestinian against the backdrop of urban rebellions in postcolonial France. In a playful subversion of the phrase *l'Intifada des banlieues*—a dehistoricized but ironically apt expression used in the media to link urban rebellions in the *banlieue* to foreign influences, in particular pro-Palestinianism and Islamism—Rouabhi's plays deploy transindigenous identification in a multidirectional critique of colonialism and racism across France, the United States, and Palestine.

CHAPTER 4

Subjects of Photography
Mohamed Rouabhi and the Colonial Cliché

Transindigenous Performance

In July 2000, the French-Algerian dramaturge Mohamed Rouabhi staged a play titled "El menfi" (The exile) in Ramallah, with a cast of some forty Palestinian and French actors. The play premiered in Paris six months later with a reduced cast: three months after the outbreak of the Second Intifada, only three Palestinian actors were able to travel to France.[1] This fraught context of production lends "El menfi" particular urgency in the story of natives against nativism, connecting anticolonial violence in Palestine–Israel to urban uprisings in postcolonial France at a time when the stakes of anticolonial solidarity felt particularly high. The Second Intifada signaled the end of an era of hope for a national solution to the Palestinian question. In France, it became a metonym for social unrest in *les quartiers populaires,* and a rhetorical weapon in an increasingly unapologetic Islamophobic climate stigmatizing "Arab-Muslim" French citizens as a fifth column undermining the French Republic from within. The events of 9/11 only exacerbated the decades-long relegation of French citizens of Maghrebi origins to their presumed ethnic-religious identity. In this context, "El menfi" was a timely, indeed urgent, intervention in both the Palestinian and migrant questions. But what makes this play especially interesting for my purposes is that it triangulates the France–Palestine connection via yet another settler-colonial context: the United States.

The product of a months-long Franco-Palestinian collaboration, "El menfi" begins and ends with the public recital of a Palestinian writer's memoir in a packed *banlieue* theater, against the backdrop of an urban uprising (in Arabic, *intifada*) raging outside the theater. Like the Beur militants of the 1980s, the youth protesting in the play are wearing *keffiyehs,* offering visual evidence of the iconic importance of Palestine for the descendants of France's colonial subjects. But "El menfi"

triangulates the relation between Palestine and France with a third figure of exile: the "Indian." As I argue below in my readings of Rouabhi's
Palestinian plays—"El menfi," *Les nouveaux bâtisseurs* (The new builders), and "Darwish, deux textes" (Darwish, two texts)—the performance
of colonial subjectivities across colonial contexts allows for a complex
articulation of antiracist critique, one that does not always correspond
to the unambiguous discourses articulated in protest literature or,
indeed, militant theater. It also gestures toward a Palestinian genealogy of transindigenous identification, which I explore in this chapter
and the next. As we will see, the figure of the Indian emerges from the
pages of Rouabhi's workshops with Palestinians, giving his Palestinian
interlocutors a sizable role in the triangulation of indigeneity that obtains in "El menfi" and in Rouabhi's subsequent work. Without indulg-
ing in a romantic vision of pro-Palestinian solidarity, Rouabhi's plays
illustrate the political stakes, as well as the risks, of transindigenous
performance: the theatrical representation of one colonial situation
(Palestine) on another (post-)settler-colonial stage (France, the United
States). They also draw attention to, and critique, the mediation of race,
and in particular the medium most closely associated with colonial representation and racial science: photography.

Like its cousin the *stereotype*, a *cliché* is a method and medium of
mechanical reproduction. In French, *un cliché* is also a synonym for
photograph. As scholars have documented, photography was, from
its beginnings, a race-making medium at the imperial frontier, a vehicle for the production and propagation of racial and ethnic identities.[2] Photography taught us to recognize Arabs, Jews, Moors, Turks,
Negroes, and Indians as discrete ethnoracial types. It also became one
the principal vehicles for the dissemination and consolidation of these
identities on a visual register. And yet, if photography is a medium that
produces race, it is also a medium that is subject to subversive remediation.[3] Drawing on Ariella Azoulay's writings on photography in the colonial contact zone, I argue that Rouabhi's plays stage indigenous critique through the subversive remediation of photography on, and for,
the stage. Against identitarian readings of Rouabhi's plays, I show that
their performance of photography is precisely meant to denaturalize
what I call the *colonial cliché*, in order to critique the production of the
indigène (the "native") via the colonial gaze.[4] But Rouabhi's transversal

approach to race does not entail collapsing France, Palestine–Israel, and the United States into one. Unlike the militants of the CSRP and the narrator of *Georgette!*, Rouabhi does not take for granted identification with Palestinians and indigenous Americans. In this sense, his plays elude the forms of identification that have proved so easily recuperable within anti-immigrant circles. The photographic encounter, I will argue, is what enables transindigenous identification against, and in spite of, naturalized racial identities.

Children of the Colonies

Born in Paris in 1965, Rouabhi discovered the theater almost by chance. At the age of fifteen, he dropped out of school and got a factory job to help his parents, Algerian migrants whose stories of combat, captivity, and exile would later serve as inspiration for his writings.[5] Eager to improve his diction, Rouabhi enrolled in the municipal theater conservatory of Drancy and fell in love with the theater: the texts first, then acting and directing. Recruited by the prestigious École nationale supérieure des arts et techniques du théâtre (ENSATT; National Insitute of the Arts and Techniques of Theater) at the age of twenty, Rouabhi became an accomplished actor, stage director, and author of some forty multimedia plays—most of them unpublished—on topics ranging from the HIV/AIDS crisis to domestic abuse, race in America, French colonial history, and the question of Palestine.

One of Rouabhi's first acting roles was in "The Story of Kufur Shamma," a play written by François Abou Salem (né François Gaspar) and Jackie Lubeck, cofounders, in 1977, of the East Jerusalem theater troupe El Hakawati (The Storyteller). The tableau of a forty-year saga to reunite all the surviving inhabitants of a destroyed Palestinian village, "The Story of Kufur Shamma" opened in the West Bank in 1987 and then toured in Europe, North Africa, Canada, and the United States.[6] The play was set to have its French premiere at la Cartoucherie, the legendary theater of Ariane Mnouchkine's Théâtre du Soleil, when one of the troupe's actors was denied permission to leave the West Bank. Still a student at ENSATT, Rouabhi was brought in as a last-minute replacement for the play's international tour. Over the course of a year and a half he performed with El Hakawati in the UK, Germany, Finland, Italy, Tunisia, and Egypt. In an hour-long interview in a café near the Gare du Nord, Rouabhi told me that the experience had been both exhilarating and disenchanting. Raised with legendary stories of the Palestinian Revolution, he found it thrilling to participate in an act of Palestinian cultural resistance. Yet he soon realized that he had been cast not only by virtue of his talent, availability, and enthusiasm but also because of his revolutionary credentials. The son of an Algerian *mujahida* (his mother was an FLN combatant) who was repeatedly told that he had an Algerian accent—he had spent countless hours listening to tape recordings to memorize his lines in Arabic, a language he could only access via his mother tongue, Darija—gave the play an imprimatur of authenticity, in Rouabhi's words, "une caution révolutionnaire" (revolutionary credentials).[7] When the troupe performed in the ruins of the amphitheater of Carthage, two months after the assassination of PLO leader Abu Jihad by Israeli agents in Tunis, the public gave Rouabhi, poised center stage in the full combat gear of a fedayee, a standing ovation. The Tunisian press congratulated this son of Algeria for devoting himself to the Palestinian cause, without once mentioning that the young actor had been born and bred in France. While his ability to pass as an authentic revolutionary was flattering, and confirmed the continued intensity of Palestinian-Algerian solidarity, it also felt staged to Rouabhi, overly caught up in the political rhetoric of Palestinian leadership and pan-Arab discourse. Increasingly uncomfortable with the highly orchestrated production of the play, he quit the troupe before it embarked on its North American tour.

More meaningful than his triumphant reception by the Arab press were Rouabhi's encounters with Palestinian refugees during the tour, in particular minors: London-based teenagers who had witnessed the siege of Beirut, refugee children in Stuttgart who dreamed of seeing a homeland they had never set foot in. The First Intifada was raging at the time, giving urgent relevance to the drama he was playing onstage. Between rehearsals and performances, Rouabhi began to think about writing a Palestine play of his own. In 1990, he started drafting the play that would be performed, and published, seven years later, *Les nouveaux bâtisseurs*. This first experiment in staging Palestine on the French stage falls short of the complex forms of transindigenous performance characteristic of Rouabhi's later plays. But it previews in interesting ways the question that animates "El menfi" and "Darwish, deux textes": how does one represent the colonized (Palestinians, indigenous

Americans) without reproducing the colonial cliché? As we will see, the remediation of audiovisual media, including film, sound recordings, textual projections, sign language and, most centrally, photography will form an integral part of Rouabhi's dramatic solution to this problem.

Like "The Story of Kufur Shamma," which imagines a destroyed Palestinian village, *Les nouveaux bâtisseurs* is a play about a place that has been removed from the field of visibility. Galmo, an international observer for an unnamed entity, wanders through the remains of a Palestinian village with his camera, addressing rock-throwing boys, bored café patrons, and a grieving elderly woman in stilted, overly formal Arabic—rendered, in the play, in flowery, obsequious French—in a frustrated attempt to locate his position on a brand-new, glossy map. A stand-in for the humanitarian expeditions that periodically attempt to document the destruction of Palestine by photographing the concrete ruins of Gaza or the uprooted trees of the West Bank, Galmo is unable to fulfill his mission. The village, he is told, does not figure on the map. All he finds in the place of milestones and monuments are ruins, abandoned houses, and a wasteland strewn with rocks. Accosted by a soldier who tells him he is not allowed to take photographs and that besides, "there is nothing to see," Galmo asks what he plans to do with "all these rocks." "I don't know. A wall, maybe," the soldier quips.[8]

When *Les nouveaux bâtisseurs* toured throughout France in 1997, it was met with mixed reviews. Negative coverage from the right-leaning press was to be expected.[9] More surprising was the resistance it drew from the Palestinians who were in the audience. Leila Shahid, who had surveyed the destruction of Sabra and Shatila with Jean Genet in 1982 and was now representative of the newly formed Palestinian Authority in France, took issue with the pessimistic tone of the play, and in particular the suggestion that Israel might build a wall to separate Jewish Israelis and Palestinians—a project that would begin in earnest five years later. The tone of the play did not accord with the heady days of Oslo and the hope that the First Intifada (*l'Intifada des pierres,* as it is dubbed in French) might pave the way for peace. Symbolically, the suggestion that the only material evidence of the destruction of Palestine, the rocks scattered across a barren no-man's-land in the final tableau, would be used to further ostracize Palestinians—literally, to wall them off—was too cruel for the Gazans in the audience, who rebelled against Rouabhi's dystopic vision in the Q&A after the play.[10]

And yet *Les nouveaux bâtisseurs* is not concerned only with de-struction. While its ambiguous title might ironically refer to the state built upon the ruins of Palestine, or the bricklayers recruited to build the wall separating it from Israel, the play also features other kinds of builders: a filmmaker, a novelist, a storyteller, a child who throws rocks but also makes drawings, Galmo the photographer, and of course, the theater troupe itself. This *mise en abyme* of representation is evidenced in the dramaturgy of the play. Here is how a contemporary critic de-scribes the play's *mise-en-scène*:

> Eight actors appear in the small window of a television set. An
> actress presents them to the public. You understand that they will
> be performing the play. Presently they leave the screen to come
> onstage. The theater is now a substitute for the image. From the start,
> the spectator is placed in the arena of play. A narrator announces
> the beginning of each scene and comments on the action. The actors
> use their skills to turn what could be a boring history lesson into
> a joyful creation. Some of them play center stage while the others
> look at them from the back of the stage, spectators of a fate they are
> witnessing.[11]

As is apparent from this description, the theater crew—the playwright, actors, and technicians—are the new builders of the play. And what are they building? A case not for the indictment of Israel—that is Galmo's mission—but for the existence of Palestine. As Rouabhi puts it in his preface to the published version of the play, theater is a way to repre-sent, through a simulacrum of traces, what has been removed from the domain of visibility:

> Everything in *Les nouveaux bâtisseurs* pertains to the theater, start-
> ing with convention. We speak about things the spectator does not
> see, because they have been erased from the stage or covered over
> by another reality that is recognizable, that is sometimes the *image*
> we have of it. But contrary to the effort to annihilate and erase the
> traces of a land existing *under* the land of the contemporary state
> of Israel—a land that this state tries at all costs to establish as a
> *reality*—the tools of the theater, the tools of poetry allow us to set
> out in a quest for these traces, these signs that are not visible to the

naked eye—we are not in the presence of an *image*—and to see that, far from being fossilized, we are talking about a living people, a people that is being buried alive.

Against the wasteland of the final tableau, the play mobilizes a wealth of documents attesting to the persistent presence of Palestine under the ruins: "There are all kinds of traces, affixed to all kinds of media: photographs, books salvaged from the fire, children's drawings, photo-copies, architectural plans, maps, a film being made, poems, testi-monies."[12] The theater, from the Greek *theasthai,* to contemplate or to behold, metonymically, an arena for viewing, offers a new mode of seeing Palestine.[13] In metatheatrical terms, *Les nouveaux bâtisseurs* also evidences something that is not legible in mainstream accounts of the Israeli-Palestinian conflict in France: the central place of the Palestinian question within the postcolonial antiracist movements that formed in the early 1970s, in the wake of May '68 and Black September. For the Palestinian question is not an exotic conflict in Rouabhi's plays. It is the sounding board for an extended critique of the legacies of colo-nialism and race-making in France.

One of the questions that puzzled critics of *Les nouveaux bâtisseurs* was the following: "Why Palestine?" This was not the play critics ex-pected from a Franco-Algerian dramaturge. When the play premiered in 1997, the First Intifada had been overshadowed by a more spectacu-lar news item, one that should have been, according to some of his critics, more pressing for Rouabhi: the Algerian Civil War, which had already killed scores of Algerian writers, playwrights, and journalists, as well as countless civilians. Even the most positive reviews of *Les nou-veaux bâtisseurs* evoke the war in some way, either by reading clues of the current violence unfolding in Algeria between the lines of Rouabhi's Palestinian play or, more directly, by asking him if he planned to write about Algeria next. Rouabhi's answers are understandably defensive: Why shouldn't an Algerian write about Palestine? But his rejoinders are also telling: he refuses to play the role of native informant for a French public avid for news from the former crown jewel of France's empire. If and when he writes about Algeria, he explains, it will be about Algeria's relationship to France, not its postcolonial debacles. "My parents are Algerian and I was born in France, at some point I'd like to approach the question from the perspective of this fraught double belonging."[14]

Perhaps in reaction to the expectation that he should write about Algeria, Rouabhi devotes the bulk of his preface to the published version of the play to the question "Why Palestine?" Titled "Enfants des colonies" (Children of the colonies), the preface anticipates the language that would be mobilized by the antiracist collective Indigènes de la république (Natives of the Republic) some ten years later. Born in France to Algerian parents who had until 1962 been colonial subjects of France, Rouabhi is not *issu de l'immigration* (of immigrant descent), as the children and grandchildren of migrants are metonymically dubbed. He is *issu de la colonisation* (of colonized descent). This is why, before he even names Palestine, Rouabhi recalls an event that constitutes proof of his paradoxical status as a postcolonial citizen of France: "In Paris it is forbidden to gather on October 17 under one of the bridges that crosses the Seine, in front of the police station, to summon the memory of the hundreds of victims of the anti-Algerian pogrom, most of them to this day uncounted, a gaping hole in the memory of fifty-five million citizens." More than thirty years after the bloodiest chapter of *la guerre d'Algérie* on metropolitan soil, the children of the colonies still cannot openly mourn their dead.[15] How, then, are they to negotiate their relationship to a country that has forgotten the conditions that brought them to France in the first place?

It is through this articulation of an agonistic postcolonial identity that Rouabhi introduces the parallel between Palestinian subjects of Israel and Algerian subjects of France, citing Mahmoud Darwish's poem "Bitaqat hawiya" (Identity card) to capture the paradoxical position of French citizens of colonized descent:

"Write on your papers, I am Arab," says a famous verse by Mahmoud Darwish. So I write, in French, on my papers that I am Arab.... The theme of the play lies in this reflection on the individual who is a stranger in his own country. My father would tell me: "Before I was Algerian, I was French." As for me, before I was French I was Algerian. There is an obvious analogy between the historical destinies of Arab peoples who have lived under occupation and colonization, a common quest for their identity, and that was my starting point: a more or less conscious process, for an Arab living in France, of writing a play that takes place in Palestine.[16]

The "more or less conscious process" by which Palestinians stand in for colonized Algerians and postcolonial French citizens requires some parsing. Like occupied Palestinians, Rouabhi's father was a subject, rather than a citizen, of France: an *indigène*.[17] His son, albeit a citizen, is likewise relegated to his origins and barred symbolic access to the Republic. In a radical articulation of transcolonial indigeneity, Rouabhi shows that racialization in postcolonial France—the perpetual designation of the children of the colonies as immigrants, and of French citizens of Maghrebi parentage as Arabs—is part of a larger history of the production of *indigènes,* from Algeria to Palestine. Speaking more than twenty years after the publication of *Les nouveaux bâtisseurs,* Rouabhi explains that Palestine was "a door through which I could return to Algeria"—a way to access the still taboo history of the Algerian War of Independence, including the memory of October 17.[18]

Dedicated to "my brothers in anger my sisters in love my fellow children of colonization born here . . . for the children of Palestine," *Les nouveaux bâtisseurs* excavates traces of Palestine for the children of France's colonies. The following year, Rouabhi would begin working on "El menfi," a play that explicitly tackles the fraught history of France-Algeria, but via a multidirectional critique of settler colonialism in Algeria, Palestine, and the United States. If Rouabhi was reluctant to address the Algerian Civil War in interviews about *Les nouveaux bâtisseurs,* this conflict would play an unexpected role in Rouabhi's second Palestine play. Unwilling to join the chorus of condemnations of Islamist violence in a postcolony still in the throes of violent wars of memory concerning the colonial past, Rouabhi instead relitigates another Algerian war, one that was raging some forty years earlier in Algeria, and also in France: *la guerre d'Algérie.* Traces, and the question of making visible, in the theater, a "living people" swallowed up in the rubble of colonial history, will play an important role in "El menfi," which remediates the colonial cliché through a photographic encounter between an indigenous American and a Palestinian refugee.

Workshops in Ramallah

In 1999, Nadine Varoutsikos, the director of la Maison du Théâtre et de la Danse in Épinay-sur-Seine, invited Rouabhi to write a play in collaboration with Épinay's sister city, Ramallah.[19] In May and June

1999, Rouabhi held writing workshops in Épinay, Ramallah, and East Jerusalem, working with school children, university students, incarcerated youth, and refugees. Upon his return to Paris, he began drafting the play that would premiere in Ramallah in July 2000, and in Épinay in January 2001: "El menfi (L'exilé)." Unlike Rouabhi's first Palestinian play, "El menfi" is the product of an extensive Franco-Palestinian collaboration, from the writing workshops, which required the services of three translators, to the typescript of the play, composed in French and translated into Arabic, and the performance of "El menfi" by a cast of some forty amateur French and Palestinian actors, including several of his students. Rouabhi's detailed account of the first writing workshop he held in the Occupied Territories, as well as several essays he wrote before and after his residency, attest to the generative nature of these Franco-Palestinian encounters. They also point to the limits and challenges of transindigenous identification, echoing some of Rouabhi's reservations about his casting in "The Story of Kufur Shamma." In particular, the inclusion of two characters, one elaborated in the course of the writing workshops and the other included against the better judgment of Rouabhi's Palestinian collaborators, exposes the complex processes of identification at work in two-way transindigenous exchanges. The final version of "El menfi" bears traces of both the potential and limits of transindigenous identification, withholding a simple narrative of anticolonial solidarity in favor of a multilayered critique of colonialism, racism, and identitarian violence. As we will see, the performance of transindigenous identification across denaturalized roles (Algerian, *banlieusard,* Palestinian, indigenous American) is precisely what makes possible indigenous critique as a political, rather than identitarian, process.

Starting in May 1999, Rouabhi began working with an eclectic mix of children and young adults, ranging from nine to twenty-three years of age: minor offenders in Al Sakakini Center, child refugees in Al Amari camp, Birzeit University students, and students at the French Cultural Center in Ramallah and the African Community in the Old City of Jerusalem.[20] The extensive notes taken by Rouabhi during and after the workshops, available as a typescript on the website of his theater company Les Acharnés, offer a candid view of the genesis of the play that would premiere in Ramallah in July 2000.[21] For the purposes of my argument, one detail stands out in the students' written work: the recurring mention of indigenous Americans as exemplars of anticolonial resistance. In a particularly succinct illustration of disidentification with another settler-colonial state, twenty-year-old Mayssa Salem, a student at the French Cultural Center in Ramallah, explains: "I hate the Americans as a poeple because they have no precise origin, they took the land from the real citizens (Indian's origins) and I feel that the USA was built like Israël, a country which is built on the massacre and killing innocent people" [*sic*].[22]

Salem's use of the word *origins* requires parsing here. On the one hand, Salem is claiming indigeneity, in the sense of first or prior occupancy, on behalf of indigenous Americans. Those we call Americans are not from the American continent; the "Indians" are. And yet I would argue that Salem's claim goes beyond a literal claim of originariness—analogous to debates over who was in historic Palestine first, the Jews or the Canaanites, and who can lay claim to sovereignty over the land in the twenty-first century—to articulate what I have been calling *indigenous critique:* a critique of the production of the *indigène,* from the Americas to Africa and Asia. Transindigenous identification, here, is based on disidentification with a nation-state founded, like Israel, on ethnic cleansing. Salem's condemnation of the United States is all the more striking because she had initially "rejected the parallel . . . between American Indians and her country," refusing the premise that Palestinians might be confined to reservations, or disappear altogether. By the time the workshop ends, she has appropriated the figure of the Indian in order to assert her continued presence in Palestine and "fight for the right to say that Palestine exists."[23]

The figure of the Indian appears again in the course of one of the most interesting writing exercises that was assigned to each group. Students were asked to choose one image from a selection of six to eleven photographic reproductions, describe the subject(s) it represents, and imagine their autobiography. Unlike previous questions about the personality, fears, dreams, and aspirations of the students—that is, questions about their identity—this question was an exercise in identification. Regardless of the photos they selected or the stories they told, students projected upon, identified with, or imagined themselves as another, even if, in most cases, this other was imagined to have a nearly identical life story. Writing about a photograph of two elderly people sitting on a bench, whom he imagines to have lost their home due to the occupation, a boy from Al Amari camp explains: "This place is Palestine because every place where there is an occupation is called Palestine."[24] Several children from Al Amari camp and Sakakini prison selected a photograph of a little girl standing alone in a desolate landscape, imagining her to be a Palestinian refugee or an orphan from Kosovo, Lebanon, or Albania, because her wretched life "is the life of all Muslims."[25] But if nearly all the photo-essays are based on identification with other Muslims or Arabs, one essay stands out by virtue of the imagined identity of the photographed subject.

Badawi Qawasmi, a twenty-year-old Birzeit University student who, like Mayssa Salem, would travel to Épinay-sur-Seine for the French premiere of "El menfi," chose to write about a close-up photographic portrait of an elderly man, his face angled *de trois quarts,* head held high, gaze cast downward, lips sealed in an upside-down smile (Figure 8). The photograph resembles the iconic clichés taken by photographers on the colonial frontier in the wake of the catastrophic conquest of North America. Though Rouabhi did not provide any captions or contextual information for the images, Qawasmi instantly recognized the photographic subject as an "American Indian."[26] Written in slightly ungrammatical but fluid English, Qawasmi's photo-essay reveals the close affinity he must have felt when he saw the face captured in the colonial cliché. For the photograph tells a story remarkably close to that of the occupied Palestinian:

irhamu 'azizan dhul [have pity on the beloved oppressed]
inspiritual leader
The face of an Indien-American tribe leader who was captured by the
   new comers
Sorrow and pain is reflected by his body language
Name: Anka Moka
Date of birth: 25/6/1826
Date of taking the photo: 25/6/1911
Place of taking the photo: downtown of the old Dallas city in one of
   the cowboys shack.

—

My story is the story of most Indien-American. We were living in peace and prosperity, our tribes we spread through the plains, hills

FIGURE 8. *Edward S. Curtis,* Lone Tree—Apsaroke, *1908. Photogravure plate. One of the photographs used by Mohamed Rouabhi during his 1999 theater workshops in Ramallah. Courtesy of the National Museum of the American Indian, Smithsonian Institution (080_F08_plate_143).*

and mountains of what we believed was our land. We had no borders, no prisons, no killing, and the only thing we thought about was
hunting and raising horses. Our civilization grew slowly and steadily
untill and at a sudden, we were confiscated from our freedom. These
new comers killed our children, stole all our possessions and most
importantly our freedom. Instead of setting down as a leader of my
tribe I am setting in the occupier's prison not knowing what is waiting for me out of this door.[27]

Like Salem's reluctant identification with the story of American colonization, Qawasmi's photo-essay captures the centrality of the figure of
the Indian in Palestine. Unlike Salem's categorical statements, however,
this text also requires us to reflect upon the mediation of indigenous
America in Palestine, and on the modalities of its translation into a
Franco-Palestinian play.

As discussed in the introduction and chapter 3, identification with
indigenous Americans is a trope common to Palestinian, Maghrebi,
and Franco-Maghrebi writers and activists. Qawasmi's autobiography
as an "Indian" activates some of the same romanticized stereotypes we
find in the writings of Farida Belghoul or Zahia Rahmani: an idealized
view of precolonial life, torn asunder by the violent intrusion of the colonizer. What interests me here, however, is the medium of identification:
photography and the photographic essay, based on a performance of
autobiography-as-imagined-other. Unlike the stereotype—a term that
derives from an early technology of mechanical image reproduction—
photography is a relational medium, involving photographer, photographed, and, as Ariella Azoulay argues in her remarkable analysis of
"photographing on the verge of catastrophe," the spectator.[28] According
to Azoulay, the photograph eludes authorship not because of its repro-
ducibility, but because of its relationality. The photograph is "always, of
necessity, the product of an encounter—even if a violent one—between
a photographer, a photographed subject, and a camera, an encounter
whose involuntary traces in the photograph transform the latter into a
document that is not the creation of an individual and can never belong
to any one person or narrative exclusively."[29] Qawasmi's appropriation
of a colonial-era photograph of an indigenous American participates in
what Azoulay calls the "citizenry of photography": a civil contract linking not only the imagined photographed subject ("Anka Moka") and

photographer (the "occupier"), but also the spectator (Qawasmi) in an unequal but potentially transformative relationship. Crucially, the photograph is not only a record of what "was there" and is no longer. It also addresses the spectator. The photographed subject speaks through the Palestinian student observing the image to address a grievance, in nonidiomatic English, to a community of empathetic spectators.[30]

To Azoulay's performative account of civil spectatorship—the kind of careful watching that makes possible an imagined citizenry of photography—we need to add an intermedial and transindigenous dimension: the remediation of spectatorship (Qawasmi's empathetic gaze) into a written grievance transposes indigenous dispossession into the terms of Palestinian occupation. For this ventriloquized account of colonization Palestinianizes the indigenous subject's experience by introducing a term, *the occupier,* not usually found in the context of Native dispossession and genocide. In this sense, it also beckons Qawasmi's gaze into the image, as if the spectator were not simply witnessing but also participating in the citizenry of photography. Qawasmi's "Indien-American" autobiography will find its way into "El menfi" in the mouth of a character whose name, Kawani, echoes that of its author, and whose photograph—which now includes a Palestinian spectator *within* its frame—will structure the play from beginning to end. The figure of the Indian will accompany the Palestinian protagonist of "El menfi" throughout the play, first as a colonial cliché and then as a spectral reminder of anticolonial resistance and endurance.

Enter the Colonial Cliché

A concatenated tableau of exilic encounters across the United States, France, Lebanon, and Palestine, "El menfi" is framed by the life story of John Walid Jaber. When the curtains open, Jaber's stenographer-turned-fiancée, Anissa, is reading his memoir in a packed municipal theater in the French *banlieue*. She turns the page, and the lights go out. The second scene, narrated by the adult Jaber and echoed, as we will see, in the play's conclusion, tells the "singular story" of his encounter-in-photography with a man named Kawani:

> My name is John Walid Jaber. When I was a boy something strange happened to me, and this event marked my childhood: I was kidnapped by a Pawani Indian. This was in New York, at JFK airport.

There was a photographer who would come up to people and ask them if they wanted to pose with a real Pawani Indian, if they wanted to bring back a souvenir photo of mythical America. I asked my mother for a dollar and sat down next to the real Pawani Indian. The man who was with him took the picture and then the Pawani Indian asked me if I wanted to hear a Pawani story, a story like no one tells them anymore, and I said yes.

Then he asked me to follow him and we left the airport, the Pawani Indian and I, and got into a black 1969 Buick with gold striped rims and we headed toward Southtown Avenue and then highway 927 and I can't remember how many hours or days we drove but it was dark when Kawani told me that we were in what used to be the land of the Pawani Indians.

Kawani and John stop at a gas station for coffee and donuts. The boy sees a newspaper lying on the counter and exclaims: "Oh look, that's you in the photo." The "souvenir photo" has been printed in the paper and now bears the double function of a missing child advertisement and wanted mug shot. But Kawani does not recognize himself in the colonial cliché:

KAWANI Why do you say that this, on this paper, is me?
JOHN, *child* Because it's true. That's you here and there it's me.
KAWANI I don't believe that I am on this paper. I'm speaking to you
    and my whole body is inhabited by life. . . . Look at my hands. My
    hands are alive, aren't they? This man on the paper does not have
    hands like mine. He has no arms and no legs and half of his face
    is missing . . . His hair is still, mine is animated isn't it? . . . I can
    speak, I can express myself, I can address this man on the paper
    if he is as alive as you say he is. But this man on the paper doesn't
    answer me. He is mute.

Against the partial, static, lifeless image presented in the photograph, Kawani evokes the living faces he has known, faces that bear the traces of the time that has engulfed his people and the imprint of the land that was theirs: "I have seen men with faces of all colors, faces of all shapes, faces wrinkled by time, grooved by time, the leather of their face pleated like the earth of our land, the land of the Pawani Indians."

Sitting at a gas station built on Pawani land, Kawani is interrupted by its new occupants:

> DOUG, *the gas station employee*
> Hey there old man why don't you stop pestering us with all that nonsense. Leave the boy alone would you.
> JOHN, *child* Tell me the story you promised me.
> KAWANI Your story has already begun. Come on, John, let's go. What do I owe you young man?
> DOUG Hey there Redskin [*Peau-Rouge*] I think I just asked you something.... Hang on a sec haven't I've seen you before ...
> KAWANI Hum hum
> DOUG, *grabbing a shotgun from under the counter.*
> Goddamn he's making fun of me hey Mike come on over here.
> KAWANI Put down your weapon.
> DOUG You're giving me orders now? ... I'm gonna skin you man [*je vais te faire la peau mec*]!
> MIKE Go on Doug, skin that Indian [*fais-lui la peau à c' t' indien*]![31]

Attested, according to the *Trésor de la langue française,* since 1850, the heyday of the conquest of the American West and of Algeria, the idiomatic expression *faire la peau à quelqu'un* (literally, to make someone's skin, figuratively, to kill them) offers uncanny evidence of the epidermic regimes of racialization operative in the quotidian racism of twenty-first-century encounters between "natives" and settlers, transposed, here, into another (settler) colonial tongue. The intrusion of a centennial racist gaze further raises the stakes of the photographic encounter between the indigenous American and Palestinian in this scene. For Doug's first interpellation—"haven't I seen you before?"—has a double valence: if he has seen Kawani before, it is not only because he has seen the photograph of the wanted child kidnapper in the newspaper, but also because he recognizes in that picture, and in Kawani himself, the cliché of the Indian popularized through the staged ethnographic photographs taken at the turn of the nineteenth century— the very sort of "souvenir photo of mythical America" that the airport photographer sells for a dollar to unsuspecting foreign tourists and, unwittingly, Palestinian refugees. But now John is in this picture too: a second racialized, occupied subject has entered the colonial cliché. The story of colonial racism told here is, as Kawani implies, also the story of Palestine: "Your story has already begun," Kawani tells John, sending him back to the car. When John awakens, Kawani is gone, the two racist men are dead, and his skin is tattooed with intricate Pawani motifs. Against racial regimes of visibility, Kawani recasts John's skin as a surface "marked" by transindigenous solidarity.

It is important to note that Pawani is the name of a fictional indigenous American nation. When I pressed him to explain why he decided to invent a tribe rather than use one of the numerous extant names still in use—indigenous Americans have not disappeared, contrary to settler-colonial fantasies of total conquest—Rouabhi responded that, for him, Kawani is a survivor of genocide, a being who should not be there but remains.[32] Though Rouabhi's comments are formulated as an indictment of settler colonialism, Jodi A. Byrd's critique of the "spectral" appearance of indigenous peoples in postcolonial theory as "past tense presences" or "melancholic citizens dissatisfied with the conditions of inclusion" still applies, I would argue, to the ghostlike presence of Kawani in the play.[33] At the same time, the paradoxical presence of a survivor of genocide brings together the conflicting temporalities of settler colonialism and exile as it usually theorized in postcolonial studies. The name *Kawani* sounds like it could be derived from the Arabic trilateral root *ka-wa-na,* which gives us both the verb *kan,* "to be, to exist," and *kan wa ma kan,* literally "there was and there was not" or, more idiomatically, "once upon a time." Like the photographs of indigenous Americans taken on the cusp of dispossession, or the tattoo that will magically appear on John's skin at the end of this scene, Kawani's presence indexes both what was and is no longer, and an impossible encounter between two heterogeneous subjects of photography: an indigenous American and a Palestinian. The restitution or invention of a Native tribe, whose spectral presence is attested in photography, is another way of "multiplying the traces" of a people displaced by colonial settlement. It also performs indigenous critique not as an empirical claim to indigeneity—the land of the Pawani Indians is fictional—but as a political articulation of anticolonial and antiracist critique, against the nativist claims of those who want to "make the Indian's skin." The indigenous American leaves the colonial cliché to haunt the Palestinian refugee as he is exiled from the United States to Lebanon and ultimately to France.

The most visible trace of Rouabhi's Palestinian workshops, the photographic encounter between John and Kawani makes legible the scenes of racism and violence in France in subsequent scenes of the play. Act 1 is devoted to Jaber's early life in the United States, from the transformative encounter with Kawani to his father's untimely death. Act 2 shuttles to a *bidonville* (shantytown) in the periphery of Paris on the night of October 17, 1961, as a young girl named Nadia awaits in vain for her father's return. Connected by the trope of paternal death, the Palestinian refugee and the Algerian immigrant never meet, although Nadia, who grows up to be a television reporter, will play an important role in the play's startling conclusion. Shuttling back and forth from the shantytown of her birth to the streets of Paris to give voice to the exiles of French society, Nadia is the repository of the memory of colonial violence on French soil. Staged in a brief scene that serves as a transition between act 1, set in the United States, and act 2, set in France, her evocation of October 17 establishes an implicit link between "the children of the colonies" and Palestinian noncitizens of Israel. It also echoes the tale of American indigeneity told in the first act of the play, articulating a radical indigenous critique of the colonial cliché, this time in postcolonial France.

The connection between France and the United States becomes evident in a scene in which Nadia interviews *banlieue* youth for a live television broadcast. The dialogue begins *in medias res* after, we presume, a question she has put to them about whether or not they feel "Arab":

NADIA . . . and what about you?

YOUTH 1 For me there's no point.

NADIA What do you mean, there's no point?

YOUTH Sure, there's a point when you go over there, but here, there's no point in being Arab. They're always asking for your ID [*tu te fais contrôler tout le temps*], they just keep busting your balls, anywhere you go that's the first thing they tell you.

YOUTH 2 They don't even tell you they don't even tell you, they think it, you can see they're thinking, *yeah, that one's an Arab we're not going to take him,* say when you go for a job that's what they do.

YOUTH 3 It's racism.

YOUTH 4 It's segregation.

YOUTH 3 Yeah it's racial segregation.[34]

Embedding a transnational antiracist lexicon in their vernacular French, these young men are keenly aware of the specific form French racism has taken in the postcolony. Blatant racial profiling and social exclusion ("racial segregation") produce what we might call the postcolonial cliché: a reified image of the racial other. It is not coincidental that *identification* is one of the means of racial profiling: in French, being asked for a photo ID is *se faire contrôler* (literally, to be controlled or surveilled). As Gérard Noiriel has argued, photographic identification was a key component of the production of migrants as racial others in Europe.[35] In France, a photograph also adorns the top right-hand corner of one's curriculum vitae, visually confirming the phenotype implied by one's proper name. Perpetually relegated to an ethnoracial category that keeps them on the margins of French society, these young men do not enjoy the rights of full citizenship. And yet, Nadia insists:

NADIA But you are French?
YOUTH 1 Honestly do I look French?
YOUTH 2 I'm not French. I'll never be French.
NADIA Why not?
YOUTH 2 Because I want to stay Arab.
NADIA Being Arab has nothing to do with your nationality.[36]

At first glance, Nadia's rebuttal might be read as an appeal to, and a performance of, republican universalism: the promise that one can be French regardless of race, ethnicity, or creed. At yet it surreptitiously articulates indigenous critique in one of the ways I have been defining it throughout this book. "But you *are* French," she exclaims. Thirty-nine years after October 17—this lapse of time is repeated in the *stage directions* at several points, framing the *petite couronne* scenes as sequels to the colonial massacre—the daughter of an *indigène* killed by the colonial state claims indigeneity to France for the descendants of colonial natives. If the *indigénat* formally ended in 1946, the extrajudicial killing of those dubbed *Français musulmans d'Algérie* on October 17, 1961, and the continued exclusion of their French-born children offer incontrovertible evidence of the enduring legacies of colonial law in postcolonial France. Staged between two scenes that establish "photographic citizenry" within the colonial cliché—the "souvenir photo" of an Indian, posing with a Palestinian child refugee in the first and last frames of the play—this scene connects France, the United States, and Palestine–Israel in a relational critique of colonialism and racism rooted in transindigenous identification and solidarity. The structure and framing of the play are crucial to Nadia's claim to indigeneity in France. The racial production of Kawani as a colonial native (*indigène*) who is not American enough to be included in the U.S. body politic finds its parallel in this scene in France, the settler postcolony.

It is important to stress that for the young men Nadia is interviewing, Arabness is a relational, situational identity, a defensive response to racist essentialism rather than an identitarian fantasy. Identified as Arabs, they disidentify with the state that refuses to recognize them as French. As a counterpoint to this subversive articulation of identity, Rouabhi stages a character who threatens to foreclose transindigenous solidarity altogether: Muhammad, an Algerian Islamist who comes to France "to wage war" against infidels and ends up killing Anissa, a spokeswoman of Palestinian cultural resistance in France.[37] Against the *banlieue* youth's reappropriation of the racial nomenclature *Arab*, Muhammad articulates a combative Muslim identity: "Before, the word *Arab* meant temerity, courage, poetry, and faith. Arabs inspired fear and respect. Today, it's an insult."[38] A stand-in for the Algerian militiamen who targeted French-language intellectuals and artists during *la décennie noire* (the "black decade," as Algeria's civil war is known), Muhammad also represents the betrayal of the Palestinian cause by Arab regimes, and its co-optation by violent Islamist groups. Anissa's murder—erroneously reported by Nadia in the final tableau as "a racist crime"—figures both the fratricidal violence of 1990s Algeria and the political recuperation of Palestine in a single dramatic action.[39] If, at the time of his first Palestine play, Rouabhi was reluctant to write about the Algerian Civil War for a French public, in the second he insists on complicating the story of transindigenous solidarity by staging intra-Arab violence onstage, at the risk of alienating his Palestinian public.

Unlike Kawani, Muhammad is nowhere to be found in the Palestinian workshops. On the contrary, his intrusion onto the scene of Franco-Palestinian solidarity—the recital of a Palestinian memoir in the French *banlieue*—provoked spirited debates among the Palestinian actors. Qawasmi, who was cast in the role of Muhammad, even threatened to quit on account of his disagreement with the inclusion of this character in the play. Why would Rouabhi risk jeopardizing

Franco-Palestinian solidarity by including a character dangerously reminiscent of Western clichés of violent Arab men? When pressed with this question, Rouabhi responded summarily, "It's to stay clear of propaganda"—perhaps the kind of propaganda exemplified in the tableau of the French-Algerian fedayee acclaimed by the Tunisian audience of "The Story of Kufur Shamma."[40] But I would go further: the inclusion of Muhammad in "El menfi" is what makes clear the difference between identitarian claims—whether Arabist or Islamist—and what I am calling *indigenous critique*. It is not coincidental that Rouabhi chose to give this controversial figure his own first name, implicitly complicating his students' immediate identification with him on identitarian grounds. In a text written in June 1999, toward the end of his first residency, Rouabhi narrates his first encounter with the incarcerated youth of Al Sakakini prison: "What's your name?—Muhammed.—So you're Arab, like us?—Yes."[41] For his Palestinian students, Rouabhi is a fellow traveler, albeit from a quasi-mythical place of revolutionary desire, Algeria: "Over there, saying you're Algerian opens all the doors."[42] The character Muhammad, however, does not correspond to the idealized image Palestinians have of Algeria. No surprise, then, if the murder of a Palestinian refugee by an Algerian Islamist did not sit well with Rouabhi's Palestinian interlocutors.

And yet, paradoxically, the introduction of a character that clashes with Palestinians' mythic image of Algeria constitutes evidence of the two-way exchange made possible in Rouabhi's Franco-Palestinian workshops. "El menfi" is in this sense a companion to *Les nouveaux bâtisseurs*. Where the latter exhumed Palestine for "the children of the colonies," the former reconstitutes traces of France–Algeria for a Palestinian public. More than Rouabhi's first Palestine play, "El menfi" also performs transindigenous exchange, the give-and-take process that produced the play in the first place. Rather than smooth out or resolve the discrepancies that emerged between Rouabhi's expectations and those of his students, "El menfi" exploits these tensions for dramatic effect. The result of this encounter between *la banlieue* and Palestine is a complex and sometimes jarring performance of indigenous critique, one that, as I suggested earlier, hinges on the introduction of a character one might not expect to appear in a Franco-Palestinian play. Abandoning the obvious articulation of Palestinian–Algerian solidarity in favor of a more complicated map, Rouabhi stages transindigenous identification through an encounter between an indigenous American and a Palestinian.

The ghostlike figure of Kawani returns to haunt Jaber during the most climactic moments of his life: after he loses his eyesight in the summer of 1982, and again after Anissa is killed in the penultimate scene of the play. Standing alone onstage, his face lit up by the flash of cameras recording the Intifada-like riot raging outside the theater— "youth protesting and throwing rocks on police officers . . . masked with Palestinian headscarves"—Jaber sees Kawani seated on a chair. "The story always picks up where it left off," explains Kawani as he beckons to him: "Come here, my little John, come." John, now a child, comes to sit on his lap, as we hear the adult Jaber reading the beginning of the memoir: "My name is John Walid Jaber. When I was a boy something strange happened to me, and this event marked my childhood: I was kidnapped by a Pawani Indian. . . . There was a photographer who would come up to people and ask them if they wanted to pose with a real Pawani Indian, if they wanted to bring back a souvenir photo . . ."[43] The flash of a photo camera illuminates the pair one last time, and the lights go out.

The encounter between the colonized photographic subject and the Palestinian spectator, turned, in "El menfi," co-subject of colonial photography, is, I have argued, what makes possible a relational critique of colonialism and racism across imperial histories and geographies. The transformation of photography into a site of anticolonial solidarity is all the more poignant given the role that photography has played in developing the cliché of race, be it that of the "Indian" or the "Arab." An instrument of racial science, the colonial cliché becomes a medium of transindigenous identification, much like the racial nomenclature *Arab* in Rouabhi's reading of Darwish: "so I write, in French, on my papers, that I am Arab." In the final section of this chapter, I turn to Rouabhi's performance of indigeneity through the poetry of Darwish, a performance that will allow him to exit the colonial cliché.

Exit the Colonial Cliché

In 1996, while he was completing *Les nouveaux bâtisseurs,* Rouabhi staged Mahmoud Darwish's "Discours de l'indien rouge" ("Khutbat 'al-Hindi al-ahmar'—ma qabl al-akhira—amam al-rajul al-abyad," translated into English as "The 'Red Indian's' Penultimate Speech to the

White Man"), a long prose poem he discovered in 1993 in the pages of *La revue d'études palestiniennes*.⁴⁴ Rouabhi would return to "Discours de l'indien rouge" on a number of occasions: in 2003, with codirector Carlo Brandt, and again after Darwish's death, in 2009 and 2010, for a solo performance titled "Darwish, deux textes," a double bill featuring "Discours de l'indien rouge" alongside Darwish's memoir of the 1982 Israeli bombing of Beirut, *Une mémoire pour l'oubli* (*Memory for Forgetfulness*).⁴⁵

Inspired by Chief Seattle's 1855 address to Governor Stevens, "The 'Red Indian's' Penultimate Speech to the White Man" was originally included in Darwish's 1992 poetry collection *Ahada 'ashara kawkaban* (Eleven stars), marking the quincentennial of the conquest of the Americas and the Reconquista of Muslim Spain. Darwish's poem is an eloquent example of transindigenous performance, mobilizing a relational, comparative understanding of coloniality: a Palestinian poet addresses the white man in the name of indigenous Americans, and in so doing, reinscribes Palestine within the *longue durée* history of European colonialism.⁴⁶ Like Qawasmi's autobiography as an Indian, "The 'Red Indian's' Penultimate Speech to the White Man" also surreptitiously smuggles in the language of Palestinian resistance, evidencing the Palestinian genealogy of transindigenous identification I alluded to earlier. In a passage I will return to in my analysis of Jean-Luc Godard's film *Notre musique* in the next chapter, the eponymous Indian's address to the white man recalls Darwish's musings, elsewhere, about the tragic irony that has irremediably tied the Palestinians to the Israelis: "isn't it time we met, stranger, as two strangers of one time / and one land, the way strangers meet by a chasm?"⁴⁷ In a 1996 interview with the Israeli poet Helit Yeshurun, who has just asked him about the meaning of exile, Darwish characterizes his own relationship to the colonizer in strikingly similar terms: "The occupier and I both suffer from exile. He is exiled in me and I am the victim of his exile."⁴⁸

"L'exilé," of course, is the French translation of "El menfi." But beyond the intertextual echoes of Darwish in Rouabhi's plays, Rouabhi's production of "Discours de l'indien rouge" is crucial to the notion of transindigenous performance I evoked at the beginning of this chapter. In theatrical terms, "an Arab living in France" plays the role of a Palestinian poet playing the role of a "Red Indian," addressing the white man from a triply (post)colonial subject position. Formally speaking, the remediation of Darwish's poem on a French stage enables the performance of indigeneity via Palestine and indigenous America: a French-Algerian man, whose only costume is the glimmering silver and bright blue turquoise bolo tie appended to the collar of his linen suit, declaims Darwish's address to the white man in eloquent French, simultaneously translating his peroration in sign language, an indigenous American gestural semantics (Figure 9). Rouabhi's embodiment of Darwish as a "Red Indian" also remediates colonial photography in a way that further illuminates the final frame of "El menfi."

In the promotional materials for "Darwish, deux textes," Rouabhi explains his decision to embody Darwish's "Red Indian" in the guise of an indigenous American posing for a studio photograph. For Rouabhi, photography simultaneously marks the obliteration of a world and, paradoxically, enables its preservation, albeit as cliché:

> With the massacre of Wounded Knee, one of the last great battles of the 19th century, and the death of the Sioux chief Big Foot at the end of 1890, it's sort of like the end of a world, the dusk of pre-Columbian America. . . . The irony is that photography, which has just seen the light of day, will forever capture on the silver plaques of its entrails the faces and bodies of those who are already little more than ghosts, halos of light impressed upon paper, winged spirits visiting our dreams.[49]

Against photography as a testament to what was and is no longer, Rouabhi performs the subject of photography, making possible a civil contract between the photographed subject, the writer or actor who imagines to be this subject, and the spectator who witnesses this transformation.

On the occasion of the 2010 performance in la Chapelle du Verbe Incarné in Avignon, Rouabhi explained the conditions under which the theater becomes a space of relationality, one that requires the spectator not only to look and listen but to enter into a sort of contract with the character seated only a few feet away.[50] Performing "Darwish, deux textes" in small, intimate settings, in a carefully composed chiaroscuro, Rouabhi calibrated the sound of his voice such that it would seem to surround the small group of listeners—no more than sixty at a time—assembled around him, as if he were whispering in their ear.

FIGURE 9. *Mohamed Rouabhi performing Mahmoud Darwish's poem "The 'Red Indian's' Penultimate Speech to the White Man." Mohamed Rouabhi, "Darwish, deux textes," Maison de la Poésie, Paris, October 2009. Photograph by Eric Legrand.*

Haloed by a spot that illuminates his face and torso, this character looks hauntingly like Kawani, sitting on the verge of the souvenir photograph of mythical America. Remember Kawani's rebellion against the reduction of his identity to a still image: "I don't believe that I am on this paper. I'm speaking to you and my whole body is inhabited by life. . . . Look at my hands. My hands are alive, aren't they?"[51] Sitting almost perfectly still, barring his hands, which trace words and images in the sky, Rouabhi embodies the "Indian" captured in colonial photography, animated in turns by the Palestinian poet, the Birzeit student, and the French-Algerian actor and director who speaks in his place, at first sitting squarely before the audience, then angled *de trois quarts,* like Qawasmi's Anka Moka, and finally upright, as if exiting the colonial cliché.

In 2009, Nadine Varoutsikos organized a screening of Godard's *Notre musique* following Rouabhi's performance of "Darwish, deux textes."[52] The tension between the colonial cliché of the Indian and the embodied performance of indigeneity in Rouabhi's play is, I will argue in the next chapter, the linchpin of *Notre musique,* which stages "The 'Red Indian's' Penultimate Speech to the White Man" in a powerful rebuke of nativism at the borders of Europe. Elias Sanbar, whose translation of "Khutbat 'al-Hindi al-ahmar'" moved Rouabhi to perform Darwish's poem, was also instrumental, as we will see, in Godard's shift from a satirical engagement with the colonial cliché to a sustained critique, through sound layering, of colonialism and nativism across imperial formations. The co-appearance of indigenous Americans and Palestinians on the set of Europe's last genocide, Bosnia, indexes indigeneity as the site of a continued contest for native belonging, and gestures in remarkably prescient ways to the so-called crisis that would climax some ten years later along the Balkan route and other itineraries of exile: the migrant question.

CHAPTER 5

Indigeneity at the Borders of Europe

Palestinians and Indians in Jean-Luc Godard's Films

Transindigenous Comparisons

In 1969, Swiss-French filmmaker Jean-Luc Godard and Jean-Pierre Gorin, his principal collaborator in the Dziga Vertov film collective, received an invitation from Fatah, the nascent Palestinian resistance movement, to film a documentary about the Palestinian independence struggle. Funded to the tune of six thousand dollars by the Arab League, with additional funding from a couple of European producers, Godard, Gorin, and their cameraman Armand Marco traveled to Jordan, Lebanon, and Syria between November 1969 and August 1970 to shoot a "political film-tract" about the Palestinian Revolution, titled "Jusqu'à la victoire" (Until victory).[1] In a brief text written before their first trip to Jordan, "Sketch for a Palestinian film commissioned by the organization El Fatah," Godard and Gorin underscored the urgency of making the film in explicitly anticolonial terms: "What happened to the Redskins [*Peaux-Rouges*] must not happen to the Palestinians."[2] The collective returned to France in August to edit the film, only to learn, a few weeks later, that most of the fedayeen they had filmed in Jordan had been killed by King Hussein's troops. The film-tract celebrating the Palestinian resistance could no longer be. After several failed attempts, the project was abandoned.[3]

Foreshadowing Black September, the massacre of thousands of Palestinian civilians and combatants in September 1970, Godard and Gorin's naive admonition that "what happened to the Redskins must not happen to the Palestinians" is the starting point in my investigation of the twin figures of the Indian and the Palestinian in Godard's films. Although this call to action is clearly based on solidarity with colonized peoples—Godard and Gorin are siding with the Indians against the cowboys—its language betrays an unselfconscious adoption of what, in chapter 4, I called the *colonial cliché*. The unproblematized use of the derogatory term *Peaux-Rouges* to speak of indigenous Americans recycles, in overtly racialized terms, the image of the Indian produced by Hollywood Western films—a cliché that is, as we will see, a recurrent motif in Godard's collectivist films, where it serves to anchor a critique of U.S. cultural imperialism (the hegemony of Hollywood cinema) rather than ongoing settler colonialism. This statement of solidarity also paradoxically implies that the indigenous peoples of North America are of the past, not of the present, locating them, in Jodi A. Byrd's apt formulation, "outside temporality and presence, even in the face of the very present and ongoing colonization of indigenous lands, resources, and lives."[4] Penned by First World filmmakers eager to make a revolutionary film in the Middle East, the simple parallelism between Palestinians and "Redskins" in Godard and Gorin's call to directorial action relegates the Indian to a mythic anticolonial past and enshrines the Palestinian as the vanguard of the revolutionary future, ensuring that, in discursive terms at least, they remain discrete rather than overlapping figures.

And yet, problematic as it may be, Godard and Gorin's formulation of solidarity with the Indians of yesteryear and the Palestinians of tomorrow represents an important moment of critique in Godard's filmography. Rooted, as I will show, in the romanticized figure of the Indian popularized by Hollywood Western films, Godard and Gorin's admonition further implicates the filmmakers in an expanded and overlapping imperial history that includes American settler colonialism in its purview. It also unwittingly gestures toward a distinctly Palestinian genealogy of the figure of the Indian in Godard's films. If the Dziga Vertov group's desire that the Palestinians not suffer the same fate as the "Redskins" is the only reference to American indigeneity in the extant archive of "Jusqu'à la victoire," this transindigenous genealogy was already palpable on the set of the film, where, according to one Palestinian observer, the fedayeen fashioned their image in the likeness of the "'brave' Indians" of Hollywood Westerns.[5]

The poetry of Mahmoud Darwish occupies a privileged role in Godard's corpus. I expand on the Palestinian genealogy of the figure of the Indian I began tracing in the previous chapter in my reading of

Godard's *Notre musique* (*Our Music,* 2004), focusing on the indigenous performance of Darwish's poem "Khutbat 'al-Hindi al-ahmar'—ma qabl al-akhira—amam al-rajul al-abyad" ("The 'Red Indian's' Penultimate Speech to the White Man"). The question of indigeneity plays a central role in the film, where, I argue, it remediates the colonial question in twenty-first-century Europe, in the aftermath of genocide (the Bosnian War) and on the cusp of the migrant crisis that would peak a decade later. Against the critical tendency to divide Godard's oeuvre into distinct periods, I read the twinned figures of the Palestinian and the Indian across Godard's filmography to think through the recuperation of indigeneity in postcolonial Europe: the deployment of nativism against former natives (*indigènes*), cast as migrants without history. Emerging from the colonial cliché that dominates Godard's early films, the indigenous Americans and Palestinians of *Notre musique* become the conduit, I argue, for a critique of nativism at the borders of Europe.

Godard is a notoriously protean and prolific filmmaker. Most of the films I assemble in this idiosyncratic archive are little-known films from his collectivist period: the unrealized documentary "One A.M.," shot with American pioneers of direct cinema, Richard Leacock and D. A. Pennebaker (1968; the footage was edited by Pennebaker and released under the title *One P.M.* in 1972); *Vent d'est* (*Wind from the East,* 1969), the "leftist spaghetti Western" around which the collective formed by Godard, Gorin, and a few others officially adopted the name Dziga Vertov;[6] "Jusqu'à la victoire," also unrealized (1970); *Ici et ailleurs* (*Here and Elsewhere,* 1974), the essay-film Godard and his Sonimage partner Anne-Marie Miéville made with the rush footage shot in the Middle East; and *Notre musique* (2004), which, albeit signed by Godard alone, is in many ways the product of his long-standing friendship with Elias Sanbar, the Dziga Vertov group's impresario in the Middle East, whose subsequent scholarship on the parallels between the colonization of indigenous Americans and Palestinians would have a decisive impact on Godard's late films, including *Notre musique* and *Film socialisme* (2010), where Sanbar makes a cameo appearance. Sanbar was also instrumental in drawing Godard's attention to the politics of representation, and in particular the use of sound as a site of critique in the audiovisual medium of film. Sound as medium of critique is the connective tissue articulating the variegated works under discussion in this chapter, from Godard's experiments in collective filmmaking at the height of Third Worldist revolutionary fervor to his late essay films on the porous borders of Europe.

In the following section, I analyze the various gradations of sound—voice, volume, sound layering, and silence—in *Ici et ailleurs* and argue that the use of sound in Godard and Miéville's montage stages a complex critique of audiovisual representation that implicates First World filmmakers in the production of a romanticized image of revolution "elsewhere." I then provide a Palestinian genealogy of the appearance of indigenous Americans in Godard's late films, before analyzing *Notre musique* as a staging ground for the contest over indigeneity at the borders of Europe. Where the Dziga Vertov group's projected film "increased the volume" to such an extent that the voices of the Palestinians were drowned out, *Notre musique* layers the sounds of indigenous American and Palestinian voices in an audiovisual montage that exposes the colonial gaze on-screen in the reified figure of the Indian, costumed, in an ironic reproduction of the colonial cliché, in tasseled suede tunic and bolo tie. The critique of representation staged in *Ici et ailleurs* makes way in Godard's later work, I suggest, for a more complex representation of indigenous Americans and Palestinians in a postcolonial Europe that continues to relegate the question of indigeneity beyond its tightly controlled borders, foreclosing any acknowledgment of its settler-colonial past and nativist present. Far from representing diametrically opposed poles in the temporal scale of coloniality found in the Dziga Vertov's sketch for "Jusqu'à la victoire"—the settler-colonial past, the revolutionary future—the co-presence of indigenous Americans and Palestinians in *Notre musique* indexes the colonial roots of Europe's nativist present, set in the ruins of Sarajevo and the landlocked borders of the European Union. Sound, as we will see, is at the heart of the question of how to represent indigenous Americans and Palestinians in both *Ici et ailleurs* and *Notre musique*.[7]

Sounds of Palestine (*Ici et ailleurs*)

Watching the rush footage of "Jusqu'à la victoire" in 1974 with Anne-Marie Miéville, his partner in the new video collective Sonimage, and Elias Sanbar, the Dziga Vertov group's Franco-Palestinian interpreter, Godard discovered that in a number of key scenes the voices of the fedayeen were muted, drowned out by the competing voices of their military superiors, or simply silent. Viewing a shot of a group of fedayeen returning from a failed nighttime raid, Godard had the "intuition" to lower the volume of the voice addressing the camera in the foreground (the filmmakers had asked one of the combatants to deliver an autocritique for the camera).[8] When Sanbar translated the fedayeen's now audible conversation in the background, what the trio discovered, in lieu of autocritique, was a heated confrontation with the leader who had sent them out to battle unprepared, resulting in the deaths of several of their fellow combatants. Describing the scene two decades after the filming of "Jusqu'à la victoire," Sanbar suggests that this collective attempt to decipher the muted voices of the fedayeen was the impetus for *Ici et ailleurs,* the film Godard and Miéville made with the rush footage shot in the Middle East. "We were in shock [*abasourdis,* literally "deafened"]," writes Sanbar, "Godard because he had not asked me to translate what these men were saying at the time, and me, whose mother tongue they were speaking, racked with guilt that I had heard absolutely nothing, so completely had these unshakable theories and convictions deafened me."[9] The failure of the revolutionary to represent Palestine in sound would be the starting point for Godard and Miéville's *Ici et ailleurs.*[10]

Conceived with his principal collaborator in the Dziga Vertov group, Jean-Pierre Gorin, filmed on location with cameraman Armand Marco, and completed with Anne-Marie Miéville in 1974, *Ici et ailleurs* is "a video about a failed film."[11] Ostensibly a documentary about the Palestinian struggle for independence—the film opens with footage of Palestinian men, women, and children in the midst of revolutionary activities—*Ici et ailleurs* splices the film footage shot in Jordan and Lebanon (*ailleurs,* "elsewhere") with a narrative film sequence set in Grenoble (*ici,* "here"), as well as still images, video montage, and "a bifurcated sound-track—one half synch sound, one half voice-over" deconstructing the original propaganda film commissioned by Fatah.[12] Critics have accordingly read *Ici et ailleurs* as a symptom of Godard and Miéville's rejection of Marxist-Leninist discourse.[13] Taking my cue from Elliott Colla and Irmgard Emmelhainz, I argue that *Ici et ailleurs* decisively poses a critique of representation—in particular, documentary film's claim to represent the other, rooted in a naturalization of

voice—as the condition for engagement with, and support for, the colonized other.[14] In this reading, *Ici et ailleurs* remains an emphatically
pro-Palestinian film, but one that refuses "the economy of identification" that would collapse "ici" and "ailleurs" in a simple equation of
First and Third World struggles.[15] Sound, and in particular the acoustic
gradations of volume, becomes the medium for a complex engagement
with the politics of representation in the film. "The sound is too loud
and covers reality," as the voice-over puts it in the film's final seconds.
Volume, here, is a metaphor for representation as substitution in the
film: speaking over, not for, as, or to, the Palestinians. The play and
modulation of volume in the film, from silence to silencing with many
gradations in between, allows us to hear sonic representation as substitution. In what follows, I show how *Ici et ailleurs* makes use of direct
sound (the Palestinians), voice-over translation (Miéville), voice-over
commentary (Godard and Miéville), and silence to deconstruct representation in sound.

From the outset, the voice-over and editing make it clear that the
Palestinian Revolution is being staged for Western viewers. The first
frame is composed of pixelated block letters flickering against a solid
black background—"my / your / his or her [sound] image"[16]—as the
voice-over of Godard intones: "In 1970, this film was titled *Victory*. In
1974, this film is titled *Here and elsewhere*." The sounds and images that
follow—women and men training with automatic weapons, a semi-
literate woman haltingly reading a Fatah pamphlet, children marching
in military formation—are sequenced according to the prerogatives
of the Palestinian Revolution, dubbed by Miéville, and commented on
by Godard: "tous les sons et toutes les images, dans cet ordre-là" (all
the sounds and all the images, in that order). But the representational
premise of Miéville's voice-over translation—already denaturalized
in her prosodic imitation of the Palestinian woman's halting Arabic—
breaks down when the same rush footage plays again, this time muted.
Instead of the sound track of "Jusqu'à la victoire," we hear Godard's
voice compute the Fatah slogans that were to structure the film, in a
nasal monotone sharply at odds with the lyricism of the Palestinian resistance: "the will of the people, plus, plus the armed struggle equals
the war of the people, plus, plus the political work equals the education of the people, plus, plus the logic of the people equals the popu-

lar war prolooonged, prolooonged, prolonged until the victory of the Palestinian people."

As Sanbar's account of the Dziga Vertov group's Middle East journey reveals, Godard's prosody is, in fact, a rendition of the intonation of a fedayee, albeit one deprived of affect in his monotone voice-over. During one of the many interviews that served as material for the Dziga Vertov group, Mahjoub, an Egyptian doctor-turned-fedayee, explains to his captive audience the importance of stretching out the vowels of *al-harb al-tawiiiila* (the loooong war) in order to *"hear"* its duration.[17] The uncredited translation of Mahjoub's elongated vowels in the voice-over is not the only moment that draws attention to the remediation of Arabic voices for Western consumption. In the first few minutes of the film, for example, we hear a Palestinian woman prompting another to read a political tract. Obviously struggling to decipher the document, the apprentice militant elicits almost constant corrections and encouragements from her invisible chaperone, whose words, in turn, are translated by Miéville, drawing attention to the scripted nature of revolutionary discourse. In a subsequent scene, we distinctly hear Godard asking, in French, a young Palestinian sympathizer in Beirut to adjust her veil as she dedicates her unborn son's life to the revolution. Here too, the focus of the scene is as much on the interviewer's offscreen voice as it is on the camera's ostensible subject, the mother of a fictional martyr-to-be (a Lebanese student who was not, in fact, pregnant when she agreed to play this role, according to Miéville's voice-over commentary). More poignantly, a shot of a little girl declaiming a poem by Mahmoud Darwish in the ruins of Karameh, the symbolic birthplace of the Palestinian resistance, is revealed to be a quintessential example of the kind of "political theater" in which, we are told, the revolutionaries of 1789 excelled. The little girl is "innocent," Miéville explains, her performance less so. But the main object of her critique is the Dziga Vertov group. "The texts speak, speak, but they never speak of silence." And indeed, Miéville's own commentary is suspect. As Rebecca Dyer and François Mulot point out, the poem recited in the ruins of Karameh is not "I will resist," as the voice-over erroneously claims in this scene, but "Azhaar al-dam" ("Roses of Blood"), a poem about the 1956 massacre of Kafr Qasim.[18] The revolution, it turns out, is scripted, by both the revolutionaries and their French documentarians. Godard and Miéville's

FIGURE 10. *Film workers stand underneath still images shot by the Dziga Vertov group in Jordan and Lebanon in 1970. Screenshot from* Ici et ailleurs, *directed by Jean-Luc Godard and Anne-Marie Miéville (1974).*

voice-over makes audible the silencing of Palestinians in a film that purports to make them speak.

Withholding all judgment, all irony from the Palestinian images and voices it renders, *Ici et ailleurs* draws attention instead to the conditions of production of the images and sounds it assembles, provoking us to question the filmmakers' motives, as well as the images and sounds they have produced. This is the function of the extended sequence of scenes that interrupts the story of the Palestinian Revolution at mid-point. In a pastiche of a master class in film that comically stages the "making of" the projected film "Jusqu'à la victoire," two women and three men in a Grenoble film studio take turns affixing photos on a blank wall as they declaim the five stages of the revolution (Figure 10). But in cinema, Godard comments in voice-over, one doesn't see all the images at once. The room goes dark, and the camera lights up each image in sequence as a voice—a different one each time—pronounces the title of the photograph, in French ("the will of the people," etc.). The

FIGURE 11. *Film workers hold up still images of the Palestinian Revolution before the camera in a pastiche of the "making-of" an agitprop film. Screenshot from* Ici et ailleurs, *directed by Jean-Luc Godard and Anne-Marie Miéville (1974).*

following shot reveals how the images are assembled in a send-up of the art of editing, as each character walks up to the camera and holds up an image, in silence. Again, we see the images all together in one frame as the film workers shuffle comically from right to left holding up a still (now moving) image, this time with an edited Arabic sound track (Figure 11). The result, Godard tells us, is a series of "images à la chaîne" (assembly-line images). A *mise en abyme* of the making of the film that was to be titled "Jusqu'à la victoire," this sequence of scenes also makes *Ici et ailleurs* suspect, drawing attention to the editing process that affixes particular sounds to particular images, assembled in the proper order ("dans cet ordre-là").

The rest of the film proceeds to critique the filmmakers' attempt to speak for the Palestinians. "We did what a lot of people do," Godard explains in voice-over. "We took images, and we turned the volume up too high." An extreme close-up shows the hand of a man, then of a woman—Godard's and Miéville's?—slowly raising the volume knob

FIGURE 12. *Close-up of Godard's hand raising the volume on a Sony sound system as the chorus of the Communist Internationale resounds. Godard comments, in voice-over, "Always the same sound, always too loud." Screenshot from* Ici et ailleurs, *directed by Jean-Luc Godard and Anne-Marie Miéville (1974).*

of a Sony sound system as we hear the chorus of the Communist anthem resound: "c'est la lutte finale" (this is the final struggle) (Figure 12). Punctuated by the Internationale, which booms out each time the volume is raised, the voice-over continues: "with just about any image: Vietnam, always the same sound, always too loud, Montevideo, May '68 France, Italy, Chinese cultural revolution, strikes in Poland, torture in Spain, Ireland, Portugal, Chile, Palestine, the sound so loud that it ended up drowning out the voice it wanted to extract from the image."

The camera cuts one last time to the close-up shot of two hands raising the volume on a sound system, immediately before the longest continuous shot in the film: this is the scene from the rush footage of "Jusqu'à la victoire," translated by Sanbar after lowering the volume of the voice in the foreground. A troop of fedayeen are discussing tactics as they rest in a banana grove near the Jordan River after an unsuccessful nighttime operation. We hear their muted voices, birds chirping, the wind rustling the leaves. Godard's voice layers over the sound track to ask Miéville what they are saying, as she resumes the role of interpreter she had at the start of the film. But now we know her translation is not unmediated. Her voice has lost the transparency it had when we first heard it. The fedayeen, she explains, "are critiquing the way they crossed the river under the fire of Israeli machine guns." What is tragic is that they are talking about their own imminent death, Godard remarks. What is tragic, Miéville retorts, is that you didn't say anything about it. The camera continues to film after the fedayeen stop talking. Godard comments: "it's true that even silence, we never listened to it in silence. We wanted to cry out victory right away, and what's more, in their stead [*à leur place*]." In literal terms, silence here is the sound that was to be edited out of the film. But it is also tantamount to silencing: it is the substitution of one sound for another.

The sound track of the film that wasn't made would have silenced the fedayeen in favor of a scripted autocritique. Instead, Godard and Miéville decompose the movements of sound, the ways in which the volume of one sound increases to cover the others. "Why is it that we were incapable of listening to and seeing these simple images," asks Miéville, "and that like everyone else we said other things about them, other things than what they nevertheless said? It's probably because we do not know how to see or hear, or because the sound is too loud, and covers reality." Unable to reconstitute the sounds of Palestine, *Ici et ailleurs* makes us hear the silence in the sound track of "Jusqu'à la victoire."

Filming as a Frenchman

In one of a handful of interviews that Godard and Gorin gave during the making of "Jusqu'à la victoire," the former New Wave auteur explained that he had conceived of a film on the Palestinian Revolution "as a French national [*en tant que Français*], as a film about the Arabs that was never made during the Algerian war."[19] This is a telling admission coming from the director of *Le petit soldat* (*The Little Soldier,* 1960), one of the first films to broach the question of torture during the Algerian War—although the scenes of torture depicted in the film are perpetrated by FLN militants, not the French army, which began systematically torturing captured militants in 1957. Set in Geneva on the day of the pro–French Algeria generals' putsch of May 13, 1958, and shot on location in spring 1960 during the long climax of the war (another putsch would follow in 1961), the film was simultaneously denounced by Algerian sympathizers, who felt it sided with the pro–French Algeria terrorists, and was censored by the French government until 1963, one year after Algerian independence.[20] That the film elicited such strong reactions from both pro-Algerian and pro–French Algeria parties is not surprising. *Le petit soldat* is precisely a film about the inability to commit, politically, to an anticolonial struggle. Shortly after the shoot, Godard chose not to sign the "Manifeste des 121," an open letter calling for enlisted soldiers to resist the draft, even though he was himself twice a deserter. "Je ne me sentais pas assez responsable" (I did not feel responsible enough), he would later explain in a public conversation with anticolonial filmmaker René Vautier.[21]

In characteristically concatenated prose, Godard's declaration that he would film the Palestinian Revolution as a French national should have filmed the Algerian War—that is to say, not the way he filmed it— clearly indicates that he considered himself to be directly implicated in the messy imperial history that had produced the Palestinian question. "We thought it was more just, politically, to come to Palestine rather than elsewhere, Mozambique, Colombia, Bengal," Godard explains in a text published in Fatah's clandestine journal *El fatah* in July 1970. "The Middle East was directly colonized by French and British imperialism (Sykes-Picot agreement). We are French militants."[22] The Dziga Vertov group's film was an act of political responsibility-taking, not a naive and detached form of benevolent Third Worldism.

This is not, however, how the unrealized "Jusqu'à la victoire" has usually been cast, including by critics who approach it through Godard and Miéville's autocritique of the project in *Ici et ailleurs*. In his biography of Godard, for example, Antoine de Baecque cites the fact that "the Palestinian revolution had become a standard-bearer for the international left since . . . the 'six-day war'" to explain Godard's interest in Palestine at the height of his "Maoist period," presumably by analogy with his interest in the other anticolonial cause of the moment, Vietnam—thereby discounting Godard's commitment, as a French national, to Palestine, and simultaneously disavowing the role France played in setting the stage for the American war in its erstwhile Indochinese colony.[23] Godard's investment in Palestine, and Vietnam before it, should, on the contrary, be read in relation to his laconic statement about filming as a French national ought to have filmed the Algerian War. His acknowledgment of his positionality as an "implicated subject" in Palestine also points to a more complex relation between the First World filmmaker and his revolutionary subject, one that acknowledges, and critiques, the filmmaker's role in the production of the colonial cliché.[24]

Thirty years after making a video essay with Miéville about the impossibility of filming the Palestinian Revolution, Godard would return to the question of Palestine, but from a new angle: that of transindigenous identification, or what Steven Salaita calls "inter/nationalist" solidarity between indigenous Americans and Palestinians, enabling a critique of postcolonial Europe from the perspective of the still colonized.[25] If, in 1969, Godard and his Dziga Vertov companions could write that "what happened to the Redskins must not happen to the Palestinians," by 2004 he seemed to suggest that what had happened, what continued to happen to indigenous Americans was, in fact, happening to the Palestinians. As I will argue, the staging of transindigenous identification in the film also implicates Godard—and the viewer—in the continued colonization of indigenous Americans, whose presence serves to underscore the transformations, stakes, and dangers of claims to indigeneity in Europe. Before turning to *Notre musique,* I provide a brief account of the Palestinian genealogy of American indigeneity in Godard's film, and of the ways in which it intersects with, and sometimes contradicts, Godard's long-standing fascination with the figure of the Indian, one nourished by a lifetime immersion in the history of cinema, including Hollywood cinema and that Hollywood genre par excellence, the Western.

"Indien de Cinéma"

Godard's early admiration for the Hollywood Western—"the most cinematographic genre of cinema," according to his superlative review of Anthony Mann's *Man of the West* (1958) in *Les cahiers du cinéma*—goes a long way toward explaining how the Western became, in Godard's political films, a metonym for Hollywood imperialism.[26] Whether it serves as model or foil, however, the settler/pioneer narrative of conquest remains intact in Godard's early engagements with Westerns. Take the contrast he sets up between John Ford's *Stagecoach* (1939) and Mann's

The Last Frontier (1956) in the abovementioned review, which adopts the point of view of the cowboy and, in Godard's appraisal, further objectifies those he persists in calling *Redskins*:

> You have only to compare the famous panoramic shot of the appearance of the Indians in *Stagecoach* and the static shot in *The Last Frontier* where the Redskins [*les Peaux-Rouges*] simply rise up from the tall grasses surrounding Victor Mature and his fellow adventurers. The movement of Ford's camera drew its force from its plastic and dynamic beauty. Mann's shot was of a *vegetal* beauty, so to speak. Its force came precisely from having nothing to do with a premeditated aesthetics.[27]

Already gesturing toward the privileging of static shots in Godard's films (Godard was shooting his first feature, *A bout de souffle*), this favorable review of Mann's cinematography offers an accurate, if woefully uncritical, interpretation of the equally static image of the *Peaux-Rouges* as an element of nature. Less clear is how Mann's shot does not rely on the premeditated aesthetics of the Western (in all senses of that term) representation of Indians, eternally emerging from a rugged landscape ripe for the taking. If Mann "reinvents the Western," it is to better capture the quintessentially "vegetal" nature of native peoples, by analogy, one might surmise, with native plants.[28]

The use of the figure of the Indian in Godard's early films has less to do with a change of point of view—one that might better align with the anticolonial positions he adopted in the mid-1960s, most notably in solidarity with Vietnam and Palestine—than with the critique of U.S. cultural imperialism he began systematically to incorporate into his films. Godard's satires of the Western genre in fact rely, I will argue, on leaving intact the form, narrative, and even casting of the Western, including the use of white American actors in "redface."

There are brief allusions to the Western genre in Godard's first political films, most notably in *Week-end* (1967), which, like *La chinoise* before it (also 1967), marks the end of Godard's auteur period: the cameo role of a little boy "playing Indian" in *Week-end*'s opening sequence, for example; the allusion to "primitive peoples" (Iroquois, Mayas, Aztecs) in the anticolonial speech delivered by a Congolese worker and his "Arab brother" (played by Hungarian actor László Szabó) in a central scene of the film; and, in its apocalyptic final sequence, the cannibal leftist militant group whose members (played by white actors) are wearing an assortment of brightly colored clothes and headbands halfway between hippie and primitivist attire. But it is the appearance of "Indian" characters in the films Godard made during his collectivist period—sympathetic albeit clichéd embodiments of the antiheroes of the Hollywood Western—that confirms the contrapuntal role the Western genre plays in Godard's critique of U.S. cultural imperialism.

In March 1968—a period of intense political involvement for Godard, who was immersed in the social and labor movements that would come to be metonymically known as May '68—American documentary filmmakers Richard Leacock and D. A. Pennebaker invited Godard to show *La chinoise* to students at the New York University. Their recently formed production company, Leacock Pennebaker Inc., had acquired the rights to the film, and the American documentarians were interested in collaborating with the icon of New Wave cinema as he embarked on a new, anti-auteurist adventure. Godard met Leacock and Pennebaker in Paris in the early 1960s, and although he had strong reservations about their methodology—in particular, direct cinema's claim to represent unmediated reality—he agreed to work with them on a film about the impending American revolution, to be titled "One American Movie" or "One A.M." Godard started filming in April 1968, and returned to the United States with Gorin in October and November 1968 to complete the shoot.[29] Dissatisfied with the rush footage shot by Leacock and Pennebaker, Godard abandoned the project to pursue other collectivist projects, in Cuba, Québec, England, Prague, Italy, and eventually the Middle East.

When Godard and Gorin returned to the United States in March 1970 to raise money for "Jusqu'à la victoire," they delivered the final postmortem on "One A.M.," declaring the film project "a corpse." Godard had already complained that during the shoot he never knew who was shooting what (Leacock was the official cameraman, but Pennebaker was filming too). After viewing the rush footage again, Gorin explained that with "One A.M." they were still trying to "fetch images" (the reality captured in direct cinema) and then edit them. The Dziga Vertov group's task, as they saw it now that they were filming the

Palestinian Revolution, was to edit before, during, and after the shoot, in order to "build images."[30] In other words, they were trying to "make films politically," not "make political films."[31]

"One A.M." was never completed. But *One P.M.* (ironically dubbed *One Parallel Movie*), Pennebaker's montage of the scenes shot with Leacock and Godard in 1968, provides us with the first Indian character in Godard's filmography, one that prefigures the appearance of indigenous Americans in *Notre musique*—with the important difference that in *One P.M.,* a white American actor plays the role.[32] In the nearly twelve-minute opening scene of the film, a shaky, handheld camera films Godard laying out his plans for "One A.M." to the film crew in the offices of Leacock Pennebaker Inc. The film was to be composed of five continuous takes, each lasting ten minutes, representing the "documentary" or "reality" part of the film, doubled by "fiction," "acting," or "art" sequences. "Each part is separated in two, A and B," Godard explains, counting off on his fingers. "The five reality parts are: 1. Wall Street Lady; 2. Eldridge Cleaver; 3. the Jefferson Airplane; 4. Tom Hayden; and 5. the little Black girl from Brooklyn, the one we saw yesterday. And all those five pieces of reality are separated by five pieces of art"—to be played alternately, and sometimes simultaneously, by a female and a male actor.

Although some of the specifics of Godard's scenario are not found in *One P.M.* (for example, the female actor), most of the scenes Godard shot with Leacock and Pennebaker are included in Pennebaker's montage: the interview with Eldridge Cleaver, minister of information for the Black Panther Party, in Oakland (filmed hours before he fled to Cuba); the interview with New Left antiwar activist Tom Hayden in Berkeley; a scene in which Hayden and the film crew listen to a recording of the interviews with Hayden and Cleaver; an interview with Carole Bellamy, a lawyer on Wall Street; a scene shot in a junior high school classroom in Brooklyn where the actor Rip Torn, in Revolutionary War costume and then in a contemporary army officer's uniform, playfully tries to rile up the students against the "business" sector claiming to "develop" them in order to "put them back onto the plantation" (like the young Bellamy tried to develop the "Natives" of Guatemala during her stint as a "community action worker"); a scene in which the same actor plays the Hayden interview on a tape deck, pauses the tape, and recites

Hayden's words as he ascends the empty shell of a high-rise under construction in an elevator; and a clandestine rooftop Jefferson Airplane concert, cut short by a police raid.

Most interestingly for my purposes, *One P.M.* also features a number of scenes of Godard directing the action on the "set" of "One A.M.," scenes that were not intended to be included in the film, as evidenced by the fact that Godard not infrequently urges Pennebaker to direct his camera elsewhere. One such scene depicts Godard playing Hayden's interview on a tape deck in the Leacock Pennebaker studios and instructing Rip Torn, already dressed for the part he will play in the high-rise scene—leather jacket and black beret—on how to modulate his voice (Godard waves his hand up and down to illustrate the movement), from whispering to shouting, and even singing, before he hands him the tape deck. This is the tape deck that Torn uses in the scene I describe next.

Although I have not been able to confirm that the Indian character that appears in *One P.M.* was part of Godard's original idea for "One A.M."—Godard does not mention this scene in his summary of the script—Pennebaker claims to have simply assembled the footage "with as little editing as possible," suggesting that the sequence of scenes in *One P.M.* roughly corresponds to Godard's plans for the film.[33] In fact, the scene that interests me here is the first to follow Godard's proposed scenario, whereby an actor plays back and recites the interviews that form the centerpiece of the documentary. A white American actor (Torn) dressed up as a Hollywood Indian (feathered headdress and tasseled suede jacket) walks through a wooded area holding a leather-bound tape deck—the one Godard handed to him in the Leacock Pennebaker studios—repeating the word "blood" in a thunderous voice as a recording plays (this, we realize in a subsequent scene, is the interview with Hayden). The "Indian" sits down and pauses the tape to repeat keywords from the recorded speech for dramatic effect, delivering a sort of telegraphic echo of Hayden's words (Torn's words are in italics):

> That's why it's so important that we fight back and why—*it's important we fight back*—the victory of Vietnam over the United States is so important because—*that's why the victory of Vietnam over the United States is so, soooo important. Important!*—The lesson that you have to—*the lesson! the lesson*—teach—*teach*—the man in the office

and the man in the factory is that he cannot win. He cannot sup-press Blacks—*he cannot suppress Blacks!*—no matter how hard he tries—*no matter how hard*—he cannot destroy the Vietnamese or the Chinese—*he cannot destroy the Vietnamese, destroy cannot, cannot destroy Vietnamese, Chinese!*

The entire scene—the second in *One P.M.*—lasts three minutes and sets up the format of the film envisioned by Godard, a commentary on the impending American revolution as imagined by two of its representatives, Hayden and Cleaver. Although there is no description in the extant archive of "One A.M."/*One P.M.* of the various characters ventriloquizing revolutionary speech, the fact that the vehicle for Hayden's call to revolution—a white American actor—alternatively dons Indian, Revolutionary, and late-twentieth-century military dress clues us in to the significance of this performative act of dubbing. In these scenes, the settler-colonial past of the United States comes to bear upon its imperial and racist present.

The anticolonial nature of this indictment of racism becomes clear in the interview with Cleaver, conducted shortly before he fled to Cuba, which serves as the centerpiece of the film.[34] In a rare example of continuity editing (Pennebaker's choice—Godard wanted as little editing as possible), Cleaver's voice is heard first on tape—Godard, Hayden, and the rest of the team are conducting an autocritique of the film project by listening to the interviews—and then, in a nearly perfect sound bridge, on camera, precisely as he begins to speak about "transposing" the "colonial analogy" between "the Algerian situation" and the "domestic colonial situation" of Black people in the United States (the sound becomes much sharper moments before the visual cut, when the film's sound track replaces the sound of the tape recording). In diegetic terms, the heterogeneous yet analogous "colonization" of Black Americans and Algerians is placed at the center of a film about the impending American revolution, relayed by a white man in Indian drag who embodies the inventory of U.S. violence in the opening shots of *One P.M.*

Characteristic of the self-reflexive mode of Godard's political cinema and a far cry from direct cinema's attempt to simply let the subject speak, *One P.M.* (*One Pennebaker Movie* in Godard's wry formulation) merits to be included in Godard's filmography.[35] Although it relies heavily on the cliché of the combative Indian popularized by the Hollywood Western, it also gestures toward the more complex representation of indigenous Americans in Godard's late films. By contrast, the Dziga Vertov group's pastiche of the Western genre, *Vent d'est,* simply inverts the Manichaean world of the classic Western. Filmed in Italy in spring and summer 1969 and "based on an original idea" (as Hollywood film credits would put it) by Daniel Cohn-Bendit, the face of the student revolts of May '68 and a friend and classmate of Godard's wife, Anne Wiazemsky, *Vent d'est* turns the pioneers of American Westerns into antiheroes of the leftist revolution. This revolution is waged by, among other archetypal characters, a barely recognizable "Indian," played by white American actor Allen Midgette, who, according to the notes from a "general assembly" held by the film crew in May 1969, embodies the role of the "oppressed minority" in the film, in counterpoint to the revolutionary (read leftist) "acting minority" (*minorité agissante*) embodied by Wiazemsky.[36] Gian Maria Volonté, a rising star of Italian cinema, plays the part of the "Unionist ranger" (*ranger nordiste*) proudly dressed in the iconic blue uniform, who nonchalantly drags the Indian (inexplicably attired in what resembles a white karate costume, complete with red belt and black headband) through the woods at the end of a short rope attached to the saddle of his horse.[37] Completely deprived of agency, the Indian of *Vent d'est* is closer to a parody of subjection than the "vegetal" but nonetheless dangerous "Redskins" of Mann's *Last Frontier.*

The most interesting scenes in this "leftist spaghetti Western" are the nondiegetic shots of the film crew preparing for action.[38] Ten minutes into the film, we see two of the actors being prepared for the shoot. A makeup artist carefully applies blush to the forehead of Cristiana Tullio Altan, who embodies the "young bourgeoisie" in the film, while Midgette slowly smears brightly colored face paint on his cheeks, nose, and forehead—evoking, one assumes, primitive war paint, although the technicolor hues he uses are a far cry from the natural tones one would recognize from Western films.[39] A female voice-over intones a critique of Western cinematic imperialism: "It is the people that makes history. But on the screens of the Western Hemisphere, it's still the reign of beautiful ladies and gentleman . . . safely hidden behind their makeup [*à l'abri de leur maquillage*]." As the camera zooms in to frame Midgette's brightly painted face, the voice-over explains: "the revolution advances, masked." A man steps into the frame with a clapperboard indicating the number of the take (42—1—Vento dell'Este), underscoring that the mode of production of *Vent d'est* is not, in fact, far removed from the "bourgeois" mode of film production denounced by the female voice-over commenting on the scene. And indeed, even anticolonial cinematography comes under fire in her wide-ranging denunciation of cinematic imperialism:

> No longer relying on their own strength, the progressive African governments entrust the making of films to Western industry and give white Christians the right to speak of Black and Arab peoples. Algiers, Pontecorvo, Klein. Conakry, Société Comasico. After the popular war and the action of the masses threw them out the door, the imperialists return by the window of the camera [*la fenêtre de la caméra*] to endanger the revolution.

In this account, two of the most iconic anticolonial films of the twentieth century, Gillo Pontecorvo's epic film *The Battle of Algiers* (1966) and William Klein's documentary about the 1969 Pan-African Festival of Algiers, are cast as double agents of Western imperialism, which has put down the gun and picked up the camera as a more effective tool of neocolonial infiltration.[40] But as the presence of the makeup artist and director's assistant in this scene suggest, the Dziga Vertov group, too, is implicated in "Western" cinematic imperialism. "You forget that this film has a name, the Western, and that this is not a coincidence," the voice-over continues in the extended autocritique delivered in the second half of the film, as the Unionist ranger reappears, leading his captive Indian through the forest. If the voice-over critiques the filmmaker's attempts at *cinéma vérité,* the illustration of Hollywood's claim that "this cinema Indian [*cet Indien de cinéma*] is more real than an Indian" is not, in fact, a Hollywood Western, but a scene from *Vent d'est.* Cinema is implicated in the production of the colonial cliché, no matter the intentions of the filmmakers. "Que faire?" (What is to be done?), the question raised in the midst of this unsparing autocritique, is the object of the subsequent films Godard made with the Dziga Vertov group, including the never realized "Jusqu'à la victoire."

A Palestinian Western

When, in November 1969, Godard and Gorin were invited to film the Palestinian Revolution, they had just completed their "leftist spaghetti Western." Notwithstanding the critique of the Hollywood production of the figure of the Indian in *Vent d'est*, for the filmmakers, the Palestinian guerilla fighter was at the antipodes of the "Redskin" as passive victim of colonization, as evidenced in the short sketch they drafted before their first trip to Jordan. And yet I would like to suggest that the simplistic view of Indian defeat that obtains in *Vent d'est*—a view informed, as we have seen, by Godard's education in American cinema, and that "most cinematographic" of genres, the Western—was transformed during the experience of filming in the Middle East. If the "Indian" in *Vent d'est* is forced into silence by the horseman who drags him along on a rope, silence becomes a strategic weapon for those who, in Sanbar's account, were acting the part of the Indians of Hollywood Westerns on the set of "Jusqu'à la victoire": the Palestinians.

In March 1970, Mahmoud Hamchari, the representative of the PLO in France, gave a mission to a young Palestinian law student in Paris. Born in Haifa in 1947 and exiled in Lebanon and then France, Elias Sanbar was to serve as guide and interpreter for the Dziga Vertov group, commissioned by Fatah to film a documentary on the Palestinian Revolution. In a touching and often funny account of his first tour in the Jordan Valley in the company of Godard, Gorin, and Marco, Sanbar recalls being struck by the sudden arrival of the fedayeen over the crest of a hill, bearing their Kalashnikovs as well as pitchforks, borrowed for the occasion in anticipation of filming a scene titled "the land belongs to those who liberate it." In Sanbar's account, the Palestinian militants cut a familiar if unexpected figure, that of the "'brave' Indians" of Hollywood Westerns, cast, this time, in the lead role:

> I had been taken aback by the sudden appearance of the militants. It was the first time, barring funeral processions, that I had seen as many combatants, *in their setting* [dans leur décor] so to speak. They seemed to come out of nowhere, like a living illustration of all the romantic images that filled the heads of adolescents of my generation. Today I suppose, in fact I am sure of it, that these men, who had been informed and knew that "cinema" was about to happen, had imagined a scene to welcome us in their own manner. They were writing

their own film, probably made up of reminiscences of Westerns and especially that archetypal scene when the horseman or convoy of pioneers suddenly see a multitude of "brave" Indians profiled against the surrounding hillcrests, silent and still. But this time, there was no chief raising his lance, no war cry to announce the onrush of pursuers, only songs and soon after, a joyful melee.[41]

Written twenty-one years after his stint with the Dziga Vertov group—this is the text in which he recounts Godard's shock upon realizing that the fedayeen's critique of leadership was inaudible in the rush footage—Sanbar's retrospective account is, like *Ici et ailleurs,* lucid about the "political theater" of the Palestinian Revolution, although his "impression" of the scene reveals an entirely different Palestinian subject. In *Ici et ailleurs,* Godard and Miéville staged an autocritique of the filmmakers' role in reifying the slogans of the revolution, to the detriment of the silenced people playing the roles outlined for them: fedayeen, apprentice militants, patriotic children, mothers of martyrs. In contrast, Sanbar gives agency to the Palestinians he describes, who choose to stand "silent and still" for theatrical effect. Informed that a film crew is on its way, they are not pawns of their commanding officers in this vignette, but actors in a film of their own making, Indians ambushing the invading "pioneers" trapped in the valley below them. In this *mise en scène,* the fedayeen have the upper hand, while the unsuspecting film crew and its native informant—convinced, until then, they were going to shoot an authentic moment in the Palestinian Revolution—play the role of the defeated settlers. This distribution of roles—Palestinians as Indians, filmmakers as aspiring pioneers—offers a gentle and ironic rebuke of the French film crew that has been invited to film the anticolonial struggle. They may think they can save the Palestinians from the plight of the "Redskins," but such a desire remains caught in a colonialist view of indigenous subjects as perpetually on the cusp of defeat. In the fedayeen's film, the terms of comparison are reversed: transindigenous identification becomes a source of strength and resilience—*sumud* is the Arabic term that corresponds to the fedayeen's defiant posture in this scene—not a harbinger of defeat.[42]

Sanbar's suggestion that the fedayeen are drawing from their memories of Western films to fashion their image as "'brave' Indians" is not as fanciful as one might think. When he wrote this text, Sanbar had already published *Palestine 1948: L'expulsion* (1984), a monograph about the 1948 expulsion of some 800,000 Palestinians to make way for the fledgling Israeli state, and the first scholarly publication, in his estimation, to establish a sustained comparison between indigenous Americans and Palestinians.[43] Sanbar would revisit this comparison in several texts, including, as we will see, those that later served as explicit intertexts for *Notre musique*. But the comparison was not new. As I showed in my readings of Mohamed Rouabhi's workshops with Palestinian students (chapter 4), identification with indigenous Americans has been a persistent leitmotiv for Palestinians. As was the case for the protagonist of Farida Belghoul's *Georgette!* (chapter 3), the ubiquitous Hollywood Western movies that aired on French television, and saturated the visual field in the Middle East as well, helped fashion the image of the "Red Indian" (*al-Hindi al-ahmar,* the Arabic term used to designate indigenous Americans) shared by formerly and still colonized subjects across the Mediterranean, from Algeria to France and Palestine.

As Steven Salaita has amply documented in his work, transindigenous identification has a vibrant textual life as well, from Robert Warrior's seminal 1989 essay "Canaanites, Cowboys, and Indians" to Russell Means's recent response to the poem staged in *Notre musique,* Mahmoud Darwish's "The 'Red Indian's' Penultimate Speech to the White Man."[44] As Salaita astutely observes, "Indians have become actors in the rhetorical battlegrounds of the Israel–Palestine conflict."[45] Although Salaita is right to caution against an instrumentalist appropriation of Native suffering as a token of authenticity for Palestinian (or for that matter Israeli) indigeneity, using a cinematic metaphor to critique the use of "Indians" as figures or *figurants* (extras) on the set of the Israeli-Palestinian drama, I propose that we recuperate the root sense of the term *actor* to analyze transindigenous identification as a reciprocal form of agency. What does it mean for Palestinians to play the role of the Indians in their own anticolonial Western? What, in turn, happens when indigenous American actors declaim a Palestinian poem composed in their name?

Without limiting my reading to one of unidirectional influence, my attempt to trace a Palestinian genealogy of the appearance of indigenous Americans in Godard's late films is driven by the question of transindigenous identification. Although, as we have seen, Godard was already deploying the figure of the Indian before his encounter with Sanbar on the set of "Jusqu'à la victoire," this encounter would have a decisive impact on the transindigenous perspective adopted in *Notre musique*. Indeed, Sanbar can be credited with inspiring, or at least enabling, Godard's most sustained representation of indigenous Americans to date, in the film *Notre musique,* which cheekily cites Sanbar in the film credits as being responsible for nothing less than "memory."

Palestinians and Indians (Shot/Reverse Shot)

My reading of *Notre musique* revolves around the co-presence in the film of three indigenous American characters, played by indigenous actors (in order of appearance, Léticia Gutiérrez, George Aguilar, and Ferlyn Brass), and Mahmoud Darwish, who plays himself. As Darwish's principal translator in France, Sanbar was instrumental in securing the poet's participation in the film, where Darwish recites, from memory, his lines from an interview with Israeli poet Helit Yeshurun, as well as the rights to include Darwish's poem, "The 'Red Indian's' Penultimate Speech to the White Man," in the film's diegesis. In one of the most important scenes in *Notre musique,* Godard, playing his own role, gives a lecture on a series of still images and photographs, one of which had recently been published in Sanbar's magisterial photo-essay, *The Palestinians: Photographs of a Land and Its People from 1839 to the Present Day,* which compares Orientalist photographs of Palestinians to nineteenth-century photographs of conquered Indians. It is Sanbar who allegedly gave both Darwish and Godard the idea of including "Indians" in their work.[46] But his role as purveyor of memory is most deeply felt, I would argue, in the way indigenous Americans are represented in *Notre musique.*

Notre musique is made up of three movements of unequal length: "Hell," a ten-minute montage of fiction and documentary films depicting battles and war atrocities, including shots from John Ford's A-list Western *Fort Apache* (1948) and Godard and Miéville's *Ici et ailleurs,* set to dramatic symphonic music; "Purgatory," which comprises the diegetic portion of the film, set in Sarajevo and, briefly, in the terrace garden of Godard's residence in Rolle, Switzerland; and "Heaven," a six-minute dreamlike sequence that follows Olga, one of the fictional characters in the film, onto a lakeside beach guarded by U.S. Marines. I focus in my analysis on "Purgatory," which offers a montage of intersecting stories in lieu of a classic plot. The diegetic pretext for this central part of the film is the convening of the European Literary Encounters in Sarajevo, where fictional characters interact with writers and artists playing their own roles, most notably Juan Goytisolo, author of a searing account of the Bosnian War, *Landscapes of War,* and *State of Siege,* a novel that splices the siege of Sarajevo with the fictional assault of a working-class, immigrant neighborhood of Paris by "ethnic cleansing brigades";[47] Darwish, who plays himself in the above-mentioned interview, conducted in the film by the fictional character Judith Lerner, a reporter from Tel Aviv; and Godard himself, who delivers a master class on the cinematic technique of shot/reverse shot to a roomful of captive film students.

To the extent that there is a plot, its heroine is Olga. After an establishing shot of the café Imperijal—chosen, presumably, for its evocative neon red sign—where Godard will meet several of the film's characters, the camera intermittently follows Olga as she runs through the streets of Sarajevo, sits in rapt attention, eyes closed, through Godard's lecture, and confides to her uncle, Ramos Garcia, a polyglot interpreter, that she is planning to commit suicide. Her final act is reported offscreen by the interpreter, who calls Godard as he is tending to his garden, three weeks after the European Literary Encounters. Bearing the red shoulder bag she lugged around in Sarajevo, Olga took hostage a cinema audience in Tel Aviv, asking if anyone wanted to join her for the cause of peace. When the IDF soldiers who shot her down examined the contents of her bag, Garcia continues, they found that it was filled with books. A slow tracking shot of Godard's flower beds and the sound of birds chirping announces the transition to the third part of the film, which follows Olga into her leafy paradise.

Most analyses of *Notre musique* focus on the centrality of the Israeli-Palestinian conflict in the film, for good reason. In a public conversation with René Vautier in 2002, Godard announced that he was working on a film that would feature a pro-Palestinian French kamikaze, confirming the centrality of Olga's final act in the diegesis of the film.[48] The film makes Olga Jewish—for added dramatic effect?—and doubles her with a second female lead, the reporter from Tel Aviv.[49] Lerner's interview with Darwish is positioned halfway through "Purgatory," placing the Palestinian question quite literally at the heart of a film set in Sarajevo, the site of a Muslim genocide that cannot but evoke the ethnic cleansing of Palestinians.

Symbolically staged at the Holiday Inn, where foreign reporters and international observers such as Susan Sontag and Juan Goytisolo witnessed the nearly four-year siege of the city (1992–96), the interview with Darwish functions as an allegory for dialogue in the wake of destruction. Lerner has come to Sarajevo to "see a place where reconciliation seems possible." "Why Sarajevo? Because of Tel Aviv, because of Palestine," she tells the French ambassador to Bosnia-Herzegovina, who hid her parents from the Vichy authorities in 1943. In a magical operation of instantaneous translation—effaced by the introduction, against Godard's wishes, of English subtitles—the interview is conducted in Hebrew and Arabic, without recourse to an interpreter (the original interview with Israeli poet Helit Yeshurun, on which this exchange is based, was conducted in Hebrew, a language Darwish mastered perfectly). The Palestinian and Israeli understand each other's languages, even though in one instance, Darwish corrects Lerner's citation of his words: "In *Palestine as Metaphor,* you write, 'If they defeat us in poetry, then it's the end." Layering the Arabic original over her faulty Hebrew translation, Darwish recites from memory what he actually said in the interview that Lerner (and Yeshurun before her) is misquoting here. "'I don't think there's an end to people, or to poetry.' There must be a mistake in this quote." Elided in the partial subtitles, which do not include Darwish's correction, the layering of Hebrew and Arabic voices in the sound track sets the published record straight, offering an audio archive of the Palestinian's rejoinder—albeit one that remains untranslated in the subtitles, and incomprehensible to Adler, who in the role of Lerner acts as if she understands Arabic but cannot, in fact, make out the meaning of her interlocutor's words.[50]

The centrality of the Israeli-Palestinian relation in *Notre musique* becomes clear in the formal and thematic parallels between this scene and the next, Godard's master class on the cinematic technique of shot/reverse shot, traditionally used to film dialogue (Godard gives the classic example of the close-up shots of Cary Grant and Rosalind Russell, engrossed in conversation in Howard Hawks's *His Girl Friday*). Formally mimicking the conventions of a shot/reverse shot encounter, the first shot of Darwish, a medium close-up framed, in *contre-jour* lighting, against the French windows of the hotel lobby, finds its visual equivalent in the following scene, which ends with a close-up of Godard's head and shoulders in silhouette, a bright light bulb shining behind him. Godard has just completed his lecture, which centers around two photographs representing Palestinian refugees and Jewish settlers in Palestine. "For example," Godard explains to his captive audience, "in 1948 the Israelites walked in the water to reach the promised land. The Palestinians walked in the water to drown. Shot and reverse shot. Shot and reverse shot. The Jewish people enters the realm of fiction, the Palestinian people, documentary."[51] Following Lerner's interview with Darwish, Godard's cryptic and, needless to say, controversial relegation of "Israelites" to fiction and Palestinians to documentary serves as a visual extension of Darwish's ironic self-presentation as the "poet of Troy."[52] The Palestinian poet's claim, in the preceding interview, "to speak in the name of the absentee [*al-gha'ib*]" comes close to what, in his study of Palestinian cinema, Kamran Rastegar describes as "the perceived need to offer testimonial evidence to [the Palestinians'] collective experiences"—the need to serve as witness "of a people that has not been recognized," in Darwish's apt formulation.[53]

In an interview published in *Cahiers du cinéma* in May 2004, Godard gives what is perhaps the clearest account of his intentions in denaturalizing the cinematic technique of shot/reverse shot. Speaking of what he calls, in inverted quotes, "'American' cinema" (America, he rightly notes, is the name of a continent) Godard ties his idiosyncratic use of the shot/reverse shot technique to a critique of U.S. imperialism's "fantasy" of origins: "Origins are linked to the desire to be unique, *to not have a reverse shot*. There is a phantasm, a psychosis of origins."[54] According to Godard, a reverse shot that simply follows the point of view established in the previous frame leaves intact the dominant gaze. In this case, the gaze is male and "American." But Godard's critique also applies to the shot of "Redskins" rising out of the grasses in Mann's *The Last Frontier,* for example, where "the gaze follows an imposed orientation" (also Godard's, at the time): that of the settler/pioneer. The Hollywood shot/reverse shot does not invite "thinking" (*la pensée*). It remains a cliché.

The most contentious shot/reverse shot in *Notre musique* is undoubtedly Godard's abovementioned montage of a color photograph of

"Israelites" disembarking in Palestine, followed by a black-and-white photograph of Palestinians "thrown into the sea" (as the photo's caption in Sanbar's book has it).[55] Implicit in Godard's critique of U.S. exceptionalism is a critique of the exceptionalist discourse that presents the Jewish genocide as a unique and incomparable event, as becomes clear in an interview Godard gave shortly after the film's release. Here he proposes the cinematic technique of shot/reverse shot as a relational method of comparison that does not, in his view, collapse the two shots, but rather "poses a question":

> I bring two situations together [*je rapproche deux situations*], people say: Godard claims that the Shoah endured by the Jews and the Nakba endured by the Palestinians are one and the same. Of course not! That's completely idiotic. Shot and reverse shot signify no equivalence, no equality, but rather pose a question.

It is precisely in the dissymmetry of the Israel–Palestine couple that Godard sees a genuine shot/reverse shot, one that underscores the differences between the two rather than their similarities. Differences that Godard presents as resolutely colonial. For the Palestinians have become, *nolens volens,* the "other" of the Israelis. "This dissymmetry constitutes a genuine shot/reverse shot, a putting into relation [*une mise en relation*] that bears more questions than the simple juxtapositions [*alternances*] that claim to establish an equivalency between two terms."

Recalling his desire to film Palestine the way a Frenchman should have filmed Algeria, Godard describes his own role, as filmmaker, in setting up this shot/reverse shot in unambiguously transcolonial terms. In a fascinating admission of the ways in which he is implicated in the European and Israeli colonial ventures, including the colonization of Palestine and Algeria, Godard expands on the significance of Israel–Palestine as shot/reverse shot:

> The Palestinians have been forced to fashion for themselves an image . . . of "others," those others that the Europeans have called Arabs since the era of colonization. I grew up, like many people, with this imagery: when I was little I ate in storied dishes that narrated the most exciting moments in the conquest of Algeria. We ate our buttered bread on the plate of General Bugeaud.

In other words, the Palestinians are the others of the Israelis, but they are also the others of the European colonizers, the reverse shot hidden beneath the storied images of the conquest of Algeria that were the daily bread of Godard's childhood. In this sense, the Palestinians are in good company. For as we have seen, indigenous Americans populate Godard's anticolonial visions, from the clichéd images lifted from Hollywood Westerns into his collectivist films, to the life-sized characters that populate *Notre musique*. "Le vrai contrechamp des Palestiniens," Godard confides in his interview with the *Cahiers du cinéma*, "c'est sans doute moins Israël que les Indiens" (The real reverse shot of the Palestinians is not so much Israel as it is the Indians).[56]

If, as Godard suggests, "Indians" constitute the reverse shot of the Palestinians, what questions does this heterogeneous montage pose? Pace Jacques Rancière, for whom *Notre musique* effaces the differences between Indians, Palestinians, and "Jews murdered in the camps," Godard's insistence on the cinematic technique of shot/reverse shot as a methodology that invites thinking demands that we take seriously the distinction introduced by the cut between the two.[57] To say that the Indians are the reverse shot of the Palestinians is precisely not to say they are the same, but to pose the question of their relationality. At the antipodes of the clichéd representations of Indians in his early films—as we will see, *Notre musique* stages an explicit critique, through shot/reverse shot, of the image of the Indian—and of the Dziga Vertov group's schematic comparison between "Redskins" and Palestinians, the encounters *Notre musique* stages between indigenous Americans and Palestinians withhold straightforward identification and invite us instead to pose the question of indigeneity at the borders of Europe.

Indigeneity at the Borders of Europe

I begin with the critique of the cliché of the Indian in *Notre musique*, even though it is the final scene in which the indigenous American characters appear in the film, because it serves to underscore the contrast between Godard's previous uses of this figure and his sustained reflection, through sound layering, on transindigenous identification in the scenes I will discuss below. In the penultimate sequence of "Purgatory," Lerner, who has just interviewed Mahmoud Darwish, takes a taxicab to the Mostar bridge, which was shelled by Croatian forces in 1993 and was being rebuilt at the time of filming. After visiting an elementary class and conversing with Gilles Pecqueux, the French engineer tasked, at the time, with rebuilding the bridge, Lerner runs down to the riverbank to take one last photograph. As she aims her camera, she hears the sound of a stuttering engine and turns around. The long shot that follows shows the three indigenous American characters getting ready to leave in a blue pickup truck. Brass is throwing stones into the water, Gutiérrez is dragging a heavy bag to the truck, and Aguilar is trying to start the engine. The engine revs up, and the three drive off before Lerner has time to snap a picture of them. With a faint smile that reveals wonder and amusement, Lerner turns her gaze toward the bridge again as the sound of the engine fades in the distance. The point-of-view shot that follows reveals an impossible montage: a long shot of the three indigenous Americans standing silent and motionless under the Mostar bridge, now dressed in Hollywood Indian garb. Brass is on horseback, and Gutiérrez and Aguilar stand by his side (Figure 13). The imperceptible movements of their hair and clothes and the flowing waters of the river reveal that this is a moving image, not a still. And yet the point-of-view shot makes it clear that this is the *cliché* ("photograph," in French) Lerner hoped to take of the three "Indians." They left before she could press the shutter, but she re-creates the scene in her imagination, swapping out their jeans for suede tunics and their pickup for a horse. The camera cuts to Lerner's face again, and then to a medium long shot of the same scene, with the symphonic music from "Hell" now drawing a link to the archive of violence in the first part of the film. The audio cue to John Ford's *Fort Apache* alerts us to the role of the Western genre as foil in *Notre musique*. But foil for what? If, as Rancière suggests, "the Redskin's horse and satirical feathers in front of the bridge at Mostar denounce the clichés of European imagery," the previous scenes staging indigenous Americans in the film go much further than a simple deconstruction of the Indian of American Westerns.[58]

Most readings of *Notre musique* take this final tableau of the cliché of the Indian as an allegory of radical otherness. Burlin Barr and Phillip Roberts, for example, argue that Godard uses the "phantasm" of the Indians in this scene as a figure of "radical alterity."[59] James S. Williams concurs, bizarrely placing the indigenous Americans of *Notre musique* in "a clear pecking order of others (Palestinians at the top, supported metaphorically by Native Americans from below)."[60] Although

FIGURE 13. *Point-of-view shot of actors Ferlyn Brass, Léticia Gutiérrez, and George Aguilar disguised as Hollywood Indians, standing before the Mostar bridge in Sarajevo. Screenshot from* Notre musique, *directed by Jean-Luc Godard (2004).*

these critics correctly identify the centrality of indigenous Americans in the film, I would argue that they nevertheless follow an "imposed orientation"—Lerner's point-of-view shot—instead of "posing a question" about what this heterogeneous montage signifies. At the antipodes of "'American' cinema," and most notably that American genre par excellence, the Hollywood Western, the indigenous American characters that populate *Notre musique* invite the particular kind of thinking made possible by Godard's heterogeneous shot/reverse shots. Kriss Ravetto-Biagioli comes much closer to the mark when she asks: "Are the Native Americans who appear in their traditional dress a symbol of the ghostly past? If so, whose past do they present: the Native Americans, Native Americans as imagined by a Palestinian poet (Darwish's "Speech of the Red Indian"), Palestinians, or the 'natives' of Mostar?"[61] Ravetto-Biagioli's insistence on the centrality of nativeness in Bosnia-Herzegovina is well taken, even though, following Byrd, I part ways with her "spectral" figuration of indigenous Indians, who are evoked, even in the most sympathetic discussions, as "past tense presences."[62] Far from representing the past, as the cliché of the Indian would lead us to believe, I will argue that the indigenous Americans in *Notre musique* serve to make the question of indigeneity—habitually circumscribed to America's past—urgently relevant to Europe's present.

This becomes clear through the use of sound layering in a scene that is usually read, as I suggest above, as an allegory of the centrality of the Israeli-Palestinian relation in the film: Lerner's interview with Darwish. The scene begins with an exterior shot of the reporter, accompanied by a film crew—we see the cameraman in the frame—and a pair of indigenous American characters (played by Léticia Gutiérrez and Ferlyn Brass) playfully chanting, hopping up on the rim of a fountain, and hugging as they approach the Holiday Inn. In a somewhat jarring sound bridge, a female voice-over introduces Darwish to his interviewer before the camera cuts from a shot of the Holiday Inn sign, which Lerner is photographing, to a shot of the same woman telling Lerner (on-screen) and Darwish (offscreen): "OK folks, it's your play." The relatively long scene of arrival, sound bridge, and slightly non-idiomatic cue ("it's your play") all draw attention to the staging of the interview for the camera crew, which remains visible throughout the scene. After the *contre-jour* shot of Darwish—also a self-reflexive shot, in the sense that it would normally be edited out of a televised interview—the cameraman comes to sit behind Darwish to film Lerner, and then continues filming from a third angle, taking a seat next to a character played by one of the most recognizable indigenous American actors in the history of Hollywood, George Aguilar of *Star Trek* fame. The camera cuts to Lerner and then to Darwish, who concludes his musings about the poetry of Troy with the line "you [the Israelis] have brought us defeat and renown." The camera cuts once more to Lerner as the sound track suddenly expands to heighten the muffled background noise, chattering of voices, and echo of laughter that provided a faint ambient sound in previous shots. We hear Darwish's last line repeated against this markedly noticeable background noise, suggesting, in diegetic terms, that the film has been edited to include a reverse shot of Darwish's words. If the framing suggests that the reverse shot is filmed from Darwish's point of view, the hotel guests previously faintly visible behind Lerner suddenly come into much sharper focus. The center of gravity of the soundscape has been definitively altered. Offering an audio echo of the cut to the shot of Aguilar moments earlier, the sound of the interview becomes fainter as well, capturing sound from the point of view of a third subject: the indigenous American witness to the Arabic-Hebrew interview. The sound of an echoing, staccato, male voice, barely distinguishable over Darwish's words, serves as a sound bridge to the following shot: two indigenous American men (played by Brass and Aguilar) in suit and tie stand in the hotel lobby, conversing in Native American English— the slightly accented speech stereotyped in Western films—as they wait for their friend (Gutiérrez). The sound track of the interview comes to the fore again as Darwish's acousmatic voice rings out, accompanying Gutiérrez as she slowly descends the steps of a marble staircase.

In diegetic terms, the final shot of this scene, a close-up of Gutiérrez smiling to her companions, explains the presence of the indigenous American couple in the establishing shot of this scene, and of Aguilar during the interview. The three indigenous Americans are staying at the Holiday Inn, where Darwish is being interviewed. And yet their presence in Sarajevo is not merely happenstance. For the indigenous Americans emerging from the sound track of Darwish's interview are the same characters who recited an unattributed poem by Darwish, "The 'Red Indian's' Penultimate Speech to the White Man," in a previous scene, set in a spacious and almost entirely empty reading room in the ruined library of Sarajevo, where an elderly man sits hunched over a rickety desk inscribing the title of books on a catalog ledger. Goytisolo walks through the frame declaiming words that might be excerpted from his novel about the destruction of "thousands of Ottoman, Persian, and Arabic manuscripts," dubbed in French by the interpreter, Garcia, while a little girl in a red jacket runs up to the desk to donate a picture book.[63] An elderly woman (a colleague or accomplice of the librarian) enters the frame, takes the girl's picture book, and carelessly throws it into a heap of books on the floor.

Although the older couple's activities are not explained, two lively fires burning in a far corner of the room, and the haphazard way the woman throws the books onto a pile, evoke the destruction by fire of what was, at the time of the bombing of Sarajevo's municipal library, one of the most distinguished collections of Islamic scholarship in Europe. The camera cuts to a series of panning shots of the empty shell of the library, following Goytisolo's footsteps, before returning to the reading room, but from a reverse-shot angle, as if to suggest an entirely new perspective on the book-burning symbolically represented in this scene. Gutiérrez enters the frame from behind the camera and walks toward the librarian, standing in the center of the frame, followed by Aguilar, who fills the left third, occupying a visual field in which the librarian, still hunched over his desk, suddenly appears much smaller. The physical presence of the indigenous American characters is imposing, although their attire is unremarkable, save a black-and-white feather stuck in Gutiérrez's hair. Aguilar begins declaiming the second stanza of Darwish's poem in a booming baritone as he approaches the man, still oblivious to the pair's presence: "The white man will never understand the ancient words / here in spirits roaming free / between the sky and the trees. Let Columbus scour the seas to find India. . . . / he can call us Red Indians . . . / but outside the narrow world of his map / he can't believe that all men are born equal." While Aguilar circles the librarian, his accomplice attempts, unsuccessfully, to wrestle a book out of Gutiérrez's hands. Gutiérrez blurts out, in a slightly Spanish-accented English: "Isn't it about time?" Aguilar shushes her and continues his recitation: "Isn't it about time, stranger, / for us to meet face to face in the same age, / both of us strangers to the same land?" (Figure 14). A camera bulb flashes unexpectedly, and the camera cuts to a close-up of Aguilar and Gutiérrez looming over the librarian, the crackle of the fire suddenly crisply audible in the background. Gutiérrez completes the recitation of Darwish's poem, slowly delivering verses that echo chillingly with the book-burning evoked in this scene: "Both of us strangers to the same land, / meeting at the tip of an abyss. . . . / Winds will recite our beginning and our end / though our present bleeds / and our days are buried in the ashes of legend."[64] In the final shot of this scene, a middle-aged woman wearing a headscarf walks into the now empty reading room and places a visibly brand-new book on the abandoned desk—perhaps a sign that after the indigenous Americans' disquisition, the book-burning will stop? The near-encounter between this Muslim Bosnian woman and the indigenous Americans provides a fresh clue to the presence of indigenous Americans in Sarajevo, as I will suggest at the close of my reading.

As critics of *Notre musique* were quick to note, nowhere is Darwish credited with this poem in the film. A viewer unfamiliar with Darwish would not know that the outraged address to the "white man" in this

FIGURE 14. *George Aguilar and Léticia Gutiérrez declaim Mahmoud Darwish's poem "The 'Red Indian's' Penultimate Speech to the White Man" in the library of Sarajevo. Screenshot from* Notre musique, *directed by Jean-Luc Godard (2004).*

scene was penned by a Palestinian, not an indigenous American, although as I suggest in my reading above, Darwish's interview in the following scene establishes a strong, if somewhat enigmatic, audiovisual connection between Palestinian and American indigeneity. The "poet of Troy" is also, readers of Darwish will know, the poet of indigenous America. "The 'Red Indian's' Penultimate Speech to the White Man" was first published in *Ahada 'ashara kawkaban* (Eleven planets), a collection that begins with a long poem titled "Ahada 'ashara kawkaban 'ala akhir al-mashhad al-Andalusi" ("Eleven Planets at the End of the Andalusian Scene").[65] Published in 1992, this volume coincided with the centenary of what Ella Shohat has dubbed "the two '1492s'": the conquest of America and the Catholic Reconquista of Spain, culminating in the expulsion of Jews in that year and, in 1609, the final expulsion of Muslims, who ruled Al-Andalus, as they dubbed the Iberian Peninsula, for nearly eight centuries.[66] In this sense, *Ahada 'ashara kawkaban* deliberately connects the expulsion of the Arabs from the West—metonymically symbolized by the fall of Granada—to the conquest of the Americas, accompanied, Darwish explains, "by a genocidal project that followed the model and spirit of the Crusades."

In preparation for writing "The 'Red Indian's' Penultimate Speech to the White Man," Darwish immersed himself in the history of resistance to U.S. settler colonialism in order to "put [himself] in the skin of the Indian." This is a telling expression for what I am calling *trans-indigenous identification,* given the role lent to skin color in the modern production of racial difference. But most interesting for my purposes is Darwish's claim to have recognized himself in the history of indigenous Americans: "Everything had already prepared me to receive the message of the Indian. . . . Having learned about his culture, I realized that he had spoken of me better than I had been able to."[67] Read in this way, the "Red Indian's" address to the white man—"Isn't it about time, stranger, for us to meet face to face in the same age, both of us strangers in the same land?"—is as much a Palestinian's address to an Israeli. The use of the nomenclature *stranger* in Darwish's poem is highly marked, given the contest for indigeneity in both Palestine–Israel and the United States. It goes without saying that Darwish is not trying to relativize indigenous American and Palestinian rights to the land of their ancestors. Both, he insists, continue to be subjected to colonial rule. But I would argue that staging an encounter between "strangers in the same land" shifts the focus from a naturalized understanding of indigeneity as priorness—I was here first—to indigeneity as the basis for a political relationship between colonizer and colonized in the present.[68] In the same interview that was misquoted by Yeshurun, Darwish clarifies what he means by calling for Palestinians and Israelis to "meet face to face": "given that this land [Palestine] has been trodden throughout History by strangers . . . I can accept that we [Palestinians and Israelis] are both strangers. But he [Israel] asks me to be the sole stranger, the sole intruder."[69] Like the Muslims of Spain, the indigenous Americans and Palestinians have been erased from the past, present, and future of the land they once called theirs.

The year 1992, of course, is also the apex of the Bosnian War, fought over the legitimacy of the very presence of Muslims in Europe. The quincentennial of the fall of Granada staged in Darwish's "Eleven Planets at the End of the Andalusian Scene" coincides with the threat of a new expulsion, by genocide, of Muslims at the landed frontier of the European continent. That indigenous Americans perform a poem written by a displaced Palestinian in the voice of dispossessed "Red Indians" in the ruined library of Sarajevo explicitly indexes the question of indigeneity at the borders of a Europe increasingly prey to *nativism:* the ethnonationalist claim that only white, Christian Europeans—not the veiled woman who donates a book to the library—can lay claim to indigeneity.

In a public conversation with Godard in 2004, Sanbar offers a somewhat different interpretation of the presence of indigenous Americans in Godard's film, reviving the derogatory formulation "Peaux-Rouges"— although, to his credit, this is perhaps an attempt to translate Darwish's "Red Indians"—to speculate on the condition of exile in *Notre musique:*

> *Our Music* is a nomadic work. Because nothing in this film is in its place. The Redskins are not at home. Juan Goytisolo is not in Catalonia. Mahmoud Darwish is not in Palestine. The Israeli journalist is not in Tel Aviv.... Even Sarajevo is not in its place.... This film shows that we can better understand [*entendre*] what is happening in a place when it is displaced.[70]

Although I take issue with Sanbar's somewhat naive understanding of "nomadism" or exile as an experience that can be shared across subject positions—as if indigenous Americans and Palestinians were displaced in a way that is at all commensurate with Goytisolo's or Lerner's pilgrimage to a site of Muslim genocide in Europe—his intuition that one understands (or hears) better from a site of displacement is worth developing. What does it mean that Sarajevo itself is not in its place? What, indeed, is the place of Sarajevo in the film?

Targeted during the Bosnian War as a symbol of multiconfessional pluralism, Sarajevo has become a metonym for the possibility of genocide at the borders of Europe. Eighty years after another international conflict—also sparked in Sarajevo—created what Hannah Arendt called "the problem of the stateless people," half a century after the first mass-scale genocide in the modern history of continental Europe, Sarajevo also marks the replacement of politics with humanitarianism, and the consequent failure of the very institutions created to safeguard against the possibility of genocidal violence in Europe.[71] Adding to a chorus of critics of humanitarianism, Rancière has argued that, unlike the Algerian War of Independence, where the stakes were clearly political—as a French citizen, one was either for or against Algerian self-determination—the Bosnian War failed to trigger a political relation to what he calls "the cause of the other."[72] But this does not explain the failure of European institutions to take responsibility for the fate of European Muslims. Godard wanted to make a film about Arabs as a French national should have filmed the Algerian War. *Notre musique* is his attempt to make a film about European Muslims as a European should have filmed the Bosnian War. That he does so by including his "others"—indigenous Americans and Palestinians—clearly implicates him in a conflict that most Europeans would consider foreign.

Nuancing Sanbar's suggestion that all the characters in *Notre musique* are out of place, I'd like to suggest, at the close of this reading, that the characters assembled in Sarajevo in the first years of the new millennium are there for a reason. As I argued above, the intersecting encounters staged in "Purgatory" inscribe the question of indigeneity at the borders of Europe: the indigenous American performance of a Palestinian poem about the Indian genocide; the indigenous American witnessing of an Arabic and Hebrew interview with the "poet of Troy"; and the near encounters between indigenous Americans and Bosnian women, first in the library of Sarajevo, where a middle-aged veiled woman donates a book moments after the performance of "The 'Red Indian's' Penultimate Speech to the White Man," and then in the streets of Sarajevo, where a pair of indigenous Americans' joyful chants echo with the sound of the muezzin as an elderly woman in hijab passes by. Against the nativist claim that Islam is foreign to Europe and must be rooted out, the co-presence of indigenous Americans and European Muslims in these scenes indexes the question of indigeneity as one that is fraught with significance in Europe today.

That the Balkan Route would become, a decade after *Notre musique* was released, one of the major sites of mass migration to Europe, and a beacon in the pan-European Crusade against the new Muslim "invasions," only lends more urgency to the staging of transindigenous identification as a critique of nativism in *Notre musique*. In the next chapter, I explore the ongoing migrant question in relation to the decades-long Palestinian question, and argue, against the ubiquitous discourse of hospitality, that we need urgently to adopt a transcolonial and transhistorical approach to migration in order to counter the nativist recuperation of indigeneity in the late twentieth and early twenty-first centuries.

CHAPTER 6

Palestine and the Migrant Question

The Migrant Question

Two decades ago, Mireille Rosello argued that "the vision of the immigrant as guest is a metaphor that has forgotten it is a metaphor."[1] The trope of the migrant as unexpected guest remains ubiquitous in current discourses about migrants, from nativist discourses on the right to liberal attempts to reframe the "migrant crisis" in humanitarian terms.[2] What I call instead *the migrant question*—the production of a dehistoricized discourse of crisis about the purported invasion of France by colonial subjects-turned-foreigners—is at the heart of the archive I have mobilized in this book, from the ephemeral publications of the CSRP and the PIR to Jean Genet's unrealized screenplay "La nuit venue," Farida Belghoul's *Georgette!*, Mohamed Rouabhi's "El menfi," and Jean-Luc Godard's *Notre musique*.[3] Central to all of these texts is a critique of the discourse of crisis that turns (post)colonial migrants into strangers/foreigners—a critique that I call *indigenous* because of its attention to the colonial history that produced the racialized identities it unravels (*indigène,* Arab, Muslim, Indian).[4] Already a key concern in the early 1970s when antiracist activists began invoking Palestine as rallying cry, the migrant question has taken on even more urgency for antiracist activists in recent years.

This chapter zooms out from metropolitan France to think about the relationship between the migrant question and the question of Palestine in the context of the ongoing mass displacements from and across the Global South. I read a range of texts that deploy Palestine in a comparative framework to show that the mass transfer of populations we are witnessing today is less a turning point—one of the etymological meanings of *crisis*—than a new iteration of what Ann Laura Stoler calls "history as recursion . . . processes of partial reinscriptions, modified displacements, and amplified recuperations."[5] In this reading, migrants are not foreigners, strangers, or unexpected guests, but what Stoler has termed the "debris" of empire, simultaneously forced into movement and immobilized in transit zones at the borders of the (former) metropole.[6]

Building on key insights delivered by Hannah Arendt and Edward Said decades ago, I turn to three recent texts that significantly expand the scope of this book to place the migrant question on a planetary scale that exceeds the bounds of the French empire. My approach here is less granular and exhaustive than in previous chapters, allowing me to foreground the very contemporary stakes of what I am calling *indigenous critique: Brûle la mer* (*Burn the Sea*), a 2014 film by Maki Berchache and Nathalie Nambot that stages a comparison between a Tunisian *harrag* ("burner" or undocumented migrant) in Paris and his occupied Palestinian friend; *Tropique de la violence* (*Tropic of Violence*), a 2016 novel by the Mauritian writer Nathacha Appanah that invokes Palestine to elucidate the abject misery of the inhabitants of "Gaza," the notorious slum of Mayotte, many of them Comorian clandestine migrants who cross the Indian Ocean to land on French overseas soil; and Ai Weiwei's 2017 documentary film *Human Flow,* which places the Palestinian question at the heart of the mass displacements of the 2010s. In different ways, these texts offer a critique of the production of the migrant as unexpected or unwelcome guest from a Southern, formerly and still colonized perspective. They also decenter the hegemony of the Mediterranean as a site of crisis by including the peripheries of empire in an expanded map of forced displacement. I conclude by reading Ghassan Kanafani's 1962 novella *Men in the Sun* as an allegory of the migrant question from a Palestinian point of view.

Sans-papiers

I begin my reading of Palestine and the migrant question with Maki Berchache and Nathalie Nambot's 2014 experimental documentary film *Brûle la mer,* which stages an encounter between a Tunisian *harrag* and a Palestinian who occupy different coordinates of the migrant experience: the Tunisian wants to stay in a country, France, that is barred to him; the Palestinian came to Paris legally but finds himself unable to return home. As the characters put it in the scene I analyze below, their stories are not the same ("mish nafs al-hikaya," in Palestinian Arabic),

FIGURE 15. *Tunisian migrant Maki Berchache and his Palestinian friend Shadi Al Fawaghra rest in a park near Maki's apartment in Bagnolet, a suburb of Paris. Screenshot from* Brûle la mer, *directed by Maki Berchache and Nathalie Nambot (2014). Courtesy of Maki Berchache and Nathalie Nambot.*

yet they nonetheless offer a complex audiovisual articulation of the shared experience of (post)colonial migration.[7] One of the most original films about the migrant question in Europe, *Brûle la mer* sets up an unexpected comparison between the situation of *harraga* (plural of *harrag*) and Palestinians, raising a set of provocative and, I will argue, urgent questions: What are the conditions that might enable us to think the Palestinian and migrant questions together? To what extent can the Palestinian question help elucidate current mass displacements? What, in turn, does the migrant question teach us about the Palestinian question?

The visual introduction to Palestine in *Brûle la mer* is a thirty-second-long continuous shot, placed eighteen minutes into the opening sequence, which narrates the protagonist's journey to France (Figure 15). Two young men are resting on a grassy knoll surrounded by pine trees, white clouds drifting through a blue sky in a tableau that might be described as pastoral, were it not for the incessant drone of highway

FIGURE 16. *Paris seen from the* banlieue. *Reverse shot of Maki and Shadi surveying the working-class suburb of Bagnolet and, in the distance, Paris* intramuros. *Screenshot from* Brûle la mer, *directed by Maki Berchache and Nathalie Nambot (2014). Courtesy of Maki Berchache and Nathalie Nambot.*

traffic and the high-rise towers jutting out in the background, which unmistakably place this scene in the *banlieue*, the working-class urban sprawl located on the other side of the ring road that circles Paris. Though they are at ease, they seem preoccupied, casting their gaze far into the distance at what we will later understand, thanks to a reverse shot in one of the final scenes of the film, is Paris *intramuros* (Figure 16). On one side of the screen, reclining in the grass, is the film's codirector and protagonist, Maki Berchache, whose itinerary from a fishing village in the south of Tunisia to a Bagnolet high-rise is retold in the film through grainy Super 8 and 16 mm color shots of the Tunisian seashore and the French *banlieue*. Sitting next to him is a character we have not yet encountered, his arms resting on his knees: Shadi Al Fawaghra, a Palestinian from the West Bank who has come to Paris to speak about "the Palestinian situation" (*wad'a filastin*) and finds himself stranded in the French capital, unable to return home.[8] The camera observes the two young men silently for several long seconds before cutting to

FIGURE 17. *The view from Maki's window. This shot returns at several points in the film, framing Maki's stories of exile from the point of view of his arrival. Screenshot from* Brûle la mer, *directed by Maki Berchache and Nathalie Nambot (2014). Courtesy of Maki Berchache and Nathalie Nambot.*

a claustrophobic shot of Maki's window in one of the high-rise towers, a framing shot that will structure the film as it shuttles back and forth between Paris and Tunisia (Figure 17).

Shadi remains unnamed in this opening scene: he is an anonymous migrant in the Parisian *banlieue*. Ten minutes before the end of the film, the camera returns to the pair to reveal the circumstances of their encounter, and the importance of this Tunisian-Palestinian friendship in the story of migration to France. Maki begins to speak softly in Tunisian Arabic (Darija). The fact that his remarks are delivered in voice-over gives them an ethereal, dreamlike imprimatur.[9] "I really like this place," he says. "You feel like you're somewhere else." His friend agrees, in Palestinian Arabic ('Amiya): from this vantage point, the city is "like an image, like a dream." In the diglossic conversation that follows, Maki and Shadi rehearse the events that brought them together, comrades in misfortune. They "arrived in France at the same time . . . not from the same country [*balad*], but from the same land [*ard*]." They share a language, Arabic (albeit different dialects), and cultural tradition. But beyond this almost clichéd articulation of pan-Arab cultural affinity lies a stark assessment of their shared political situation. As Shadi explains, neither he nor Maki was allowed to leave his country of birth. "Visa sa'ban" is Shadi's concise explanation: visas are hard to come by, but also passports, *laissez-passers,* all the documents that the *sans-papiers,* the undocumented, are lacking. Their trajectories are exemplary of the paradoxical condition of refugees, who cannot move freely and yet find themselves forced into perpetual movement, unable to return home or make a new one in the place they have come to. "To travel [*safar*] is a dream," muses Shadi. "Yes," agrees Maki, "to travel is a dream." The shot closes with the pair still gazing at the faraway image of a city inaccessible to those who seek refuge there.

Closer attention to the dialogue and its translation, however, reveals that Maki's and Shadi's experiences of migration are not the same. It is telling, for example, that Berchache, who was responsible for translating the conversation he had with Shadi for the French subtitles, renders *safar* (travel) as *partir* (leave), projecting his desire to leave his homeland behind onto the Palestinian's desire for mobility and return. At this point in the film, we know that Maki has acquired legal residency.[10] He lives in an apartment in the Cité La Noue in Bagnolet, one of the rapidly gentrifying low-income communities surrounding Paris; he speaks French fluently, and is now a filmmaker, as well as the protagonist in his own story. Unlike Maki, one of the 25,000 Tunisians who fled the country during the revolution, Shadi came to Paris legally and now finds himself unable to return to a home under military occupation.[11] He is the stateless subject of a colonial occupation that bars him access to his native land. What Shadi says next foregrounds this important distinction between the two migrants, providing an aural corrective to Maki's mistranslation that is only discernible to the Arabophone viewer. "I wanted to travel [*safar*]," insists Shadi, "not leave my country [*ma batruk baladi*]." In spite or perhaps because of his strong sense of identification with Tunisians when the revolution began—"we were all with the revolution . . . we felt that we were the same people [*nafs al-sha'b*]"—Shadi does not share Maki's telos. "It's not the same story [*mish nafs al-hikaya*]," he explains, in Palestinian 'Amiya. "No, it's not the same thing [*mish kif kif*]," Maki agrees, in Tunisian Darija. The aural difference in the friends' Arabic tongue gives an acoustic materiality to the divergence in their trajectories of exile.

And yet, the audiovisual language of this scene blurs the distinction that is made here in narrative, linguistic, and affective terms, resulting in a transcolonial articulation of indigeneity—*baladi* is one way to translate *indigenous* in Arabic—rooted not in the same colonial experience but in the same metaphoric land, expanded to include Tunisia, Palestine, and France. As Shadi recounts the uprooting of olive trees in his village, Wad Rahal, the camera pans around in a 360-degree handheld panoramic shot of Bagnolet and the semi-industrial outskirts of Paris, gradually zooming in, as if to extend the view from Maki's apartment in the opening sequence of the film. Maki's narrative of migration finds an echo in Shadi's trajectory of exile, resulting in the audiovisual layering of an occupied Palestinian village onto the drab grayness, factory chimneys, and high-rise towers of the *banlieue*. The image, the dream that Shadi invoked at the start of this scene, loops back to his imagined Palestine, projecting home onto the site of exile, and Palestine onto the postcolonial metropole. "My body is here," he confesses, "but I left my heart in the country [*fil-balad*]."

As if fulfilling Shadi's wish for return (*'awda*), the following sequence, set in Tunisia, shows Maki and his parents walking through an olive grove, whipping the branches with thin rods to make the fruit fall. Maki's father reaches up to pick an olive, and the camera zooms in on the ripe fruit in his father's open palm, a visual offering, through montage, for the Palestinian friend Maki has left behind in Paris (Figure 18). But this scene is also, in a sense, a wish fulfillment for Maki, who is able to travel back home now that he has obtained legal residency in France. Instead of being deported, he has won the privilege of mobility. The manifest pleasure Maki takes in being reunited with his family and his land complicates the story he has been telling in the film: that life in Tunisia was a slow death, that he had no choice but to leave. Poised between the home he has left and the dream of mobility he shares with his Palestinian friend, Maki seems to occupy an ambivalent position at the close of the film, torn between a desire for travel and a yearning for home. And yet, without effacing the very real differences between Maki and Shadi, *Brûle la mer* allows their itineraries to intersect in meaningful ways. The final sequence of the film foils our

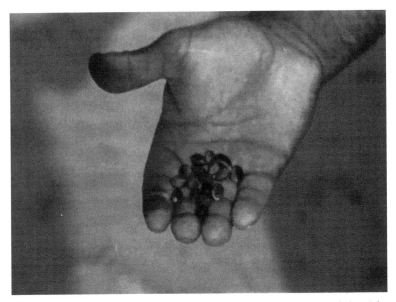

FIGURE 18. *An 8 mm close-up shot of a hand holding olives from Maki's family's olive grove in the south of Tunisia. Now a permanent resident of France, Maki is able to visit with his family back home. Screenshot from* Brûle la mer, *directed by Maki Berchache and Nathalie Nambot (2014). Courtesy of Maki Berchache and Nathalie Nambot.*

desire to understand the migrant question in simple terms, inviting us to widen our geographical and historical frame of analysis to include the Palestinian question in the story of migration. In the audiovisual chiasmus of the closing sequence, an imagined Palestine takes root in Tunisia while the working-class communities of postcolonial France echo with the sounds of Israeli bulldozers.

The complex audiovisual grammar of *Brûle la mer* is the starting point in my investigation of the migrant question from a Palestinian point of view. Despite the stark differences registered by Maki and Shadi in this scene—the Tunisian desires to stay in a country that does not want him; the Palestinian wants to go home but cannot—*Brûle la mer* sets up a startling parallel between Palestinian refugees and contemporary migrants and invites us to explore the resonances of the Palestinian question in a world that continues to be shaped by forced exile and violent expropriation. What does the ongoing migrant crisis reveal about the decades-old Palestinian question, and what can Palestine teach us about the human tragedy that continues to wash up on the shores of imperial nations?

Displacements

To fully grasp the ways in which the migrant question articulates itself with the Palestinian question, we need to begin much earlier than 2010, the date of the Tunisian Revolution, which is usually taken as the starting point of current mass migrations to Europe. As I argued in chapter 1, the palimpsestic juxtaposition of Maghrebi migrants and Palestinians in the CSRP's newsletter *Fedaï* was aimed at historicizing postcolonial migration in 1970s France. This is also one of the principal aims of the texts I read in this chapter, which present the current migrant question as the culmination of a modern history of mass displacements that includes the transfer of colonized subjects in the two great European wars of the twentieth century, and what Ilan Pappe has called, in no uncertain terms, "the ethnic cleansing by Israel of the Palestinians that started in 1948 but continues, in a variety of means, today."[12] Though distinct, the histories of displacement to Europe and from Palestine intersect at key points, and together mark the discursive reemergence of what, at the height of the European Jewish refugee crisis, Arendt called "a new kind of human being": the stateless refugee.[13]

Arendt's key insights into the paradigmatic condition of the refugee, exemplified, in the 1940s, in the figure of the European Jew, have direct bearing on my interpretation of Palestine and the migrant question. As Said argues in his reading of Arendt in *The Question of Palestine,* European Jews are exemplary of the modern state's production of statelessness, but they are not exceptional. On the contrary, the paradigmatic nature of the Jewish question is what allows Arendt to recognize the Palestinian question as one of statelessness.[14] The question of Palestine, in turn, has become exemplary of the migrant question. Here is how Said characterizes the Palestinian question in his photo-essay *After the Last Sky:* "Our truest reality is expressed in the way we cross from one place to another. We are migrants and perhaps hybrids in, but not of, any situation in which we find ourselves."[15] In the final chapter of *Culture and Imperialism,* Said extends his analysis of the Palestinian question to a global imperial map:

It is one of the unhappiest characteristics of the age to have produced more refugees, migrants, displaced persons, and exiles than ever before in history, most of them as an accompaniment to and, ironically enough, as afterthoughts of great post-colonial and imperial conflicts. . . . Insofar as these people exist between the old and the new, between the old empire and the new state, their condition articulates the tensions, irresolutions, and contradictions in the overlapping territories shown on the cultural map of imperialism.[16]

The widened frame Said offers here is not simply meant to accommodate a moving map of mass displacements. If the Palestinian question is, for Said, a classically colonial question, it is part of a messy postcolonial map that has produced "hybrids in, but not of" new sites of exile—the intersecting trajectories of a Tunisian migrant and an occupied Palestinian in Paris, for example. What this long view reveals are the discontinuous, overlapping, and recursive histories of imperialism that continue to produce today's mass displacements.

To be clear, the history of the Palestinian question does not match up exactly with the history of the migrant question. The scale (Israel–Palestine versus Europe and its former colonies) is incomparable, as is the direction of movement: from the colony in the first case, to the metropole in the second. And yet even a cursory look at these twinned chronologies of displacement underscores the belabored temporality of what the Western media have dubbed the *migrant crisis*—as if the mass movements of people from South to North in the 2010s were unprecedented. The staggering number of migrants and the velocity of displacement, to be sure, are new: over one million migrants entered Europe in 2015; more than 82 million persons were forcibly displaced across the globe in 2020. But numbers, here, are a distraction.[17] When placed in the context of the centennial displacement of colonial and postcolonial subjects, the current migrant crisis suddenly acquires a history, one that parallels the production of the Palestinian refugee crisis, even if it does not match it exactly. Products of different but overlapping histories, the Palestinian and migrant questions have only grown in urgency in the ensuing decades.

Against alarmist discourses that make the current mass displacements a turning point and existential litmus test for the future of Europe and the West, this chapter takes a long view, placing the current migrant question in a decades-long history of displacement that makes visible the production of a naturalized discourse of crisis. I use the expression *migrant question* instead of *migrant crisis* in order to delink current forms of coerced displacement from the dehistoricized discourses that have produced the very notion of crisis. The expression *migrant question* also deliberately echoes what Said analyzed some forty years ago under the name *the question of Palestine:* "something to be thought through, tried out, engaged with—in short . . . a subject to be dealt with politically."[18] Addressing the migrant question politically, in turn, requires that we place current mass displacements in a decades-long history that includes the Palestinian question in its purview.

The North in the South

I have argued that attending to the *longue durée* history of colonial and postcolonial displacements forces us to place recent migratory movements in what Said calls "the overlapping territories shown on the cultural map of imperialism," including Palestine. Paradoxically, the invocation of Palestine in my second textual example, Nathacha Appanah's *Tropique de la violence,* decenters the exceptional status of the Mediterranean on the moving map of (post)colonial displacements. If *Brûle la mer* forces us to rethink the dehistoricizing exceptionalism that portrays migrants as not only unwanted but unexpected guests, *Tropique de la violence* introduces a critique of the geographic exceptionalism that sites migration to Europe on the maritime and land borders of the continent. In recent years, critics have convincingly argued that the European Union has undergone a process of deterritorialization, erecting walls across its global extensions.[19] And yet the trope of Mediterranean crisis remains ubiquitous in the emerging field of migrant studies. Against the Mediterranean exceptionalism of migrant studies, I propose that we expand the "cultural map of imperialism" beyond Palestine and the Maghreb to the farthest reaches of Europe's overseas territories.

Tropique de la violence drags the coordinates of the migrant crisis south of the equator to Mayotte, France's minuscule island outpost in the Comoros archipelago. One of France's Indian Ocean colonies, Mayotte is, with La Réunion, France's sole remaining overseas territory in the region. Since 1975, the date of Comorian independence, tens of thousands of migrants from the three other islands in the archipelago and, increasingly, from the African continent and Madagascar have attempted to cross onto this tiny French island, a tropical avatar of Ceuta and Melilla, the Spanish enclaves nestled between Morocco and the Mediterranean. The introduction of stringent visa requirements in 1994 led to an uptick in clandestine crossings. Today, a third of the population is "foreign-born" (for the most part, from France's former Comorian colonies) and approximately 50 percent of migrants are undocumented. As occasionally happens with France's remote outposts, Mayotte made national headlines in 2016 when Mahorais militias set out to *décaser* (literally, remove from their homes, dislodge) migrants, adding to the already impressive official number of deportations by the border police: 15,000 to 20,000 per year, for a total population of 210,000.[20]

In order to draw our attention to this neglected frontier of migration to Europe, it would have sufficed to set the novel in Mayotte. But Appanah introduces another coordinate of displacement in her novel: the Gaza Strip, the tiny rectangle of land to which three generations of refugees are confined, sealed off from occupied Palestine through land and sea borders controlled by the Israeli and Egyptian states. The triangulated map that obtains in the novel stretches our understanding of the migrant question further to include both the Palestinian question and what Myriam Cottias dubs the *Black question,* yet another "question" produced in the colonial crucible.[21] For many of the migrants denied access to France are descendants of the enslaved and indentured populations from France's lucrative Indian Ocean colonies: Madagascar, Réunion, and other *poussières d'empire*—specks of imperial dust, as France's tiny island–colonies are poetically dubbed. The Indian Ocean migrants of today bear the history of the greatest forced mass displacement in modern history, a practice not restricted to the Western reaches of Europe's imperial dominion.[22]

"Mais c'est la France ici quand même!" (Come on, this is France!), exclaims one of the well-meaning metropolitan residents of Mayotte. Freshly minted as an NGO volunteer posted to this far-flung overseas department to open a cultural center for impoverished youth, Stéphane is touring Kaweni, the decrepit shantytown that sprawls north of the capital, Mamoudzou. "I'd been told it was like an inner-city housing project [*une cité*], with youngsters hanging around, dealing on the black market, steeped in boredom, with no prospects, no jobs, drugs galore." But Kaweni looks nothing like the *banlieue*. In its place Stéphane discovers a wretched shantytown made of "cases" (huts), mud, and trash. The only familiar sight is a group of disaffected young men, standing before a concrete wall bearing the tag "GAZA." Gaza is the unofficial name of this slum, and the only one the inhabitants of Mayotte use to refer to it. Stéphane takes a picture of the graffiti and sends it to his NGO friends posted in far-flung locations across the Third World, including, for the most intrepid volunteers, the Gaza Strip itself. "La bonne blague," he adds: LOL.[23]

Stéphane's sardonic invocation of humanitarian work in Gaza is the only explicit reference to the Palestinian question in the novel. But the name *Gaza,* reiterated every few pages as the climax of the novel, the murder of Bruce, "the chief of Gaza," is recounted in tightly wound prose, functions as a constant reminder of the colonial genealogy of the migrant crisis depicted in the novel. Tellingly, it is the second sympathetic white character in the novel, the policeman to whom Moïse (Mo), Bruce's murderer, surrenders, who first comments upon the naming of Kaweni:

> I don't know who it was who gave that nickname to Kaweni, the run-down neighborhood on the outskirts of Mamoudzou, but it hit the nail on the head. Gaza is a shantytown, a ghetto, a trash pile, a bottomless pit, a favela, a vast encampment of illegal immigrants, open to the skies. It's a vast steaming garbage dump that can be seen from a long way off. Gaza is a violent no-man's land where gangs of kids high on drugs make the law. Gaza is Capetown, it's Calcutta, it's Rio. Gaza is Mayotte, Gaza is France.[24]

What the representatives of state and humanitarian institutions fail to note, however, is the historical irony that makes Kaweni coeval with Gaza to begin with. It is not a coincidence that humanitarian and police discourses are, literally, vehicles for "Gaza as metaphor" in the novel.[25] The industry of human rights is implicated in the production of the discourse of crisis surrounding both the Palestinian and migrant questions.[26] But Gaza, I argue, is more than just a metaphor for poverty in the novel. It also anchors the migrant question at France's furthermost borders to the colonial question par excellence, Palestine.

The tragic tale of a Comorian who is adopted by a French woman only to give up the privileged life of a French citizen to fulfill his predestined fate as an outlaw, *Tropique de la violence* places Mayotte within a global imperial map dotted with shantytowns, ghettos, and migrant camps. Ironically, the undocumented child-turned-citizen winds up killing "the only real Mahorian" of Gaza, the citizen-turned-outlaw Bruce, a crime that surreptitiously reveals the colonial genealogy of Kaweni, whose destitute inhabitants, citizens and stateless both, are the products of colonization and slavery. "I'm not ashamed to say I'm descended from slaves," intones Mo's victim from beyond the grave, counterposing his Black pride to Mo's tragically hybrid identity.[27] That Bruce's ancestors were enslaved by Mayotte's Muslim rulers before being emancipated by the island's new French owners in 1846—two years before the second and final abolition of slavery—serves as an ironic reminder of the history of France's lucrative slaveholding Indian Ocean colonies, now points of departure for clandestine migration to Mayotte (since 2011 a French *département* whose administrative status makes it a de facto part of the European Union, though not of the Schengen Area).

In a final twist of fate, the naturalized Mo shares his jail cell with an undocumented migrant deemed "too unstable" for the Police aux frontières (Border Police), until he splits his head open against the walls that confine him.[28] Mo, an undocumented foundling turned French citizen who winds up in jail because he crossed over into Gaza, shares his cell with a man whose destiny—deportation—could have been his own. If the Gaza Strip is an open-air prison, the network of camps, jail cells, and detention centers located on France's island colony turn Kaweni ("Gaza") into a metaphor for France: "Gaza c'est la France."[29] It is not coincidental that this metaphor rewrites the colonial mantra, "l'Algérie c'est la France" (Algeria is France). Although the *gendarme* utters this phrase to critique the French state's neglect of its marginalized borderlands, it surreptitiously evokes another disavowed colonial contact zone, and the North African migrants who cross the Mediterranean to reach the former metropole. The tropic of violence is the southern frontier of a postcolonial nation-state that has forgotten the colonial history that produced the "migrant crisis" in the first place.

Are Palestinian Refugees Migrants?

One of the principal aims and effects of indigenous critique, as I have argued throughout the pages of this book, is to expose the production of the migrant as an *étranger* (foreigner/stranger). The migrant texts of the 2010s are part of a decades-long critique of the dehistoricization of (post)colonial displacement. Appanah's representation of migrants as the washed-up flotsam of colonial empires bears striking resemblance, for example, to Jean Genet's description of the Palestinian camps, seen from above as he flies over Jordan en route to the Fatah base in Baqa. In a remarkable articulation of the paradox of migrant (im)mobility, Genet portrays the contemporary "nomad" as simultaneously coerced into movement and confined to what he describes, in visceral terms, as the cesspits of the "'settled' nations," the camps:

> Who, reading this page towards the middle of 1984, when it was written, can help but wonder if the colloquial expression "they've multiplied" [*ils ont fait des petits*] applies to the Palestinian camps? As they did perhaps four thousand years ago or more, they seem to be resurfacing all over the planet, in so many places—Afghanistan, Morocco, Algeria, Ethiopia, Eritrea, Mauritania—entire populations are becoming nomads, and not by choice or because they can't keep still. We see them through the windows of airplanes or as we leaf through luxury magazines whose glossy pages lend the encampments an appearance of peace that reverberates in the cabin, whereas really they are just the detritus of "settled" nations [*les nations "assises"*]. Not knowing how to get rid of their "liquid waste," they discharge it into a valley or onto a hillside, preferably somewhere between the tropics and the equator. . . . We shouldn't have let these elegant images persuade us there was happiness there, under all the ornamental fantasy, just as we shouldn't be taken in by sunny photographs on the glossy pages of luxury magazines. A gust of wind blew everything away, the canvas, the tiles, the zinc, the sheet metal, and I saw misery in plain daylight.[30]

In an aerial view of a planet riddled with camps, nodes or blockages in routes of forced displacement that funnel the "liquid waste" of "'settled' nations" south of the equator, Genet placidly indicts the Global North in the production of the camp as the ambiguous metonym of entrapment and forced mobility.[31]

The liquid metaphors of Genet's aerial view of the camps find a startling echo in a recent documentary about the migrant question, Ai Weiwei's *Human Flow*, which gives Palestinians a central place in the story of migration while refusing to confine itself to the Mediterranean. In a disconcerting montage of drone's-eye views, handheld, moving camera close-ups, and documentary-style interviews, *Human Flow* orchestrates an ex-centric narrative of migration and enforced immobility that includes migrants fleeing destitution, fugitives from war, ethnic cleansing, and climate disasters, and colonized subjects: Syrians, Iraqis, Afghanis, Rohingya, Eritreans, Ethiopians, South Sudanese, Mexicans, Palestinian refugees in Lebanon, and occupied Palestinians in Gaza. The tension between the two starkly different visual poles that organize the film—aerial takes versus the kind of intimate portrait I discuss below—elucidates the double function of Palestine as a particular story that is nevertheless exemplary of the migrant question.

Ai Weiwei has been criticized for borrowing a military vantage point—the point of view of the drone—to represent migrants, reinforcing, in the view of his critics, the mechanistic, panoptic, and surveillance-based image of migrants as threats to Europe and the West.[32] For his part, Ai Weiwei has argued that the drone's-eye view has the paradoxical effect of humanizing the migrant: everyone looks the same from that far away.[33] Viewing *Human Flow* with Genet's aerial survey of the camps in mind, however, introduces another dimension, one that complicates both the particularistic and humanistic views offered by Ai Weiwei and his critics. I would like to suggest instead that the planetary scope of Ai Weiwei's airborne camera—from Bangladesh to the U.S.–Mexico borderland via Sudan—weaves the stories lumped together in the alarmist expression *migrant crisis* into a narrative that insists on a global history of forced displacement. Instead of drowning out historical specificity and migrant singularity, the aerial view is what allows Ai Weiwei's camera to travel across heterogeneous yet overlapping trajectories of displacement, before zooming in to film particular cases which, taken together, form the fabric of a planetary history of displacement. Palestine plays a central role in this story not because it is exceptional, but because it is exemplary of the migrant question. Like Genet's prose, which stretches across millennia from past to future to present, and from the Palestinian camps to the spread of camps across "the surface of the planet," *Human Flow* reintroduces history into the anthologizing gaze via Palestine.

One of the most striking leitmotifs in *Human Flow* is the camp, and indeed some of the shots in the film resemble what Genet describes as "sunny photographs on the glossy pages of luxury magazines," except that in Ai Weiwei's film the refugee camps have "multiplied" and expanded yet further.[34] Montage is one of the elements that make legible the importance of Palestine as a historical anchor in the film. In interviews and on social media, Ai Weiwei has suggested that the inclusion of Palestine in a film about the contemporary migrant crisis is meant to underscore the decades-long history of forced displacement—to insist that the ongoing crisis is not, in fact, new.[35] The form and figure of the camp is what ties together the individual migrant stories of the film, beginning, in diachronic terms, with the Palestinian camps.

I focus on a scene near the end of *Human Flow*, which films ten young women seated in two staggered rows on the concrete ruins that litter the Gaza seashore, as if they are posing for a photograph. As in *Tropique de la violence*, Gaza is the name of the migrant question, except that here the camp is no longer a metonym for the migrants forced to live there. Gaza itself is a camp. As one of the young women interviewed in the film explains, "We're in a prison" (Figure 19). Echoing Shadi's wry observation in *Brûle la mer* (*"visa sa'ban"*), she explains that her "dream is to travel [*safar*]." But travel, one of her friends explains, is "very difficult . . . impossible" (*sa'b jiddan . . . mustahil*). It is a luxury for citizens with papers, not refugees, undocumented migrants, and stateless Palestinians displaced by war, hunger, and other disasters. The inability to travel is what makes Palestine emblematic of the paradox of the migrant/refugee, who is simultaneously forced into movement and immobility.

Paradoxically, Ai Weiwei chose not to film this scene in what the viewer might expect a camp to look like. In Gaza, camps take the form of palimpsestic concrete structures that have been built up since 1948 with each new wave of Palestinian refugees, and destroyed with alarming regularity since the Israeli withdrawal in 2005.[36] Instead, Ai Weiwei films the Gaza scene on the seaside border of the strip, by the placid waters of a warring sea. But even here, concrete ruins and twisted metal encroach upon the tiny possibility of a horizon that opens up an

FIGURE 19. *Palestinian refugees posing on concrete rubble on the seashore of Gaza. Gaza is "like a prison cell, just slightly bigger," they explain to Ai Weiwei and his film crew. Screenshot from* Human Flow, *directed by Ai Weiwei (2017).*

impossible dream behind the young women in the frame. Like Maki's trip to his family's Tunisian olive grove, Ai Weiwei's film is an attempt to make the Palestinians' wish come true—return for Shadi, travel for the *Gazans*—even as it bears witness to the futility of the gesture.

Perhaps unwittingly, *Human Flow* tracks the recent convergence of the escalating Palestinian question and the mass displacements of the 2010s, even as it inscribes the latter in a decades-long history that begins with the Palestinian question. In this sense, the film reverses the terms in which Palestine is usually framed in discourses about the migrant crisis, when Palestine is discussed at all. Indeed, Palestinians have gained paradoxical visibility as a result of the Arab uprisings and their violent aftermath, joining the ranks of those who aspire to the status of refugees and the protections it might afford from a European nation-state. The dehistoricized image that obtains in stories about Palestinian "migrants" robs them of the political identity that made them exemplary of the refugee question for Arendt, and of the colonial question for Said: from stateless subjects barred from their native land, they have become *sans-papiers* striving for European citizenship. Witness the lists produced in an attempt to count the number of undocumented migrants who have entered Europe since 2011, which always include Palestinians, the vast majority from Syria, where 120,000 Palestinian refugees have been displaced, mostly to neighboring countries, but also to Europe.[37] Against the mediatic erasure of the Palestinian question, drowned in the staggering numbers of the displaced and disappeared, *Human Flow* insists on the foundational place of Palestine in the story of contemporary mass displacement.

The Migrant Question from a Palestinian Point of View

In closing, I take this recent discursive transformation—from Palestinian refugee to undocumented migrant—as an invitation to rethink the Palestinian question from a migrant point of view. What happens if we consider the post-1948 Palestinian refugee crisis as a migrant question? This is, in uncannily prescient fashion, what obtains in Ghassan Kanafani's 1962 novella *Rijal fil-shams* (*Men in the Sun*). Most often read as a critique of Arab quietism if not complicity in the Israeli occupation (*ihtilal*), *Men in the Sun* is a classic example of what Kanafani himself theorized as "resistance literature."[38] As Barbara Harlow reminds us in a recent essay, *Men in the Sun* had the paradoxical effect of a call to arms on its contemporary readers, shocked by the image of Palestinians as clandestine migrants: "Why should Palestinians be represented as the unwanted, unwarranted detritus of a dominant narrative, an international process that had fatally turned its Palestinian protagonists into hapless refugees and unfortunate economic migrants, seeking menial, hardly remunerated, labor in Kuwait?" But if Kanafani's aim was to move the Palestinians to action in what Harlow qualifies as "the emergence of the modern Palestinian history of struggle," his novella also exposes the production of the Palestinian refugee as "the detritus of 'settled' nations"—in this case, the detritus of the settler colony of Israel.[39] Slightly revising the terms of Harlow's analysis, I'd like to suggest, in closing, that the Palestinian question has always been a migrant question.[40]

It is chilling, in the face of unrelenting statistics on migrant fatalities, to read the story of three stowaway Palestinians smuggled across the Iraqi desert, not only because their fate—death by suffocation—resembles that of too many migrants today, but also because the "dream" that propels them finds an eerie echo in the audiovisual chiasmus I began this chapter with. If, in *Brûle la mer*, two characters are necessary to capture the paradox of migration—forced displacement in the case of Shadi, clandestine mobility in the case of Maki—here it is contained in a single figure, the Palestinian refugee who cannot return home and is compelled to escape "slow death," whatever the cost. Haunted by the image of "ten trees with twisted trunks that brought down olives and goodness every spring," Abu Qais, Assad, and Marwan climb into the empty water tank of a truck crossing the Iraq–Kuwait border under a blistering August sun. The suspense of the narrative is unbearable, even if, or perhaps because, we know they will not survive the crossing. But the most harrowing part of the tale is the fact that nothing keeps them back but a "fantasy" of what they have lost and a halfhearted "dream" of what they might find. Shadi's vision of uprooted olive trees in the French *banlieue* and Maki's fulfilled wish of traveling back to his family's olive grove find a visual echo in the opening sequence of Tawfiq Salih's film adaptation of Kanafani's novella, *Al-Makhdu'un* (*The Duped,* 1972), which translates Abu Qais's memories of life before the camps into a montage of windswept olive groves in pre-1948 Palestine, before cutting to the cactus-lined refugee camp to which he is now confined. "The trees exist in your head," mutters Abu Qais to himself, before resolving to attempt a journey he expects will kill him.[41]

As in Genet's aerial description of the Palestinian camps and the "glossy" images of Ai Weiwei's film, the refugee camps are the unnamed backdrop in Kanafani's story of forced displacement—a contextual element so crucial to the plot that Salih includes a two-minute montage of archival footage and photographs of refugee camps in the opening sequence of *The Duped,* as if to visually explain the protagonists' otherwise incomprehensible decision to cross an unforgiving desert (Figure 20).[42] Splicing archival footage with shots of Abu Qais and his family in a filmic reenactment of the camps, this rapid-fire montage (some of the still images last no more than a second) is triggered by the question posed to Abu Qais by his friend Saad, freshly returned from Kuwait where he has made a small fortune: "What are you waiting for?" Shot in 1971, in the wake of the Israeli occupation of the West Bank, Gaza, and East Jerusalem and the massacre of Palestinian fedayeen and refugees by the Jordanian army, *Al-Makhdu'un* frames the Palestinian question as a migrant question that began with the Nakba of 1948 and is reiterated with each new Israeli incursion and Arab betrayal. Fifty years later, the promise of return seems more elusive than ever. The stateless

FIGURE 20. *Archival image of Nahr el-Bared camp, used in the opening sequence of Tawfiq Salih's film adaptation of Ghassan Kanafani's novella* Men in the Sun *(1962). Copyright 1952 UNRWA Archive Photo by Jack Madvo. Courtesy of the United Nations Relief and Works Agency for Palestine Refugees in the Near East.*

Palestinian, torn between forced immobility (the camp) and forced mobility (exile), becomes the quintessential figure of the migrant when read from the vantage point of the present.

Let me reiterate, in closing, that like the Palestinian question, the migrant question demands our attention not as a crisis but, precisely, as a question: "something to be thought through, tried out, engaged with . . . politically."[43] In turn, the migrant literature of the past fifty years reveals that the Palestinian question has been central in articulating migration as a (post)colonial question, one that must be historicized and placed on a global scale. Against the ubiquitous discourse of crisis, the texts I have analyzed in this book offer a critique of the colonial and postcolonial production of mass displacement in the twentieth and twenty-first centuries, replacing the trope of invasion with a call to historicize the present. The right of return, *'awda*, at the beating heart of the ongoing question of Palestine, might then offer a more productive point of departure for an investigation of the migrant question as a question for Europe. "Après tout, les réfugiés ne font que *revenir*" (After all, the refugees are simply *returning*), in Georges Didi-Huberman's poetic formulation.[44] Absent the possibility of return, migrants and refugees will haunt the place that set in motion their displacement.

EPILOGUE

On June 13, 2020, tens of thousands of protestors descended into the streets of French cities to demand police accountability and equal treatment for France's postcolonial citizens. Organized by the Comité Adama—named after Adama Traoré, who died in police custody on July 16, 2016—the Paris march drew some fifteen thousand protestors, despite the stringent stay-at-home orders imposed to contain the Covid-19 pandemic. Citing health concerns, the Paris police denied the protestors permission to march to Place de l'Opéra as planned. Confined to its starting point, Place de la République, the mass rally became the site of an unexpected standoff between antiracist protestors and a handful of militants from the far-right organization Génération identitaire (GI; Generation Identity).[1] Perched atop the roof of an imposing Haussmanian building framing one of the most symbolic sites in post-Revolutionary France—the statue of Marianne towering over the rapidly gentrifying working-class neighborhoods of the 10th and 11th arrondissements—GI activists unfurled a giant banner stamped with the slogan "Justice pour les victimes du racisme anti-blanc—#White Lives Matter" (Justice for the victims of anti-white racism—#White Lives Matter). Several residents of the building in question came out onto their balconies to tear down the banner. Antifa activists climbed up onto the roof to finish the job, egged on by the cheers, applause, and taunts coming from the sea of protestors below.

The confrontation was short-lived. By 7 p.m., the crowd had dispersed and only a handful of combative protestors and a squad of CRS could be seen facing off among clouds of tear gas. But the standoff between antiracist and white identitarian activists in the summer of 2020 captures, almost too neatly, the contest for indigeneity I have been analyzing in this book. A twenty-first-century equivalent of the "battle of the palisades" scene in Jean Genet's unrealized film script

"La nuit venue," where pro-Palestinian militants, African migrants, leftist activists, and white nativists plaster the construction sites of working-class Paris with competing posters, the June 13 protests offer fresh evidence of the ways in which indigeneity has been recuperated to nativist ends in postcolonial France. A transparent parroting of the now global hashtag #BlackLivesMatter, GI's counterslogan is not simply a weak echo of postcolonial antiracism. More significantly, it usurps the place of the postcolonial migrant and the subject position of racialized citizens. Antiracism has become a weapon for nativist activists who present themselves as the defenders of an imperiled "white minority."

Alongside news reports and social media posts about the standoff between antiracist and GI activists on June 13 appeared a fortuitously related news item: the death of Jean Raspail, icon of a growing nativist movement warning against the "counter-colonization" of France, and more broadly the West, by migrants. Author of a best-selling novel, *Le camp des saints* (1973; *The Camp of the Saints*, 1975), Raspail has become the darling of the anti-immigrant right, in France but also in the United States, Australia, and beyond. A heavy-handed and poorly written allegory of the "invasion" of France by a fleet of migrants from the Indian subcontinent, *The Camp of the Saints* is required reading for the nativist right, particularly since the peak of migration into Europe in 2015, which crossed the symbolic million mark and turned Raspail into a prophet of the "submersion" of the continent by Muslim migrants.[2] Tellingly, Raspail has claimed that he chose to make the invaders "come from the faraway Ganges rather than the shores of the Mediterranean" in order to sidestep "the sham debate [*le débat truqué*] on racism and antiracism in France."[3] But the ambiguity of the designation *Indien* in French, where the preferred term for indigenous Americans is *les Indien.ne.s d'Amérique,* or simply *les Indien.ne.s,* reveals a continued fascination with the "Indian" as a figure for the *indigène*, as France's colonial subjects were termed.

Published one year after the founding of the far-right, anti-immigrant party Front national (renamed Rassemblement national, or National Rally, in 2017), Raspail's novel attests to the emergence of a distinctly postcolonial form of nativism, one that rewrites decolonization as a principle of separation and replacement ("We left Algeria, now you leave France"). As discussed in the Introduction, these new forms of nativist discourse have managed to take the place of the colonized, in rhetorical terms at least: migrants are the ones who are now "invading" France. In 1978, New Right theorist Alain de Benoist would call for "reciprocal decolonization," citing none other than racial supremacist Arthur de Gobineau in support of a global segregation of the races.[4] Today, white nativist organizations have added antiracist legislation to their arsenal. In 2008, the far-right organization AGRIF took Houria Bouteldja, spokesperson of the antiracist collective Mouvement des indigènes de la république, to court for "racial injury" against whites. AGRIF did not win that case, but the decades-long campaign to recuperate antiracism in defense of what I am calling the *white minority* has now pervaded the French public sphere in previously unimaginable ways.

The term *indigène,* coined at the height of the French empire to legally define France's colonial subjects, has made a surprising return to the lexicon of racial injury in postcolonial France, albeit divorced from the colonial context of its production. Marine Le Pen, president of the Rassemblement national at the time, took to Twitter to criticize the June 13 protest, condemning "the inaction and cowardliness of the authorities [*le pouvoir*] in the face of the anti-cop *indigénistes* and far-left."[5] Tellingly, the video Le Pen uploaded as visual evidence of violence against the police—masked and hooded protestors throwing tear gas grenades back at police officers in full riot gear—is credited to @YBOUZIAR, a journalist and activist who clearly situates himself in the camp of the protestors. The caption that accompanies the video on Yazid Bouziar's Twitter feed reads "a police charge is violently repelled by black-blocs at the Place de la #Republique," placing the blame for the scuffles on the CRS, not the protestors.[6] In the age of memes and retweets, appropriation is nothing new. But the remediation of an antiracist visual archive to reframe the police as victims of violence speaks volumes to the recuperation of antiracism to nativist ends. In a thinly veiled attempt to ethnicize the protest, Le Pen redeploys a colonial term that has been appropriated by antiracist activists to emphasize the colonial genealogy of anti-immigrant racism—*indigène,* the legal identity enforced upon France's colonial subjects in the late nineteenth century—and tacks on the "ist" of ideological discourse, by analogy, one might surmise, with the "leftists" she denounces in her tweet (note that *droitiste,* "rightist," is not a word in French; *gauchiste* is). Problematically used by anthropologists and sociologists to designate "traditionalism" and, tellingly, Islamism, the term *indigéniste* becomes, in Le Pen's tweet, a covert way to portray antiracist activists as enemies of the police.[7] This is quite a tour de force, given that the June 13 rally was convened to protest police violence against the descendants of France's colonial subjects, those that Bouteldja and others dub *les indigènes de la république.*

Bouteldja resigned from the PIR on October 6, 2020. Although she has declined to attribute her decision to a single event or cause—the PIR continues to exist, and she remains active in the antiracist struggle—it is undeniable that she has borne the brunt of anti-*indigéniste* ire across the political spectrum, particularly since the publication of her provocative book, *Whites, Jews, and Us,* in 2016.[8] The violent backlash against Bouteldja, which continues unabated, offers a paradoxical testament to the very high stakes of indigenous critique in postcolonial France, particularly in the context of ongoing attempts to stifle discussions around colonialism, race, and racism in the French academy and the frequent denunciations of "Islamo-leftism" in the public sphere. An ill-defined amalgam of Islamism (and, according to the term's critics, Islam) and leftism, "Islamo-leftism" is a performative designed to curtail speech that is perceived as anti-republican in any way: critiques of *laïcité* (republican secularism), in particular government attempts to enforce it, from the headscarf ban to the burqini affair; criticism of the war on terror, including the increasingly repressive security and surveillance measures taken in the wake of the 2015 terror attacks in Paris; and, in the academic sphere, postcolonial and critical race studies, branded as U.S. imports in a disingenuous attempt to foreignize fields that have been profoundly shaped by the writings of Aimé Césaire, Frantz Fanon, Édouard Glissant, and other anticolonial theorists from the four corners of France's empire.

The decades-long debate around the purported encroachment of Islamo-leftism in France reached an apex after the October 16, 2020, murder of Samuel Paty, a middle school teacher who had displayed cartoons of the prophet Mohamed in a class on free speech. On October 22, the minister of national education, Jean-Michel Blanquer, denounced the "Islamo-gauchisme" making "ravages" in the university. On October 31, one hundred academics published an editorial alleging that "indigenist, racialist, and 'decolonial' ideologies (transferred from North American campuses) are well implanted [in our universities], feeding a hatred of 'whites' and of France; and [that] a sometimes violent militantism attacks those who still dare to confront the anti-Western doxa and the multiculturalist vulgate [*prêchi-prêcha multiculturaliste*]."[9] On February 16, 2021, Frédérique Vidal, the minister of higher education, research, and innovation, who had initially downplayed Blanquer's statement, announced on CNews, a rightist news corporation, that she would launch an inquiry into "Islamo-leftism" in the universities, to the surprise and dismay of the Centre national de la recherche scientifique (CNRS), the national research institute she claimed to have recruited for the task.[10]

As of writing, the controversies over Islamo-leftism have not died down. A website launched in January 2021, the Observatoire du déco-lonialisme et des idéologies identitaires (Observatory of Decolonialism and Identitarian Ideologies), continues to publish articles tracking the purported Islamo-leftist cabal in French scholarship, with the open support of publications like the center-right *Le Point,* which has dedi-cated an open-access rubric on its website to the publications of the Observatoire.[11] A quick look at the site's publications confirms the Observoire's main areas of concern: studies of French empire, critiques of *laïcité,* gender and sexuality studies (in particular anything having to do with intersectionality), critical studies of *la blanchité* (as white-ness is poetically termed in French), cancel culture, *le wokisme,* pro-Palestinian activism, and anything that looks remotely like a critique of the State of Israel.[12]

One of the principal targets of the witch hunt against Islamo-leftism is pro-Palestinian activism. Coined by the sociologist Pierre-André Taguieff—a founding member of the Observatoire—to characterize what he diagnosed as a "new Judeophobia" in the context of 9/11 and the Second Intifada, the term *Islamo-leftism* was initially deployed to equate anti-Semitism and anti-Zionism: "I used the expression in sev-eral talks I gave in 2002, as well as in articles about what I termed the 'new Judeophobia,' which is based on a radical anti-Zionism whose aim is the elimination of the Jewish state," Taguieff explains in a recent in-terview about the current fortunes of his neologism.[13] As discussed in chapter 3, outspoken anti-Semites like Dieudonné M'bala M'bala are proud to call themselves anti-Zionist and pro-Palestinian. But to say that pro-Palestinian activists are by definition "Judeophobes" is a met-onymic sleight of hand of enormous proportions. Any criticism of the Zionist project as a colonial venture becomes tantamount, in Taguieff's

writings, to a call for the elimination of the Jewish state, defined in ethnonationalist terms as coextensive with the Jewish people. Even more
remarkably, the project to create a nation-state for all past and present
inhabitants of historic Palestine, irrespective of religion or ethnicity—
the so-called one-state solution, long the stated aim of Palestinian anticolonial movements—is reduced to an ethnocidal project.

Without denying the reality of resurgent forms of anti-Semitism
in France that use the continued colonization of Palestine as an ideological alibi, it is easy to see that Taguieff's methodology produces the
thesis he wishes to defend: that pro-Palestinianism is an anti-Semitic
ideology imported from the Muslim world. Aside from a few anecdotal examples of anti-Semitic slogans overheard in the ranks of pro-
Palestinian activists, the bulk of the evidence Taguieff offers in his writings, most notably *La nouvelle judéophobie* (2002; translated as *Rising
from the Muck* in 2004), are statements made by non-French Islamists
and Muslim leaders (bin Laden and the Taliban are privileged sources
in the book). In other words, Taguieff's conflation of anti-Zionism and
anti-Semitism in France is based on a study of the convergence of anti-
Semitic and pro-Palestinian discourse in Islamist movements outside of
France. *L'Intifada des banlieues,* as urban rebellions have been dubbed
in twenty-first-century France, is but the first act in a global war
against the West, to paraphrase Taguieff's incendiary statements in
La nouvelle judéophobie. Take his denunciation of "the professionals of
youthist demagogy [*les professionnels de la démagogie jeuniste*]," that is
to say, the "leftists" in the hyphenated term *Islamo-leftists:* "And a subtle, indirect, symbolic Judeophobia emanates from this ideological con-
figuration, at once Islamophile, idolatrous of the Palestinians [*palesti-
nolâtre*], and 'Beurophile.'" Taguieff parses out this "new Judeophobia"
in a telling, if no less subtle, mathematical formulation: "Jews = Zionists
(= Israelis); Zionism = colonialism, imperialism, and racism; Sharon =
Hitler (or a fascist); Israeli = Nazis (or fascists)."[14] QED: anti-Zionism =
anti-Semitism.

The equation of anti-Zionism and anti-Semitism is not confined
to academic circles. On February 20, 2019, at the annual dinner of the
Conseil représentatif des institutions juives de France (Representative
Council of Jewish Institutions of France)—an umbrella organization of
Jewish associations that lists "solidarity with Israel" as one of its core
missions—President Emmanuel Macron announced that he would adopt

the expansive International Holocaust Remembrance Alliance's definition of anti-Semitism, which includes "denying the Jewish people their
right to self-determination, e.g. by claiming that the existence of a State
of Israel is a racist endeavor."[15] A nonbinding resolution was narrowly
adopted by the Assemblée nationale on December 3, 2019. Although, as
of writing, no one has successfully been brought to court for the offense
of "denying the Jewish people their right to self-determination," the climate in France has become increasingly hostile to any manifestation of
support for Palestinian self-determination.[16]

Contra Taguieff and fellow republicans for whom the Palestinian
question is an imported conflict, the premise of this book has been that
the question of Palestine is also a French question. As evidenced in the
archive of grassroots antiracist activism from the early 1970s to the present, the Palestinian question has been mobilized to critique the figure
of the migrant as unexpected or unwelcome guest, divorced from the
colonial history that turned *indigènes* into immigrants. "I am here because I was thrown up by History [*j'ai été vomie par l'Histoire*]," writes
Bouteldja in one of the most eloquent passages of *Whites, Jews, and Us*. "I
am here because white people [*les Blancs*] were in my country, because
they are still there. What am I? A *native of the republic* [*une indigène de
la république*]."[17] To "name" white people is, of course, to defy the color-
blind ideology of French republicanism. Bouteldja has frequently been
accused of *communautarisme* (U.S.-style identity politics) when it is not
"anti-white racism." But whiteness, like indigeneity, is a political identity,
as she insists at the outset of her book: "Why am I writing this book? Because I am not innocent. I live in France. I live in the West. I am white."[18]

It goes without saying that Bouteldja is not considered white in
French society, least of all by the identitarians who have accused her
of anti-white racism. Her articulation of indigeneity in France manages to capture what was at stake in the confrontation between antiracist and nativist activists at the Place de la République on June 13,
2020. To those who deny the descendants of colonized subjects the right
to demand equal treatment in postcolonial France, the natives of the
Republic reply, "We are here because you were there." "To declare oneself *indigène*," writes Bouteldja, "is a victory against the *indigénat*."[19]
There is no small degree of irony in this statement. For if indigeneity
was invented in the colony, it has become a weapon in the battle of
natives against nativism.

ACKNOWLEDGMENTS

This book is inspired by the activists, artists, and writers whose work I engage with in these pages. I have had the good fortune to be in dialogue with many of them over the years, including Bouchra Khalili, Philippe Tancelin, Mohamed Rouabhi, Elias Sanbar, and Nathalie Nambot, who dedicated time, resources, and ideas. I am grateful for their interest and trust, and hope that my readings do some justice to the complexity and beauty of the texts, films, and archives they so generously shared with me.

My thinking has been profoundly shaped by conversations with friends and colleagues over the years. My first thanks go to Keith P. Feldman, Gil Z. Hochberg, and Michael Rothberg, who gave me extensive feedback on the manuscript. Beyond their pointed and generative comments, their work continues to inspire mine. I am also deeply grateful to the friends and colleagues who read chapter drafts at various stages of production: Anna Bernard, Maria Boletsi, Maya Boutaghou, Lia Brozgal, Rachel Colwell, Muriam Haleh Davis, Arne De Boever, Madeleine Dobie, yasser elhariry, Leah Feldman, Abdellali Hajjat, Priya Jaikumar, Neetu Khanna, Peter Limbrick, Françoise Lionnet, Mehammed Mack, Jessica Marglin, Liesbeth Minaard, Lydie Moudileno, Béatrice Mousli, Aamir R. Mufti, Ethan Pack, Ben Ratskoff, Alison Rice, Thomas Serres, Guilan Siassi, Julie Van Dam, and Eszter Zimanyi. It has been immensely rewarding to write this book in their company.

I am particularly pleased that this book found a home at the University of Minnesota Press. Sohail Daulatzai and Junaid Rana, the editors of the Muslim International series, supported the project from the beginning. Jason Weidemann was a strong advocate for the book at the Press and answered countless queries about matters of substance and style. I thank the entire production team for the meticulous care they gave to the manuscript, including Zenyse Miller, who shepherded the manuscript to production; Jonathan Lawrence for his thoughtful copyedits; Mike Stoffel, who saw the project to the finish line; and Rachel Moeller, whose design team was able to produce exactly the cover I'd imagined.

I was fortunate to have two sabbatical leaves while I was working on this book, the latter thanks to the University of Southern California's Advancing Scholarship in the Humanities and Social Sciences Sabbatical program. The USC Dornsife Office of the Dean sponsored a manuscript review in fall 2021 and helped defray indexing costs. The Francophone Research and Resource Center and the Department of French and Italian at USC provided generous subventions toward the publication of this book. Several chapters began as talks and conference papers, and I am grateful to the institutions and individuals who hosted me at the University of California, Berkeley, Tulane University, Columbia University, Smith College, the University of Notre Dame's Rome Global Gateway, Roskilde University, and the European School of Visual Arts. I am particularly thankful to the librarians and archivists of the Institut des mémoires de l'édition contemporaine, La contemporaine, the Université Gustave Eiffel, and USC Libraries, who greatly facilitated my research despite the constraints imposed by the Covid-19 pandemic. Michael Turcios, who was a doctoral candidate in Cinema and Media Studies at USC at the time, conducted invaluable research for me in summer 2019, before the archives closed. Without his assistance, I would quite simply not have been able to write the first chapter of this book. For their help in tracking archival documents and other sources that were difficult to locate from afar, I thank Hajer Ben Boubaker, Albert Dichy, Abdellali Hajjat, Alicia Harrison, Léopold Lambert, Olivier Neveux, Michael Renov, Rocé, Julie Simon-Titécat, Susan Slyomovics, and Hocine Tandjaoui. Michael Bonnet, from USC's Dornsife Technology Services, produced several of the high-resolution images reproduced in this book. I am also deeply grateful to Faouzia Bouziri, Yannis Tritsibidas, Bouchra Khalili, Mohamed Rouabhi, Maki Berchache, Nathalie Nambot, and the staff of La contemporaine and the National Museum of the American Indian for their kind permission to reproduce images from their collections and works.

My most heartfelt thanks go to my partner, Arne De Boever, and to our children, Ada and Louise, who have taught me a thing or two about love. I dedicate this book to my mother, Chantal Dubertret Harrison, who brought me into a world of books and ideas.

NOTES

Prologue

1. Deloria, *Custer Died for Your Sins*, 166.
2. For a thorough investigation of French colonial doctrines of "extermination" and racial warfare, largely inspired by the U.S. example, see Le Cour Grandmaison, *Coloniser, exterminer.*
3. Hugonnet, *Souvenirs d'un chef de bureau arabe*, 119. All translations are my own unless otherwise noted.
4. Mamdani, *When Victims Become Killers*, 14, emphasis in original.
5. Spitz, "Traversées océaniennes."

Introduction

1. The Code de l'indigénat was a separate penal code first adopted in Algeria in the 1870s and applied to the rest of the empire, with minor variations, until 1946. See Le Cour Grandmaison, *De l'indigénat.*
2. "Nous sommes les indigènes de la république!," Parti des indigènes de la république, January 2005, www.indigenes-republique.fr. I retain the term *native*, rather than *indigenous*, in my translation of *indigène*, in order to clarify the colonial and racial genealogy that continues to structure representations of postcolonial French citizens and immigrants, and to make visible the ironic appropriation of indigeneity (nativeness) against white nativist claims that have sought to delink the question of immigration from the colonial question since the end of the French empire in the 1960s. The PIR-affiliated Decolonial Translation Group translates *indigène* as *indigenous*. "We Are the Indigenous of the Republic," translated by Roberto Hernandéz, www.decolonialtranslation.com.
3. For a thorough overview of the context in which the PIR emerged, see Martin, "Anti-racism, Republicanism, and the Sarkozy Years"; and Zobel, "The 'Indigènes de la République.'"
4. The law expressing the nation's "gratefulness" to French citizens repatriated from the colonies after decolonization was nevertheless approved on February 23, 2005, without the offensive article. "Loi no. 2005–158 du 23 février 2005 portant reconnaissance de la Nation et contribution nationale en faveur des Français rapatriés," last modified December 31, 2018, www.legifrance.gouv.fr.
5. "Nous sommes les indigènes de la république!"
6. According to François Gèze, the appeal was published online on January 11, 2005. Gèze, "Les 'indigènes,'" 124. Although the appeal is no longer available on Oumma.com or TouTEsegaux.net (the latter site is no longer active), they can be retrieved via the Internet Wayback Machine. "'Nous sommes les indigènes de la république!' . . . Appel pour les assises de l'anti-colonialisme post-colonial," January 19,

2005, www.web.archive.org. The charge of *communautarisme* is not surprising, in the hegemonically secular context of republican France, given that the Collectif des Musulmans de France (Collective of Muslims of France) is listed as an "initiator" of the appeal and that it was signed by the controversial figure Tariq Ramadan. Accusations of anti-Semitism were fueled by the pro-Palestinian sympathies of founding members of the collective (the appeal explicitly supports the Palestinian "struggle for emancipation") as well as a sensational and, it turned out, fabricated story about an anti-Semitic attack in the *banlieue*, the notorious "RER D affair." On the "RER D affair," see Robine, "Les 'indigènes de la République,'" 124–26. The first article to raise the specter of anti-Semitism was published in the center-left daily *Le Monde*. Philippe Bernard, "Des 'enfants de colonisés' revendiquent leur histoire," *Le Monde*, February 21, 2005, www.lemonde.fr. The far-left party Ligue communiste révolutionnaire published a critique of the PIR's founding appeal soon after it was published, although it can no longer be found online. Ligue communiste révolutionnaire, "Réponse à l'appel post-colonialisme," La Brèche numérique, April 12, 2005. For a republican rebuttal to the PIR, see "Des indigènes très peu républicains," *Marianne*, April 5, 2008, www.marianne.net.

7. Benjamin Stora, a historian of the Algerian War known for his public engagements (for example, against the 2004 law recognizing the "positive aspects" of French colonization), has criticized what are according to him facile historical equations between colonial and postcolonial subject positions. For Stora, the PIR's positions are identitarian and factually "wrong." Stora, *La guerre des mémoires*, 76–79. The anthropologist-turned-prophet of "the ethnicization of France," Jean-Loup Amselle, is even less diplomatic in his critique of the PIR's alleged racial essentialism. Amselle, *L'ethnicisation de la France*, 31. In a recent publication, Amselle goes so far as to equate the PIR's identity politics with the French far right, evoking an unholy alliance between the Third Worldist left (the red in his title) and neofascists (the brown). Amselle, *Les nouveaux rouges-bruns*, 48–52.

8. Sopo, *S.O.S. antiracisme*, 33, 98.

9. Bruckner, *Le sanglot de l'homme blanc*. The reference to Bruckner's books is so well known that Sopo does not feel the need to cite him in a chapter titled "Du long sanglot de l'homme blanc à l'enfermement victimaire." Sopo, *S.O.S. antiracisme*, 16–25. For a critique of "colonial repentance," see Lefeuvre, *Pour en finir avec la repentance coloniale*.

10. *Les quartiers* (*populaires*) is a metonym for low-income housing communities in the periphery of French cities.

11. "Nous sommes les indigènes de la république!"

12. My critique is somewhat different from that of scholars like Eve Tuck and K. Wayne Yang, who warn against the risks of applying an anticolonial framework to advance an antiracist agenda in the settler colonial context of the United States. For Tuck and Yang, such discursive slippages are, by default, complicit in maintaining settler colonial structures. Tuck and Yang, "Decolonization Is Not a Metaphor." The activists of the PIR, in contrast, are explicit in their condemnations of French colonialism overseas, which they link with U.S., Israeli, and other ongoing imperial projects.

13. Hajjat, *Les frontières de l'"identité nationale,"* 21.

14. Houria Bouteldja, "Si nous sommes ici c'est que vous étiez là-bas . . . ," *Montray Kréyol*, July 16, 2018, www.montraykreyol.org.

15. Bouteldja, *Whites, Jews, and Us*, 118–20.

16. Among the plethora of online comments of this nature, YouTube user Conrad

Bunton's remarks are telling in their simple conflation of Frenchness and whiteness: "if she doesn't like white people she can just leave [*se casser*]." Bunton posted these comments under Camille9340's upload of a televised interview with Bouteldja. Camille9340, "Souchiens," YouTube video, 5:33, July 5, 2007, www.youtube.com.

17. I borrow the term *transindigenous* from Chadwick Allen to refer to practices of identification across heterogeneous indigenous positions, broadly defined here to include both formerly and still colonized peoples. "Similar to terms like *trans*lation, *trans*national, and *trans*form, *trans*-Indigenous may be able to bear the complex, contingent asymmetry and the potential risks of unequal encounters borne by the preposition across. It may be able to indicate the specific agency and situated momentum carried by the preposition through. It may be able to harbor the potential of change as both transitive and intransitive verb, and as both noun and adjective." Allen, *Trans-Indigenous*, xiv–xv, emphasis in original. Transindigenous identification expands on Léopold Lambert's temporal and spatial notion of a "French colonial continuum" to encompass European and Eurocolonial imperial formations in the *longue durée*. Lambert, *États d'urgence*, 42–43.

18. There is now a sizable literature on the centrality of the Palestinian question in France. See Kassir and Mardam-Bey, *Itinéraires de Paris à Jérusalem;* Sieffert, *Israël-Palestine;* Debrauwere-Miller, ed., *Israeli-Palestinian Conflict;* Hecker, *Intifada française;* Mamarbachi, "Émergence, construction, et transformations." Maud Mandel and Ethan Katz have unearthed important documents attesting to the importance of the Palestinian question in Maghrebi migrant circles. Because they consider debates around Israel and Palestine in light of the fraught history of Maghrebi Jews and Muslims in France, however, their work tends to solidify the very identities that were produced in the colonial laboratory, enshrined in colonial law, and transformed in the postcolony. Mandel, *Muslims and Jews in France;* Katz, *Burdens of Brotherhood.* My approach to the Palestinian question in France is closer to the work of scholars who situate French pro-Palestinianism within the context of its emergence, the migrant rights movement in 1970s France. Maatouk, "Le théâtre des travailleurs immigrés." Hajjat, "Les comités Palestine."

19. See, for example, an article linking the conquest of the Americas to the colonization of Palestine. "Le Columbus Day ou la Nakba des Amérindiens," Parti des indigènes de la république, October 12, 2010, www.indigenes-republique.fr.

20. Chakrabarty, *Provincializing Europe.*

21. Bouteldja, *Whites, Jews, and Us,* 118. The PIR was not the first antiracist group to look to indigenous American struggles for sovereignty as a source of inspiration. According to Abdellali Hajjat, the 1983 Marche pour l'égalité et contre le racisme was partly modeled after the 1978 American Indian "Longest Walk" from San Francisco to Washington, D.C. Hajjat, *The Wretched of France,* 10, 104.

22. I use the term *indigenous critique* to refer to a critical deconstruction of the colonial production of indigeneity from 1492 to the present. Jodi A. Byrd uses the terms *indigenous critiques* and *indigenous critical theory* in a more circumscribed way to speak of anticolonial writings by indigenous persons, loosely defined as those who were present at the time of colonial conquest. Byrd, *Transit of Empire,* xxvi–xxxv.

23. Guène, *La discrétion,* 135.

24. Bouamama, *Dix ans de Marche des Beurs,* 23. I borrow the formulation *postcolonial hospitality* from Mireille Rosello. Rosello, *Postcolonial Hospitality.*

25. Kateb, "Mohamed prends ta valise"; Kettane, *Droit de réponse,* 34.

26. Harrison, *Transcolonial Maghreb.* Françoise Lionnet and Shu-mei Shih coined

the term *transcolonialism* to describe the network of relations between formerly and still colonized sites across heterogeneous imperial formations. Lionnet and Shih, "Thinking Through the Minor," 11.

27. *Indien* is the masculine form, *Indienne* the feminine. I follow the current gender-inclusive practice of using median points (*Indien.ne*) rather than defaulting to the masculine form, as is the norm in French. I place the term *Indian* in quotation marks to clarify that I am speaking of the mythic figure popularized by Hollywood rather than actual or specific indigenous Americans. It should be clear that this is how I use the term throughout the book. See Jodi A. Byrd's eloquent articulation of "Indianness [as] a site through which U.S. empire orients and replicates itself by transforming those to be colonized into 'Indians' through continual reiterations of pioneer logics, whether in the Pacific, the Caribbean, or the Middle East." Byrd, *Transit of Empire*, xiii.

28. For a critique of recuperative uses of the figure of the Indian in Palestine–Israel, see the work of Steven Salaita, who also reminds us that all racial nomenclatures are suspect, including *indigenous*. Salaita, *Inter/Nationalism*, 14–23, xiv.

29. I avoid capitalizing *indigenous* to make clear that mine is a critical and relational rather than an empirical or taxonomic approach to indigeneity. Byrd similarly takes issue with "this transformation of more than five hundred and sixty indigenous nations into a single racial minority within the national borders of the United States," which turns colonial subjection into a scene of racial interpellation. Byrd, *Transit of Empire*, 125. Glen Sean Coulthard provides an important critique of the politics of recognition along similar lines. Coutlhard, *Red Skin, White Masks*. See also Mahmood Mamdani's provocative claim that to call the original inhabitants of the lands colonized by the British *Native Americans* is to erase the history of the colonization of what was to become the United States of America, construed through this act of naming as an indigenous polity. Mamdani insists on using the overtly colonial nomenclature *Indian* instead: "The United States is an ongoing conquest—of 'Indians,' not 'Native Americans.'" Mamdani, *Neither Settler nor Native*, 339. Although I am sympathetic to the insistence by scholars of settler colonialism and indigeneity that "anti-racism is not the same as decolonization," it seems clear to me that decolonization cannot dispense with a rigorous critical analysis of race and racism. Mamdani, *Neither Settler nor Native*, 95. For a nuanced approach to the "regimes of race" that support colonialism, writ large to include "the heart of the metropolis," see Wolfe, *Traces of History*, 18–19.

30. Founded in 1984 by Bernard Antony, a former sympathizer of the pro–French Algeria Organisation armée secrète (OAS; Secret Armed Organization) and Front national (FN) militant, AGRIF purports to "struggle against all racisms and in particular anti-French and anti-Christian racisms." "À propos de nous," Alliance générale contre le racisme et pour le respect de l'identité française et chrétienne, www.lagrif.fr. The OAS was a clandestine pro–French Algeria paramilitary group founded during the waning years of the Algerian War.

31. I base my translation of Bouteldja's remarks on an excerpt of the debate posted online. enzo bateau, "Souchiens," Daily Motion video, 6:43, www.dailymotion.com.

32. Shepard, *The Invention of Decolonization*, 51–52. The term *Français musulman d'Algérie* replaced the nomenclature *indigène* after the extension of (partial) citizenship to colonized subjects in Algeria in 1944. Le Cour Grandmaison, *Coloniser, exterminer*, 272.

33. Le rider fou posted these comments under XRolan's video upload of Bouteldja's televised interview. XRolan, "Bouteldja: 'il faut éduquer les souchiens: les blancs,'"

YouTube video, 0:36, July 13, 2007, www.youtube.com. As of writing, comments have been disabled.

34. The July 1, 1972, law (dubbed loi Pleven) sanctions "incitement to discrimination, hatred or violence against a person or group of persons in reason of their origins or their belonging or non-belonging to a specific ethnicity, nation, race or religion." "Loi n° 72-546 du 1er juillet 1972 relative à la lutte contre le racisme," www.legifrance .gouv.fr. In 1991 the courts recognized AGRIF as an antiracist association, adding anti-French and anti-white racism to the repertoire of hate speech. On the history of appeals to "anti-white racism" in France, see Charrieras, "Racisme(s)?"

35. The study of nativism in France presents an interesting and perhaps symptomatic translation problem: there is no obvious cognate for *nativism* in French, even though it is a Latinate term. The closest expression in usage is the adjective *identitaire*, based on the substantive *identité* (identity), as in *la droite identitaire*, which I translate as "the nativist right." Recently, nativists have started to use the terms *indigène* (native) and *indigéniste* (a more literal translation of *nativist*) to refer to their movements. These derivatives of *indigène* have the advantage of exposing the colonial genealogy of nativism, but they have also been used pejoratively to refer to the colonized and, today, to their descendants, some of whom have appropriated the colonial identity *indigène* for antiracist purposes. The study of natives against nativism is also an attempt to historicize these fluid and ever-shifting semantic fields.

36. Bodichon, *Études sur l'Algérie et l'Afrique*, 150, quoted in Le Cour Grandmaison, *Coloniser, exterminer*, 121.

37. Tocqueville, *Democracy in America*, 376; Tocqueville, *Writings on Empire and Slavery*, 144, 70–71. On Tocqueville's shifting and sometimes contradictory positions on what he called the "unfortunate necessities" of colonial warfare in both the United States and Algeria, see Le Cour Grandmaison, *Coloniser, exterminer*, 91–92, 112, 193.

38. Le Cour Grandmaison, *Coloniser, exterminer*, 18, emphasis in original.

39. Mbembe, *Critique of Black Reason*, 57. This is particularly true of settler colonies like South Africa, which Mbembe takes aim at here, Algeria, and of course Palestine–Israel. Indigenization is part and parcel of what Patrick Wolfe calls "settler colonialism [as] a project of replacement." Wolfe, *Traces of History*, 33.

40. Tocqueville, *Writings on Empire and Slavery*, 89.

41. Tocqueville, 139–40, translation modified; Toqueville, *Sur l'Algérie*, 196. (Here and in subsequent chapters, I quote the original French alongside the published translation when I feel compelled to make modifications.) If Algerians were indeed subjects rather than citizens of France, they were, since the annexation of Algeria to France in 1834, de facto French nationals, not foreigners.

42. Tocqueville, *Writings on Empire and Slavery*, 19, translation modified; Tocqueville, *Sur l'Algérie*, 50.

43. Guha, "Not at Home in Empire."

44. Fanon, *The Wretched of the Earth*, 5, translation modified; Fanon, *Les damnés de la terre*, 43.

45. Fanon, *The Wretched of the Earth*, 1, translation modified; Fanon, *Les damnés de la terre*, 39.

46. Fanon, *The Wretched of the Earth*, 5.

47. Camille9340, "Souchiens," YouTube video, 5:33, July 5, 2007, www.youtube.com. A French euphemism for racialized subjects, *minorités visibles* (visible minorities) simultaneously occludes race as an analytical category and draws attention to what Cécile Bishop calls the visuality of race. Bishop, "Photography, Race, Invisibility," 197.

48. *Bled*, from *balad*, in the sense of "town" or "village," is one of the many Arabic

words that has made it into the French language via French Algeria. Although in contemporary French colloquial speech it can be used affectionately to refer to one's hometown, Faldo Itlehr's tone echoes its colonial use to speak of a purportedly backward Algerian hinterland.

49. French colonial nationality law is a particularly convoluted matter, nowhere more so than in French Algeria. The indigenous inhabitants of Algeria were decreed *French subjects* when Algeria was annexed in 1834. The 1865 Sénatus-Consulte officially recognized indigenous Algerians as French nationals and allowed them access to citizenship under the condition that they give up their personal status or customary law—in this case, Koranic and rabbinic codes governing marriage, inheritance, and other civic matters. In practice, this meant that very few indigenous Algerians became fully French until the 1870 Crémieux Decree, which extended French citizenship to most Algerian Jews. Muslim Algerians had to wait until the implementation of the 1946 Lamine Gueye law extending citizenship to French colonial subjects (without the attendant universal suffrage rights, however—Muslim Algerians had their own electoral college, not proportional to their numbers). For a succinct overview of nationality law in French Algeria, see Weil, "Le statut des musulmans."

50. Shepard, *The Invention of Decolonization.*

51. Quoted in Comtat, "From *Indigènes* to Immigrant Workers," 267.

52. Benoist, *Salan devant l'opinion* (1963); Benoist and d'Orcival, *Le courage est leur patrie* (1965); Benoist and Fournier, *Vérité pour l'Afrique du Sud* (1965).

53. Benoist, *Europe, Tiers Monde, même combat,* 67, emphasis in original.

54. Benoist, *Vu de droite,* 25. Benoist's writings have had a considerable impact outside of France. Previously translated into German, Italian, and Portuguese, *Vu de droite* is now available in a three-volume English translation thanks to a crowd-sourced alt-right press. Benoist, *View from the Right.* As of writing, the Kickstarter campaign that launched this translation project is still live. Arktos, "View from the Right by Alain de Benoist," last modified May 9, 2019, www.kickstarter.com.

55. Benoist, *Vu de droite,* 263, emphasis in original.

56. Benoist, 527.

57. Taguieff, *The Force of Prejudice,* 7. Taguieff was not the first to make this observation. Antiracist activists were quick to note the anti-immigrant recuperation of the "right to difference." See Kettane, *Droit de réponse,* 88; Bouamama, *Dix ans de Marche des Beurs,* 87, 156. I should note that there is some irony in quoting Taguieff in a book about grassroots antiracism in postcolonial France. A leading expert on the Nouvelle droite, Taguieff is best known today for coining the term *islamo-gauchisme* (Islamo-leftism) to denounce "decolonialism and identitarian ideologies" in France. Taguieff, *L'imposture décoloniale.*

58. Jean Raspail offers a classic example of the trope of reverse colonization in his 1973 novel *Le camp des saints* (*The Camp of the Saints*). Faced with the sudden arrival of a million migrants, one of the novel's many minor characters has this to say: "Nobody has yet pointed to the essential risk, which stems from the extreme vulnerability of the white race and its tragic status as a minority. I'm white. White and Western. We are white. But what do we amount to in total? Some seven hundred million souls, most of us packed into Europe, as against the billions and billions of nonwhites, so many we can't even keep count." Raspail, *Camp of the Saints,* 93, translation modified; Raspail, *Le camp des saints,* 112. Renaud Camus, the author of the "great replacement" theory according to which Europeans are being steadily replaced by non-Europeans, is not circumspect about identifying the threat: Muslims are colonizing France.

Camus, *Le grand remplacement;* Camus, *You Will Not Replace Us!* On Camus's influence on the alt-right, see McAuley, "How Gay Icon Renaud Camus."

59. Benoist, *Vu de droite,* xxii.

1. Palestine as Rallying Cry

1. I borrow this formulation from Emmanuelle Comtat, who analyzes "the persistence of settler colonial culture following the end of colonisation and the removal of the settler population" in her sociological study of *pied-noir* (repatriated settler) communities in postcolonial France. Comtat, "From *Indigènes* to Immigrant Workers," 263.

2. I have found only two mentions of "Indians" in the literature on and about migrant workers of the 1970s. In his 1973 testimonial, an Algerian migrant dubbed "Ahmed" uses a "vocabulaire tiré des westerns" (a vocabulary drawn from Westerns, according to a footnote by his anonymous scribe) to recount episodes from his impoverished childhood ("I threw the axe in the tree, like an Apache"). Ahmed, *Une vie d'Algérien,* 18. In his 1979 dissertation on migrant theater troupes, Frédéric Maatouk draws a much more explicit comparison between the deculturation of postcolonial migrants in France and indigenous Americans: "Like in America, where the Indians and Incas were deprived of their memory, the immigrant today is cut off from his true roots." Maatouk, "Le théâtre des travailleurs immigrés," 18.

3. Contra the media recuperation of the appellation *Beur* to demarcate the "second generation" from their migrant parents, Nacer Kettane insists that "the term 'Beur' does not divide generations: it is not the case that immigrants of a certain age are foreigners and little Beurs [*petits Beurs,* a pun on the name of a beloved French butter cookie] are French." Kettane, *Droit de réponse,* 21. On the "confiscation" of the grassroots antiracist movement that coalesced around the Marche pour l'égalité et contre le racisme by the Socialist Party and SOS racisme, see Abdallah and the Réseau No Pasaran, *J'y suis, j'y reste!,* 68. In his detailed sociohistory of the 1983 march, Hajjat shows that the *marcheurs* themselves were wary of the "recuperation" of their cause by the humanitarian and ecumenical organizations that helped publicize their cause. Hajjat, *The Wretched of France,* 109. For a damning view on the inner workings of SOS racisme, see Malik, *Histoire secrète.*

4. Tancelin, personal communication with the author, July 17, 2021.

5. I borrow the figure of reactivation from Bouchra Khalili. Khalili, "The Tempest Society. Video. 2017," www.bouchrakhalili.com.

6. Several of the militant pro-Palestinian documentary films produced in the early 1970s have recently been made available online. Francis Reusser, "Biladi," Vimeo video, 1:05:54, April 22, 2020, www.vimeo.com; Idioms Film, "L'Olivier, by Groupe Cinéma de Vincennes 1976," Vimeo video, 1:32:47, June 24, 2020, www.vimeo.com. *Compter sur ses propres forces* is one of dozens of documentary and fiction films about migrant workers that were made during this period. For a non-exhaustive list of French militant films about migrant workers and Palestinians, see Hennebelle, *Guide des films anti-impérialistes.* On the collaborations between pro-Palestinian filmmakers in the 1970s and the fledgling Palestinian cinema industry, see Yaqub, *Palestinian Cinema.* The Moroccan director Moumen Smihi's 1971 short fiction film, *Si Moh, pas de chance* (*Si Moh, the Unlucky Man*), includes a short scene, shot in a *foyer* (a state-run boardinghouse for migrant workers), in which the film's protagonist, a Moroccan migrant who cannot find work, listens to a comrade read an article from the Arab press on Palestine. Although the mention of Palestine is laconic, it offers rare audiovisual

testimony of the importance of the Palestinian Revolution among migrant workers in France. On Smihi's films, which include frequent references to Palestine, see Limbrick, *Arab Modernism*.

7. Yannis Tritsibidas, "Compter sur ses propres forces, documentaire militant 1972," YouTube video, 52:39, May 3, 2019, www.youtube.com. All translations from the film are my own.

8. For an account of the first French delegation to the Palestinian military bases in Jordan by GP activists Alain Geismar and Léo Lévy, see Hajjat, "Comités Palestine," 60. Geismar has denied allegations that Fatah offered military training to GP militants. Hecker, "Un demi-siècle de militantisme," 200.

To my knowledge, Edward Said was the first to use the expression "Palestine as rallying cry" in describing the catalyzing effect of the Palestinian Revolution in popular revolts across the Middle East. Said, *The Question of Palestine*, 125. In his study of migrant movements in France, Rabah Aissaoui similarly speaks of Palestine as "the rallying cry of all oppressed people, whatever their national or ethnic origins." Aissaoui, *Immigration and National Identity*, 213. See also Mandel, *Muslims and Jews in France*, 105.

9. Attesting to the alliances between the New Left and the movement for migrant rights in 1970s France, the title *Compter sur ses propres forces* is drawn from a chapter of Mao Zedong's "Little Red Book," translated into English as "Self-Reliance and the Arduous Struggle" (the full title, in French, is "Compter sur ses propres forces et lutter avec endurance"). Zedong, *Quotations from Chairman Mao Tsetung*, 194–202.

10. I borrow the expression from Abdellali Hajjat: "Writing the history of the Comités Palestine and the MTA as a footnote of the GP's history would completely impair the object of research." Hajjat, "Comités Palestine," 57. In her study of Jewish-Muslim relations in France, Maud Mandel draws extensively from state and police archives to argue that "Hajjat downplays Fatah's role in the establishment of the Comités Palestine [CSRP]," even though she notes factual errors in, for example, a police report she consults to make this claim, and acknowledges that such reports "often portrayed foreign laborers as passive." Mandel, *Muslims and Jews in France*, 113, 215–17nn37–56. I have made the deliberate choice to tell the story of the CSRP on the basis of the movements' own archives, rather than the state and police archives evidencing attempts to control it.

11. Comité de soutien à la révolution palestinienne, "Un communiqué et un appel à tous les travailleurs en France!," December 1970 tract, ARCH/0057/01, Fonds Saïd Bouziri, La contemporaine [hereafter FSB-LC].

12. "Dis-moi mon frère," *Fedaï: Journal de soutien à la Révolution Palestinienne* 6 (February 11, 1971): 1, ARCH/0057/04, FSB-LC.

13. For a list of Palestine committees extant in France and elsewhere in Europe at the time of the founding of the CSRP, see Hajjat, "Les comités Palestine," 19.

14. Maatouk, "Le théâtre des travailleurs immigrés," 118.

15. "Palestine—Maghreb: Même combat," *Fedaï: Bulletin des Comités de soutien à la Révolution Palestinienne* 6 (September 25, 1970): 2, ARCH/0057/04, FSB-LC.

16. Hajjat, "Comités Palestine," 56.

17. The CSRP was founded at the Maison du Maroc (the "Moroccan House" at the Cité universitaire) shortly after Black September, by Arab students and "Arab Maoists," including the Tunisian students Saïd and Hamza Bouziri, and the Palestinian Ezzedine Kalak, president at the time of the General Union for Palestinian Students (active in France since 1965), and future representative of the PLO in Paris. Other founding members, many of them known only by their pseudonyms, included the

Franco-Syrian student Gilles "Fathi," the Franco-Lebanese student Thérèse, the Algerian migrant worker Mohammed "Fedaï," and the Moroccan migrant worker Mohamed "Mokhtar" Bachiri, whose performance collective Al Assifa I discuss below. Hajjat, "Comités Palestine," 62.

18. As noted in the Introduction, the founding role of the CSRP has been largely occluded in the historiography of grassroots antiracist movements in France, which tends to start with the 1983 march. Broadcast via print journalism, photography, and television, the Marche pour l'égalité et contre le racisme, popularly if problematically dubbed Marche des Beurs, is to this day the standard-bearer for grassroots antiracism in France. Hajjat has shown that many of the *marcheurs* were new to the political field and suspicious of party politics, even as they adopted anticolonial tactics like the hunger strike in their struggle. Revolutionary aesthetics played a non-negligible role in the ubiquitous donning of the *keffiyeh*. Hajjat, *The Wretched of France*, 38–63; Hajjat, personal communication with the author, August 9, 2021. The PIR is very active on social media, and the party's spokesperson Houria Bouteldja was, until recently, a darling of French televised debates (Bouteldja resigned from the PIR in October 2020). For a critical take on the PIR's "dependency" on the mainstream media, see Hajjat, "Révolte des quartiers populaires," 257–59.

19. Christian Riss, one of the militants involved in throwing Molotov cocktails into the Jordanian embassy the day of King Hussein's visit to the Elysée Palace on July 23, 1971, was shot and gravely wounded during a police interpellation. Hajjat, "Comités Palestine," 66. Riss, who began a hunger strike on January 28, 1972, in solidarity with Sadock Ben Mabrouk and José Duarte, summarily fired from Renault-Billancourt, was later hailed as a symbol of the unity between French and Arab workers. See "Palestine vaincra," undated tract, ARCH/0057/01, FSB-LC; "Grève de la faim pour l'unité pour la dignité," *Fedaï: Journal de soutien à la Révolution Palestinienne* 15 (February 23, 1972): 4, ARCH/0057/04, FSB-LC. The film *Compter sur ses propres forces* includes a lengthy interview with Mabrouk and Duarte.

20. "Avec les fedayins tu résiteras," undated tract, ARCH/0057/01, FSB-LC. The "newspaper of the fedayeen" is undoubtedly *Fedayin*, a magazine launched by PLO representative Mahmoud Hamchari in 1969, staffed by Arab Maoists, and distributed by the GP. Hamchari's *Fedayin* and the CSRP's *Fedaï* shared several contributing editors. Hajjat, "Comités Palestine," 63.

21. Letter from police prefect to Saïd Bouziri, December 29, 1976, "Correspondance reçue de la préfecture de Police," ARCH/0057/03, FSB-LC. On the "wave of expulsions" targeting pro-Palestinian migrant activists, see the Secours rouge tract, "Commission centrale immigrés. Note aux comités de base," March 1971, ARCH/0057/01, FSB-LC. The Secours rouge was a Maoist migrant rights organization allied with the CSRP. *Fedaï* was banned on February 25, 1972, and three thousand copies of the journal were seized. Hajjat, "Eléments pour une sociologie historique," 43.

22. Di-Capua, "Palestine Comes to Paris."

23. Kassir and Mardam-Bey, *Itinéraires de Paris à Jérusalem,* 2:157.

24. "Tous unis nous vaincrons," February 1971 tract, ARCH/0057/01, FSB-LC. The Organisation armée secrète (OAS), a paramilitary organization intent on blocking Algerian independence, carried out a number of terrorist attacks in France in the final years of the war of independence, and remained active after independence.

25. "Plan de travail de la rentrée," *Peuples en lutte: Bulletin du Mouvement Anti-Impérialiste des Comités Indochine Palestine* 7 (September 6, 1973): 2, F/DELTA/RES/0579/26, FSB-LC.

26. "Déclaration d'Hamza Bouziri," ARCH/0057/01, FSB-LC.

27. Hamza Bouziri, "Grève de la faim," *Fedaï: Journal de soutien à la Révolution Palestinienne* 6 (February 11, 1971): 2, ARCH/0057/04, FSB-LC.

28. To the best of my knowledge, Hamza Bouziri was the first postcolonial immigrant to go on hunger strike in France, inaugurating the *sans-papiers* (undocumented) movement that would culminate with the occupation of the Saint Bernard Church in 1996. For an overview of hunger strikes in the early 1970s, including Hamza's brother Saïd Bouziri's much more publicized 1972 hunger strike, see Gordon, *Immigrants and Intellectuals,* 126–32.

29. The Marcellin-Fontanet circulars of January and February 1972 required immigrants to have proof of employment and "decent housing" in order to gain residency in France.

30. The murder of Djellali Ben Ali, a fifteen-year-old Algerian boy killed by a white Frenchman in the working-class neighborhood of la Goutte d'Or (Paris 18e) on October 27, 1971, was the first racist crime to mobilize migrant workers en masse since the October 17, 1961, protest against a racist curfew targeting French Muslim Algerians during the final months of the Algerian War of Independence. A rally convened by the CSRP drew four thousand protestors to Barbès on November 7, 1971, including French writers and intellectuals such as Jean Genet, Jean-Paul Sartre, Michel Foucault, and Claude Mauriac. Hajjat, "Alliances inattendues," 525–26. The Saïd Bouziri archives contain extensive profiles of some of the targets of racially motivated violence in the 1970s, including Djellali Ben Ali and Mohamed Diab. The Djellali affair inspired an anonymous 152-page film script, also included in the Bouziri archives. "Crimes racistes. Scénario du film *Les ambassadeurs* inspiré par l'affaire Djellali," ARCH/0057/15, FSB-LC. For a painstaking reconstitution of racist murders from 1970 to 1991, see Giudice, *Arabicides.* Tahar Ben Jelloun offers a more summary, if equally harrowing, list of the victims' names in his classic analysis of anti-immigrant discourse. Ben Jelloun, *French Hospitality,* 47–51.

31. See the undated manuscript issue of *Fedaï* subtitled "Pour des logements déscents! [*sic*]," which includes a call to occupy vacant buildings. "Vive la résistance des mal-logés contre la misère," *Fedaï: Journal de soutien à la Révolution Palestinienne* (n.d., c. April 1972): 5, ARCH/0057/04, FSB-LC.

32. "Le journal 'Fedaï' réapparaît," *Fedaï: Journal des travailleurs arabes,* n.s., 1 (July 15, 1972): 1, ARCH/0057/04, FSB-LC.

33. Each issue of *Fedaï* was bilingual. A similar argument could be made about the Arabic front page, which overlays the call to protest racist crimes in France with a different photograph of Palestinian boys marching in military formation.

34. "Pour arrêter les crimes racistes descends dans la rue!," *Fedaï: Journal de soutien à la Révolution Palestinienne* 15 (February 23, 1972): 1, ARCH/0057/04, FSB-LC.

35. Unlike Driss El Yazami, who cites the front cover of *Fedaï* 15 as evidence that the CSRP was shifting its attention from the Middle East to "matters relating to migration," I am interested in the complex ways in which the movement mobilized Palestine to advocate for migrant rights in France. El Yazimi, "France's Ethnic Minority Press," 120.

36. I am borrowing the neologism *indigéniser* (to make indigenous) from the PIR. "Nous sommes les indigènes de la république!," Parti des indigènes de la république, January 2005, www.indigenes-republique.fr. In the PIR's manifesto, *indigéniser* carries the sense of relegating someone who does not "hail from the colonies" to the status of a second-class citizen. Here I am using the term to speak of the reactivation of colonial-racial regimes against yesterday's *indigènes* in the postcolonial metropole.

37. "Pour la première fois depuis la guerre d'Algérie, nous étions 2,500 dans la

rue le 17 juin contre les racistes," *Fedaï: Journal des travailleurs arabes,* n.s., 1 (July 15, 1972): 2, ARCH/0057/04, FSB-LC.

38.   The term *pied-noir,* initially a pejorative epithet for *indigènes,* was used by metropolitans to designate settlers during the Algerian War of Independence, and was reclaimed by repatriated settlers after 1962. Pervillé, "Comment appeler les habitants de l'Algérie." The origins of the term *pied-noir* remain controversial, with some claiming that the nationalist anticolonial movement Parti du peuple algérien coined it in 1946, while others maintain that it was first used by the OAS to rally the support of settlers. Guy Pervillé, "Pieds-noirs: La valise ou le cercueil," Pour une histoire de la guerre d'Algérie, November 23, 2007, http://guy.perville.free.fr; Hassane Zerrouky, "OAS 'la valise ou le cercueil,'" *L'Humanité,* October 28, 2004. www.humanite.fr.

39.   I am quoting four separate texts here: "Aujourd'hui nous disons que les CP doivent se dissoudre. Ils doivent se dissoudre dans les masses," n.d.; "Bilan politique de deux semaines de travail," n.d.; "Rapport d'orientation des Comités de soutien à la Révolution Palestinienne," May 1971; and "Textes de réflexion comités Palestine," all in ARCH/0057/01, FSB-LC.

40.   There is no consensus on the exact date of the creation of the MTA. I follow Abdellali Hajjat, Rabah Aissaoui, and Daniel A. Gordon, who give June 1972 as the likely launch date of the MTA. Hajjat, "Comités Palestine," 72; Aissaoui, *Immigration and National Identity,* 212; Gordon, *Immigrants and Intellectuals,* 128, 270n34. MTA militants continued to use the signature CSRP or CP (Comités Palestine) well into 1973. See, for example, Comité de soutien à la Révolution Palestinienne, "Appel au meeting du 5 novembre 1972," ARCH/0057/01, FSB-LC.

41.   "Construisons le Mouvement des travailleurs arabes," *Al Assifa: La voix des travailleurs arabes* 2 (n.d.): 2, ARCH/0057/04, FSB-LC. Signed Mouvement des Travailleurs Arabes, this opening editorial is part of a "Supplement to Assifa no 1," whose director of publication is listed as Michel Foucault. A founding member of the Djellali Ben Ali committee and an activist in the Comité de défense de la vie et des droits des travailleurs immigrés (Committee for the Defense of the Life and Rights of Migrant Workers), Foucault lent his name to the publication, though he was not, to my knowledge, involved in its production. "MTA. Publications: El Assifa, Fedaï, La voix des travailleurs arabes," ARCH/0057/04, FSB-LC.

42.   Clancy and Tancelin, *Les tiers idées,* 19. Clancy and Tancelin were active in the Union des jeunesses communistes marxistes-léninistes (UJCML; Union of Marxist-Leninist Communist Youth) and affiliated with the UJCML publication *La cause du peuple.* Bachiri was involved in the CSRP and early efforts in militant theater. Other members of Al Assifa include Farid Aïchoune, Heddi Akkari, Ahmed Bouraka (alias "Djillali"), Fawzia Bouziri, Mustapha Charchari, Kheira, Ali Majri (alias "Ali Clichy"), and Salem Younsi. Hajjat, "The Movement for Arab Workers," 64.

43.   Clancy and Tancelin, *Les tiers idées,* 29.

44.   "Qu'est-ce que Assifa?," undated tract, ARCH/0057/18, FSB-LC.

45.   Clancy and Tancelin, *Les tiers idées,* 195.

46.   Clancy and Tancelin, 158–59. According to Bachiri, the first attempt to mobilize migrant workers through the theater was a play on Palestine, performed at the Cité universitaire. Clancy and Tancelin, 153. As early as November 1970, the CSRP was discussing the need for a revolutionary theater on the Palestinian Revolution. "Comités de soutien à la Révolution Palestinienne. Bilan des CSRP en région parisienne, nov. 1970," ARCH/0057/01, FSB-LC. In the 1976 pro-Palestinian film *L'olivier,* which includes footage of migrant protests in 1970s Paris, the camera reveals a shot of Bachiri playing the *bendir* in front of a poster advertising a Palestinian theater festival in support of

the PLO. The overhead light rail bridge identifies the location as Barbès, the working-class neighborhood where the CSRP and MTA were most active.

47. Neveux, "Apparition d'une scène politique," 340. As Maatouk notes, the stakes were just as high when performances took place in the street, where migrant workers risked being charged with "troubles sur la voie publique" (disturbing the peace). Maatouk, "Le théâtre des travailleurs immigrés," 41.

48. The political mobilization of migrant workers is itself, of course, a performative act. In the midst of the *sans-papiers* hunger strikes of 1973, an undocumented MTA activist and Al Assifa member launched a symbolic presidential campaign under the pseudonym Djellali Kamal to draw attention to the plight of migrant workers. "Candidature Djellali Kamal, élections présidentielles 1974," ARCH/0057/18, FSB-LC.

49. For a chronology of Al Assifa's plays, see Clancy and Tancelin, *Les tiers idées,* 157, 224–29. Tensions between members of the MTA, some of whom felt that Al Assifa was losing sight of the movement's political aims, contributed to the de facto dissolution of the MTA and Al Assifa in 1976. "Crise ouverte dans le MTA à Paris," ARCH/0057/02, FSB-LC; Hajjat, "Eléments pour une sociologie historique," 91. Bachiri, Tancelin, and Clancy, the founders of Al Assifa, remained invested in aesthetic experimentation, and continued to work under the umbrella organization Collectif Assifa after the dissolution of the troupe in 1976. Tancelin, personal communication with the author, July 17, 2021.

50. "La troupe Al Assifa présente: 'Ça travaille, ça travaille et ça ferme sa gueule,'" undated tract, ARCH/0057/18, FSB-LC.

51. Clancy and Tancelin, *Les tiers idées,* 159. Fatna Diab was the sister of Mohamed Diab, gunned down in a police station on November 29, 1972. Several of Al Assifa's members were active in the comité Mohamed Diab. Clancy and Tancelin, 167. The CRS (Compagnies républicaines de sécurité; Republican Security Companies) are France's national police force.

52. Clancy and Tancelin, 197.

53. Clancy and Tancelin describe Al Assifa's process of collective creation in a chapter of their memoir titled "Lumières." As they note, Al Assifa's plays "were never written down." Clancy and Tancelin, 187–99, 188. In his 1979 dissertation on migrant theater, Maatouk includes excerpts from "Ça travaille, ça travaille et ça ferme sa gueule" (presumably transcribed on the basis of performances he attended) and explains that the editors he contacted were not interested in publishing a play that had already been performed more than 250 times. Maatouk, "Le théâtre des travailleurs immigrés," 435.

54. Clancy and Tancelin, *Les tiers idées,* 159.

55. Clancy and Tancelin, 161.

56. Clancy and Tancelin, 165.

57. Clancy and Tancelin, 163.

58. Clancy and Tancelin, 181.

59. See in particular Khalili's video installation on the migrant experience, *Mapping Journey Project,* and her multimedia installation on revolutionary Algeria, *Foreign Office.*

60. Khalili, *The Tempest Society,* 165.

61. Khalili, "The Tempest Society."

62. Khalili, *The Tempest Society,* 162. Khalili is one of several artists, activists, and archivists who have recently made the scattered archives of Al Assifa available to a wider public. Others include Hajer Ben Boubaker, oral archivist and founder of the podcast Vintage Arab, and the rapper Rocé, who digitized excerpts of "Ça travaille, ça

travaille et ça ferme sa gueule" for an album titled *Par les damné.e.s de la terre.* See Ben Boubaker's four-part France Culture podcast on the history of the MTA. Hajer Ben Boubaker and Angélique Tibau, "Une histoire du Mouvement des travailleurs arabes," France Culture, October 21, 2021, www.franceculture.fr. France Culture recently re-broadcast a 1976 program on Radio Assifa, a pioneering effort in "free radio" launched by Al Assifa and other MTA militants in the 1970s, which includes a rare audio record-ing of a sketch on immigration. Marie-Dominique Arrighi and Jean-Marc Fombone, "Courant alternatif: Court-circuit—Radio Assifa (1ère diffusion: 21/03/1976)," France Culture, April 1, 2020, www.franceculture.fr.

63.   Khalili collected Al Assifa documents over the course of ten years of indepen-dent research. Khalili, personal communication with the author, September 10, 2021. Philippe Tancelin also shared his personal archive with Khalili, including black-and-white photographs of Al Assifa performances as well as a short Super 8 film by a mi-grant worker who attended a performance of "Ça travaille, ça travaille et ça ferme sa gueule" at the striking auto factory of Chausson. Tancelin, personal communication with the author, July 17, 2021. Anne Quesemand's film on militant theater, *Entre la foule et le désert,* includes footage of performances by several troupes in the Collectif Assifa, the Bendir déchiré (or Bendir déchaîné) and the Groupe salve.

64.   Kauffmann, Khalili, and Tancelin, "On Bearing Witness," 80.

65.   Kauffmann, Khalili, and Tancelin, 80.

66.   Kauffmann, Khalili, and Tancelin, 78.

67.   Kauffmann, Khalili, and Tancelin, 78.

68.   Tancelin visited the ruined camps of Sabra and Shatila in May 2012 and made a film-essay about the experience, *Les camps oubliés,* available on his blog. "Les camps oubliés: Film documentaire," *CICEP-Paris8 Centre international de créations d'espaces poétiques et de recherches,* Philippe Tancelin and Serpilekin Adeline Terlemez, www.cicep.canalblog.com. See also Tancelin, *L'ivre traversée.*

69.   Genet recurs across several of Khalili's works. In her video installation *Speeches—Chapter 1: Mother Tongue,* a Senegalese woman in the *banlieue* of Paris re-cites a text by Mahmoud Darwish about Genet in her native Wolof.

70.   Khalili, "The Radical Ally," 22.

2. Jean Genet and the Politics of Betrayal

1.   Comité de soutien à la Révolution Palestinienne, "Un communiqué et un appel à tous les travailleurs en France!," December 1970 tract, ARCH/0057/01, Fonds Saïd Bouziri, La contemporaine.

2.   Genet, *Prisoner of Love,* 12; Genet, "Four Hours in Shatila," 10.

3.   Genet, *The Declared Enemy,* 244.

4.   Critics have tended to read Genet's last published work as a taking stock of his life, a way of settling accounts with society. Because Genet to all intents and pur-poses abandoned literature after being canonized by Jean-Paul Sartre—author of the monumental *Saint Genet, comédien et martyr,* published in 1952 as the first vol-ume of Genet's complete works—they also interpret his posthumous book as a final provocation directed against the French literary establishment. See Guattari, "Genet retrouvé"; Cixous, *Entretien de la blessure;* Durham, "The Deaths of Jean Genet." As captivating as these analyses are, Palestine remains, for the most part, an analytic, a hermeneutical tool to decipher the work of an unclassifiable writer. My analysis hews closer to the important studies of the politics of betrayal in Genet's Palestinian writings. See Khatibi, *Figures de l'étranger;* El Maleh, *Jean Genet;* Said, *On Late Style;* Laroche, *Le dernier Genet;* Gourgouris, *Does Literature Think?*

5. Genet, *The Declared Enemy*, 125–26.

6. Genet, *Prisoner of Love*, 15.

7. According to Edmund White, Philippe Sollers of the journal *Tel quel* introduced Genet to Hamchari. White, *Genet*, 549. Other sources claim that he met Hamchari through Panther activists in Paris, not an unlikely scenario given the Black Panthers' ties to the PLO. Genet, *The Declared Enemy*, 313. On the Black Panthers and Palestine, see Feldman, *A Shadow over Palestine*, 59–101.

8. For a chronology of Genet's activism on behalf of the Black Panthers, see E. White, *Genet*, 521–39.

9. Founded by Michel Foucault and presided by the writer Claude Mauriac, the comité Djellali held office once a week in a room of a local church on the rue Saint Bruno in the Goutte d'Or neighborhood. For an account of the activities of the comité Djellali, including tensions with the CSRP and the Maoist Secours rouge, see Mauriac, *Et comme l'espérance est violente*, 279–522; von Bülow and Ben Ali, *La Goutte-d'Or*, 97–197.

10. E. White, *Genet*, 520–21; Gordon, *Immigrants and Intellectuals*, 101. In December 1972, Genet was booked while protesting the police killing of Mohamed Diab on December 16, 1972. Giudice, *Arabicides*, 88.

11. Here I part ways with Edmund White, who claims, without citing any sources, that "Genet's only interest in the Djilali affair was to win support for the Palestinians." *Genet*, 569.

12. Genet, *The Declared Enemy*, 71–72, translation modified; Genet, *L'ennemi déclaré*, 89–90.

13. Éric Marty cites Sartre's paradoxical assessment—"Genet is anti-Semitic. Or rather he plays at being so"—at the outset of a text that seeks to demonstrate that "the primary target [of Genet's Palestinian writings] is, therefore, the Jewish people." Marty, *Bref séjour à Jérusalem*, 91, 156. Sartre makes this assessment in his magnum opus on the young Genet, and further speculates that if the vagabond writer dislikes the Jews, it is because, like them, he is a martyr. Sartre, *Saint Genet, Actor and Martyr*, 203. Citing Genet's novels as his only evidence, Ivan Jablonka goes even further than Marty, comparing Genet's stance to that of Drieu de la Rochelle and other Nazi collaborators. Jablonka, *Les vérités inavouables*, 155–227.

14. E. White, *Genet*, 559. For a more nuanced approach to the charge of anti-Semitism in Genet's Palestinian writings, see Laroche, *Le dernier Genet*, 194–235. See also Tahar Ben Jelloun's indignant response to Jablonka, originally published in *La repubblica*. Ben Jelloun, *Jean Genet*, 200–205. In an interview with Ben Jelloun, Genet explicitly condemns anti-Semitism, correctly identifying the common roots of anti-Arab and anti-Jewish ideology in nineteenth-century racist discourse. Ben Jelloun, *Jean Genet*, 195. A truncated version of this interview was published in *Le Monde* on November 11, 1979, though Genet's remarks on the persistence of anti-Semitism in France were not included in the excerpt. Genet, *The Declared Enemy*, 179–81.

15. Genet, *The Declared Enemy*, 80, translation modified; Genet, *L'ennemi déclaré*, 98–99.

16. In his letters to the writer and editor Andrée Plainemaison (pen name Pragane or Ibis), written when he was in his twenties, Genet spoke frequently of his time in the colonial army, and even claimed that he killed Chleuh rebels during the "pacification" of Morocco. Genet, *Lettres à Ibis*, 26. On Genet's service in the colonial army, see E. White, *Genet*, 84–95.

17. Genet, *The Declared Enemy*, 43.

18. In May 1955, Genet signed a petition in favor of Algerian and Moroccan inde-

pendence, although he did not sign the "Manifeste des 121," the 1958 manifesto calling for conscripts to desert. In a letter to his editor and translator Bernard Frechtman, Genet explained that as a former deserter and convicted thief, he did not think his signature would help the Algerian cause. Bellity Peskine and Dichy, *La bataille des "Paravents,"* 26; E. White, *Genet,* 411. The publication of his 1961 play, *Les paravents,* offers a preview of Genet's interest in the plight of migrant workers. The protagonist, Said, is set to emigrate to France when the conflict between the French and the Arabs erupts. "If I cross the sea, it's to make more money. My cousin told me I can get a job and that I'll be able to save." Genet, *The Screens,* 30. The "battle of the *Screens,*" as the controversy over the play is known, further established Genet's anticolonial credentials. On the polemical and often violent reception of *Les paravents* when it premiered in France in 1966 (Jean-Marie Le Pen was one of its most vocal critics), see Bellity Peskine and Dichy, *La bataille des "Paravents"*; and E. White, *Genet,* 491–95.

19. According to Albert Dichy, the first version of "Le bleu de l'oeil" (The blue of the eye), as the script was originally titled, is dated August 1975. Dichy, personal communication with the author, July 23, 2021. All extant versions of the script are held at the Institut des mémoires de l'édition contemporaine (IMEC), which is currently in the process of reorganizing its Jean Genet archive based on newly found materials. I base my interpretation of "La nuit venue" on the manuscripts formerly numbered GNT 7.3, 7.4, 7.5, and 7.6, as well as on two recently discovered bound typescripts: one identical to GNT 7.5, but with handwritten corrections and additions, the other corresponding to GNT 7.6, the version of the script that was submitted to the Centre national de cinématographie. These are the call numbers I use for all cited manuscripts in my notes below, although they are no longer in use. Jean Genet, "La nuit venue [1977?]," GNT 7.3, Fonds Jean Genet, Institut des mémoires de l'édition contemporaine [hereafter FJG-IMEC]; Jean Genet, "Le bleu de l'oeil [197?]," GNT 7.4, FJG-IMEC; Jean Genet, "Le bleu de l'oeil [1976?]," GNT 7.5, FJG-IMEC; Jean Genet, "La nuit venue [197?]," GNT 7.6, FJG-IMEC.

20. My summary is based on scenes that run through several of the extant manuscripts of "La nuit venue." The dramatic ending whereby A. is arrested on his return to Morocco (or, in another variant of the scene, the Spanish port city of Algésiras) is found only in the manuscript numbered GNT 7.3. The note attached to this file gives this version of the script as the definitive one, with a tentative date of 1977. Careful comparison of the extant versions of the script sheds some doubt on the classification of this version as the last one, however. In addition to the fact that GNT 7.6 is (also) listed as the "last version of the script" in the IMEC catalog I consulted, GNT 7.3 is a more narrative and tentative version of the script than GNT 7.6. But its dramatic ending makes it in some ways the most militant version of the script (other versions have happier endings). Jean Genet, "La nuit venue [1977?]," GNT 7.3, FJG-IMEC; Jean Genet, "La nuit venue [197?]," GNT 7.6, FJG-IMEC. The practice of sharing intelligence about migrants was well documented when Genet wrote "La nuit venue." As discussed in Chapter One, migrant workers were in some instances deported, arrested, and tortured in their home country for offenses committed in France. See Mauriac, *Et comme l'espérance est violente,* 298.

21. For a detailed synopsis and production information for "La nuit venue," one of Genet's many unrealized film projects, see E. White, *Genet,* 587–91. The archival traces of "La nuit venue" are scant, and those involved in the project have differing accounts of what happened. In his book about Genet, with whom he worked on several Palestine-related articles in 1974, the Moroccan writer Tahar Ben Jelloun recalls that Genet asked him to write the Arabic dialogue for the film script. Ben Jelloun, *Jean*

Genet, 85–90, 181. Genet's codirector Ghislain Uhry, however, denies that Ben Jelloun was involved at all. Uhry, "Tahar Ben Jelloun refait le film de Jean Genet," *Libération*, December 1, 2010, www.liberation.fr. Genet's handwritten notes about the film project reveal that he was exasperated with the whole production team, and in particular his codirector, Uhry. Genet, "Notes relatives au projet de film 'La nuit venue' [1977?]," GNT 7.7, FJG-IMEC.

22. Genet's handwritten marginalia about where to introduce elements of "stylization" (police officers on stilts, white characters with stockinged faces . . .) are found in the (most likely) final version of the manuscript. Genet, "La nuit venue [197?]," GNT 7.6, p. 44, FJG-IMEC.

23. Genet, 79.

24. The scene with the sex worker might have been inspired by Tahar Ben Jelloun's dissertation, which Genet read carefully and tried to place, unsuccessfully, with his editor at Gallimard. Ben Jelloun, *Jean Genet*, 51–55. On the notion of "sexual misery," see Ben Jelloun, *La plus haute des solitudes*. *La réclusion solitaire*, the novel Ben Jelloun was working on when Genet was drafting "La nuit venue," offers unexpected solace for the sexual misery of the migrant worker in the mythic "image" of a female Palestinian refugee. Ben Jelloun, *La réclusion solitaire*, 127–33.

25. Genet, *The Screens*, 97.

26. Jean Genet, "La nuit venue [197?]," GNT 7.6, p. 93, FJG-IMEC. The scene I am dubbing the *battle of the palisades* is found only in the manuscripts numbered GNT 7.5 (as a handwritten insert) and GNT 7.6.

27. Genet, "The Palestinians," 8. Not to be confused with Genet's eponymous text in *Zoom*, "The Palestinians" is based on Genet's handwritten notes about a 1972 conversation with seven Palestinians in Paris, first published in an Arabic translation in *Shu'un Filastiniya* in December 1972, and then in English in the *Journal of Palestine Studies* in October 1973.

28. Scattered throughout the pages of *Un captif amoureux*, Genet's reflections on what drew him to the Palestinians are best summarized in his description of Black Panther leader David Hilliard's conversation with Black students at the University of Connecticut. "The links between them all were political, but that was not the explanation of their solidarity: also present was a very subtle but very strong eroticism. It was so strong, so evident yet so discreet, that while I never desired any particular person, I was all desire for the group as a whole. But my desire was satisfied by the fact that they existed." Genet, *Prisoner of Love*, 300.

29. The political and racial implications of Genet's critique of social functions is already apparent in a 1964 interview about his biting satire of colonialism in *Les paravents*: "Je me fous de la fonction" ("I don't give a damn about [social] position"). Genet, *L'ennemi déclaré*, 23; Genet, *The Declared Enemy*, 13.

30. Genet, *The Declared Enemy*, 229–31, translation modified; Genet, *L'ennemi déclaré*, 265–67. In a 1979 interview for *Le Monde*, Genet clarified his critique of de-historicized anti-immigrant discourses with the pithy observation that in 1914, "the natives [*les indigènes*] had the honor of spilling French or assimilated blood." Genet, *The Declared Enemy*, 181. For the full text of the interview, see Ben Jelloun, *Jean Genet*, 187–97.

31. Genet, *The Declared Enemy*, 235.

32. For the official UN report on the Israeli invasion of Lebanon, see MacBride, *Israel in Lebanon*. For a history of the events leading up to the massacres of Sabra and Shatila, see Khalidi, *Under Siege*, 167–82. On the circumstances that led Genet to write "Quatre heures à Chatila," see E. White, *Genet*, 608–14. Richard Dindo's documentary

film *Genet à Chatila* includes an interview with Leila Shahid about Genet's visit to the camps, footage of the aftermath of the massacre, and several of Bruno Barbey's photographs of fedayeen.

33. Genet, "Four Hours in Shatila," 22; Genet, "Quatre heures à Chatila," 19.

34. E. White, *Genet*, 609; on *Le langage de la muraille*, see 70–72, 605–7.

35. Said, *On Late Style*, 81.

36. Genet, "Four Hours in Shatila," 19.

37. Said, *On Late Style*, 81.

38. Genet, *Prisoner of Love*, 377.

39. For a detailed account of Israel's role in the massacres, and U.S. knowledge of the imminent attack, see Anziska, *Preventing Palestine*, 194–237.

40. Genet, *The Declared Enemy*, 72.

41. Genet, "Four Hours in Shatila," 10.

42. Genet, 16, translation modified; Genet, "Quatre heures à Chatila," 14. Genet plays on the near homophones *justice* and *justesse* (justice, rightness) in his posthumous memoir: "Ce n'est pas la justice de cette cause qui m'aura touché mais sa justesse" ("It's not the justice of their cause that moves me—it's the rightness"). Genet, *Un captif amoureux*, 582; Genet, *Prisoner of Love*, 409. On love as a figure of radical political solidarity rather than humanitarian compassion, see Bernard, "'They Are in the Right.'"

43. Genet, "Four Hours in Shatila," 13, translation modified; Genet, "Quatre heures à Chatila," 11.

44. On the "ironic vision" required to seize the historical paradox that turned Jews into colonists in Palestine, see Said, *The Question of Palestine*, xxxix.

45. Genet, *The Declared Enemy*, 243.

46. Said, *On Late Style*, 85.

47. Laroche makes a related point: "By confronting the terms identity, nation, and language—national and mother tongue—Genet questions the very principle of nativeness [*le principe même de la nativité*]." Laroche, *Le dernier Genet*, 255. For a powerful reading of Genet's "identicide," see Gourgouris, *Does Literature Think?*, 249–91.

48. Genet, *The Declared Enemy*, 244, 251.

49. Genet, *Prisoner of Love*, 428–29, translation modified; Genet, *Un captif amoureux*, 609.

50. Genet, *Prisoner of Love*, 15; Genet, *Un captif amoureux*, 25. Barbara Bray's elegant translation of Genet's expression "les nations 'assises'" (literally, the seated nations) fortuitously reintroduces the specter of colonialism into Genet's lexicon via the image of *settlement*.

51. In his recollections of a conversation with "seven young Palestinians one evening in Paris" in September 1972, Genet speculates that "fantasy, in the case of Palestine, is to some extent a blessing. . . . While its land was being drawn from under its feet, the Palestinian nation was finding itself in fantasy, but for it to be able to exist, it had to discover the revolutionary necessity." Genet, "The Palestinians," 5.

52. Genet, *Prisoner of Love*, 388; Genet, *Un captif amoureux*, 553. Genet died while he was correcting the proofs of his manuscript. In the final chapter of his study of the figure of the stranger in French literature, written a few short months after Genet's death and the posthumous publication of *Un captif amoureux*, the Moroccan writer Abdelkebir Khatibi speculates that Genet's decision to be buried in Larache, Morocco, rather than his native Paris was a way to "rob [his death] from France and transplant it in a foreign land." Khatibi, *Figures de l'étranger*, 193. Echoing the ending of the version of "La nuit venue" in which A. returns to Morocco accompanied by the coffins of

migrant workers, Juan Goytisolo makes an even more fitting comparison, noting that Genet was "repatriated in secret like one of the many migrant workers who died in Europe." Goytisolo, "Le poète enterré à Larache," 104. See also Goytisolo, *Forbidden Territory*, 298. According to Leila Shahid, Genet's coffin was, in fact, labeled "travailleur immigré" when it was unloaded from the plane. E. White, *Genet*, 634.

53. Genet, *Prisoner of Love*, 105; Genet, *The Declared Enemy*, 80.

54. Said, *The Question of Palestine*, 124.

55. "This is *my* Palestinian revolution," Genet writes in *Un captif amoureux*. Genet, *Prisoner of Love*, 355, emphasis in original.

56. Genet, *Prisoner of Love*, 17–20. Following closely on the heels of the Fatah victory at Karameh (Jordan) in March 1968, the occupation of the Sorbonne in May 1968 provided, for the first time, a space for pro-Palestinian activism in the French public sphere, albeit a fleeting one. The Palestinian stand at the Sorbonne was quickly taken down to avoid confrontations with Zionist students. Kassir and Mardam-Bey, *Itinéraires de Paris à Jérusalem*, 2:167.

57. Genet, *Prisoner of Love*, 127, translation modified; Genet, *Un captif amoureux*, 182–83.

58. Genet, *Prisoner of Love*, 128, translation modified; Genet, *Un captif amoureux*, 183–84.

59. Genet, *Prisoner of Love*, 165, translation modified, 163; Genet, *Un captif amoureux*, 237, 235.

60. Genet, *Prisoner of Love*, 159.

61. Guattari, "Genet retrouvé," 27.

62. Genet, *Prisoner of Love*, 382–83, translation modified, emphasis in original; Genet, *Un captif amoureux*, 545.

63. Genet, *Prisoner of Love*, 383, 385, 386, translation modified; Genet, *Un captif amoureux*, 545, 548, 550.

64. Edmond El Maleh similarly reads Genet's Palestinian writings through the lens of his time in mandate Syria: "Genet will find that same colonial order in the 'dirty war' that was displaced, decentered to fall upon Beirut, the Palestinian villages and camps." El Maleh, *Jean Genet*, 57.

65. Genet, *Prisoner of Love*, 287. On the capitulation of France as a form of "vengeance," see Genet, *The Declared Enemy*, 125–26.

66. Genet, *Prisoner of Love*, 387, translation modified; Genet, *Un captif amoureux*, 550–51.

67. "We should always remember that the Palestinians have nothing, neither passport not territory nor nation, and if they laud and long for all those things it's because they only see the ghosts of them." Genet, *Prisoner of Love*, 84. Mobility is, Genet reminds us, a privilege that he enjoys by virtue of his nationality, making him complicit in the statelessness of the Palestinians: "Meager though it seemed at the time, I'd had the privilege of being born in the capital of an empire so vast that it circled the globe, while at the same time the Palestinians were being stripped of their lands, their houses and even their beds." Genet, *Prisoner of Love*, 12, translation modified; Genet, *Un captif amoureux*, 21.

68. Genet, *Prisoner of Love*, 387–88, translation modified; Genet, *Un captif amoureux*, 552.

69. Genet, *The Declared Enemy*, 72, translation modified; Genet, *L'ennemi déclaré*, 90.

70. On the "contrived ignorance" of imperial discourse, see Stoler, *Along the Archival Grain*, 247, 237–78.

71. Genet, *Prisoner of Love,* 174.

72. E. White, *Genet,* 24.

73. Genet, *Prisoner of Love,* 74–75, translation modified; Genet, *Un captif amoureux,* 107–8.

74. Genet, *Prisoner of Love,* 386, translation modified; Genet, *Un captif amoureux,* 550.

3. The Contest for Indigeneity in Postcolonial France

1. "Nous sommes les indigènes de la république!," Parti des indigènes de la république, January 2005, www.indigenes-republique.fr. Adama Traoré died of asphyxiation in a police van in July 2016. Activists' demands for a full inquiry into his death have gained traction in the wake of the massive, global antiracist protests of summer 2020 following the police killing of George Floyd.

2. On the "racialization of urban rebellions," see Hajjat, *The Wretched of France,* 65–66. Historian Gérard Noiriel is also critical of what he calls "the ethnicization of the discourse on immigration," including the appropriation of the *verlan* term *Beur* (*Arabe*) to speak of the activists of la Marche pour l'égalité et contre le racisme, redubbed Marche des Beurs in both left- and right-leaning media. According to Noiriel, the result of this discursive shorthand is to reduce the political demands of the *marcheurs* to an identitarian claim, relegating them to a communal, rather than political, identity. Noiriel, *Immigration, antisémitisme, et racisme,* 588–667.

3. I use the term *French alt-right* in this chapter to capture the eclectic, centrifugal, and often ideologically confounding nature of the statements emanating from an increasing number of fringe organizations and parties that are in some way tributary to the nativist discourses that emerged in the wake of decolonization, even if some of its most eloquent representatives (for example, Farida Belghoul and Dieudonné M'bala M'bala) are themselves of colonized descent. First used during the Trump years in the United States, the term *alt-right* also highlights the now well-documented transnational solidarities between fringe right-wing movements across Europe, North America, and beyond.

4. Published in 1983, Mehdi Charef's *Le thé au harem d'Archi Ahmed* inaugurated the genre known as Beur literature: writings by the children of Maghrebi migrants to France, most of whom grew up in the 1970s and 1980s and were instrumental in placing antiracism at the heart of public discourse. Less often studied than their male counterparts, women writers were central to the rise of the Beur novel. In 1985, the Belgian-Moroccan novelist Leïla Houari published *Zeida de nulle part.* Belghoul's *Georgette!* was awarded the Prix Hermès du premier roman in 1987, the year another remarkable text by a French-Algerian woman was published, Sakinna Boukhedenna's memoir *Journal "Nationalité: Immigr(é)e."* Born and raised in colonial Algeria by her Algerian father and French mother, Leïla Sebbar does not easily fit the *Beur* label, although the novels she began publishing in the early 1980s are considered foundational of the genre. Sebbar, *Shérazade.*

5. On the French alt-right's use of social media and alternative publication platforms, see Albertini and Doucet, *La fachosphère.*

6. Sayad, *The Suffering of the Immigrant,* esp. 177–215.

7. Until recently, Soral's video presentation of *Georgette!* was embedded in his website's promotional page for the Kontre Kulture edition of the novel. *"Georgette!,"* no date, Égalité & réconciliation, www.egaliteetreconciliation.fr. It was also accessible on Soral's YouTube channel ERTV Officiel, until YouTube banned him from the platform in July 2020.

8. The French state's attempts to censor Dieudonné's shows, while successful in court, have only made him more popular. For a non-exhaustive list of legal suits against Dieudonné, see "Depuis 2006, la longue liste des condamnations contre Dieudonné," *L'express*, March 19, 2015, www.lexpress.fr.

9. In 2013, Vincent Peillon, minister of education under François Hollande, commissioned two separate reports on gender equality and homophobia in schools. These reports led to the creation of a new teaching module for preschool, "Les ABCD de l'égalité." Although the Peillon reforms stalled due to massive resistance against "gender theory," gender equality remains a priority for the administration of Emmanuel Macron, which has announced that preschool and elementary school teachers will be trained "to deconstruct sexist representations" while middle school teachers will focus on "combatting pornography and cyber bullying." "Égalité des filles et des garçons," last modified November 2017, www.education.gouv.fr. For a thorough account of French resistance to queer theory, including passing reference to Belghoul, see Perreau, *Queer Theory*, 17–74, esp. 66–67.

10. Belghoul's first experiments in homeschooling her children are the subject of a documentary short, Samia Chala, *Sauve qui peut!*, Vimeo video, 37:00, May 15, 2008, www.vimeo.com.

11. The Journée de retrait de l'école was renamed Justice et respect pour l'enfance in 2017. Although the JRE's website has been suspended, it can be retrieved on the Internet Archive Wayback Machine. Journée de retrait de l'école, last modified December 23, 2013, www.web.archive.org.

12. Although Alain Soral has been banned from YouTube, E&R's televised interview with Belghoul was reposted on YouTube by the user Catholique de France. "Farida Belghoul sur la théorie du genre," YouTube video, 40:03, January 30, 2014, www.youtube.com. On May 19, 2016, Dalila Hassan, a JRE correspondent, and Farida Belghoul were condemned for defamation after producing a video accusing a preschool teacher of "education à la sexualité." As of writing this video is still available on YouTube. JRE 2014, "Ecole maternelle de Joué-les-Tours: un enfant traumatisé," YouTube video, 10:44, March 29, 2014, www.youtube.com.

13. For more information on la Route de la fidélité, see Belghoul's YouTube channel, which contains numerous videos posted during the pilgrimage, including a trailer that offers a montage of photographs and title cards representing abortion, sex education, topless Femen protesters, and other evangelical nightmares, set to a dramatic orchestral crescendo that culminates with a GoFundMe appeal. Belghoul, "La route de la fidélité," YouTube video, 2:48, August 5, 2017, www.youtube.com.

14. Citing another passage from the novel, PIR activist Houria Bouteldja concludes that "what Georgette's father is saying is that between white people and us [*indigènes*], there is race. It is constitutive of this Republic. It will always rise between us." Bouteldja, *Whites, Jews, and Us*, 116.

15. I have not been able to find any indication that Belghoul disagreed with Soral's use of an unattributed segment of her video on "gender theory," or with his presentation of the novel, although their very public break suggests that she might have regretted her decision to allow Kontre Kulture to reprint *Georgette!* See note 17 below.

16. No doubt due to Belghoul's anti-Semitic comments, enhanced in the video with alarmist photographs of UEJF members, E&R's televised interview with Belghoul has been removed from Soral's website. If Julien Dray was indeed active in the UEJF when he founded SOS racisme in 1984, Belghoul's comments offer a modern twist on the well-worn cliché of the alleged Jewish monopoly on French media and politics, still prevalent in far-right discourse but increasingly so in the amorphous, conspiracy-

theory-driven circles of the French alt-right, including figures like Renaud Camus, Soral, Dieudonné, and Belghoul. As early as 2009, Belghoul was claiming that SOS racisme was a fabrication of the UEJF to counter pro-Palestinian sentiment in the *banlieue*. Belghoul, interview by Kleppinger, October 13, 2009. Antiracist militants were quick to denounce Belghoul's rewriting of history, including those most critical of SOS racisme. Mikael Corre and Julien Wagner, "Farida Belghoul marche-t-elle pour le racisme?" Presse & Cité, *Le Journal Officiel des Banlieues*, January 6, 2014, www.presseetcite.info; Houria Bouteldja, "A Farida Belghoul et aux héritiers de la Marche des 'beurs': Du bon usage d'un héritage," Parti des indigènes de la république, September 17, 2013, www.indigenes-republique.fr.

17. Belghoul's association with Dieudonné and Soral was short-lived. She now paints them in much the same light as the UEJF and SOS racisme, accusing them of recuperating minority voices for their own lucrative and political interests. On the imbroglio of affairs that have recently plagued Dieudonné and Soral, including their tiff with Belghoul, see Willy Le Devin and Dominique Albertini, "Après la Quenelle, le temps des querelles," *Libération,* December 5, 2014, www.liberation.fr.

18. See, for example, Belghoul's statements on the Tariq Ramadan affair. A prominent academic whose writings on Islam in Europe have sparked a number of controversies in France, Switzerland, and the United States, Ramadan was accused of multiple counts of aggravated sexual assault starting on February 2, 2017. Belghoul begins her defense of Ramadan by reminding viewers of her long-standing anti-Zionist positions to prove that she is not "an agent of Israel"—implying that Ramadan's opponents are. Farida Belghoul, "Autour de Tariq Ramadan," YouTube video, 1:41:22, November 11, 2017, www.youtube.com.

19. Mamdani, *Good Muslim, Bad Muslim,* 15–16; Alsultany, *Arabs and Muslims in the Media,* 1–17. It is significant in this regard that Belghoul identifies her father as Kabyle rather than Algerian in the 2013 video interview discussed above. One of the indigenous populations present at the time of the Muslim takeover of North Africa, the Kabyles were reified in colonial anthropology as a pre-Arab, sedentary, superficially Islamized and thus assimilable *indigènes*. Without getting into the complex history of the political nomenclature *Kabyle* and the politicization of indigeneity in the North African context, it is important to note that Kabyle remains a more palatable, assimilable identity in France today than Arab or Muslim. It is also of note that, while Belghoul presents herself as a devout Muslim, she does not wear a headscarf or hijab, a sartorial expression of faith that would present an insurmountable obstacle to many of her Catholic and alt-right fans.

20. A self-avowed anticleric, Boualem Sansal received the Grand prix du roman de l'Académie française for his dystopian novel about an Islamist state, set one hundred years after George Orwell's *1984. Sansal, 2084.* A prolific journalist who won the Goncourt's first novel prize for *Meursault, contre-enquête,* a postcolonial riposte to Albert Camus's *L'étranger,* Kamel Daoud sparked controversy in France for an article denouncing the repression of sexuality in the Muslim world. Kamal Daoud, "The Sexual Misery of the Arab World," *New York Times,* February 12, 2016, www.nytimes.com.

21. "Ça se voit que t'es l'arabe comme tu marches!" (It's obvious you're the Arab the way you walk!), exclaims her friend Mireille, a few pages into the novel. This is the only indication that the unnamed narrator of the novel is of Maghrebi origins. Belghoul, *Georgette!,* 12. Subsequent page references to the 1986 edition of *Georgette!* will be included in the text in parentheses.

As discussed in the introduction, examples of transindigenous identification with indigenous Americans are plentiful in Beur and *banlieue* literature. The protagonist of Nacer Kettane's 1985 novel, the son of Kabyle migrants to France, discovers his solidarity with "Indians" in the cinema: "Brahim no longer enjoyed war films or Westerns in which the cowboys massacred the Indians. By instinct, he was on their side. After all, they were at home, and the white man was taking their land and assassinating their language." Kettane, *Le sourire de Brahim*, 52. In her 2006 memoir, Zahia Rahmani similarly describes a romantic identification with indigenous Americans. Looking at an old photograph of her maternal grandmother, she imagines her to be "the granddaughter of a great Indian chief. A Cherokee far away from his American lands" who sees in the Algerians "a certain resemblance to his brothers." Rahmani, *France*, 53–54. For other examples of the use of "a vocabulary drawn from Westerns," see Ahmed, *Une vie d'Algérien*, 18; Boudjedra, *Topographie idéale*, 143; Begag, *Le gone du Chaâba*, 185.

22. Most readings of *Georgette!* revolve around this scene of writing, and the confrontation between home and school in the novel. The most convincing, to my mind, is Laura Reeck's articulation of writing to the question of race in the novel, including, briefly, indigeneity. Reeck, *Writerly Identities*, 51–72.

23. Gil Hochberg, in discussion with the author, annual meeting of the American Comparative Literature Association, April 1, 2018. In her own reading of *Georgette!*, Hochberg argues that "Georgette fails, or refuses, to understand her reality as the product of a clash between two cultures," and interprets the narrative as a form of resistance, through the child's imaginary, to the symbolic order of (adult) narratives of integration. Hochberg, "The 'Problem of Immigration,'" 162. Ironically, Belghoul's well-founded resistance to the reduction of Beur novels to the identity of their authors may also have facilitated the recent recuperation of her novel. On Belghoul's refusal of the label *political novel*, see Kleppinger, *Branding the "Beur" Author*, 80–120. I am grateful to Kleppinger for sharing an unpublished interview she conducted, which reveals that as late as 2009 Belghoul continued to shy away from political interpretations of her work, even as she insisted that France was structured by the afterlives of colonialism, from racist crimes to France's failing schools. Belghoul, interview by Kleppinger, October 13, 2009. For a representative example of postcolonial readings of *Georgette!*, see Hargreaves, *Voices*, 75–77.

24. Reeck, *Writerly Identities*, 63, 72n13.

25. Rosello, "*Georgette!* de Farida Belghoul," 44. See also Rosello, "The 'Beur Nation.'" On the productive co-optation of racial stereotypes, see Rosello, *Declining the Stereotype*, 1–20.

26. The PIR has denounced Dieudonné's *dérive fasciste* on several occasions. Bouteldja, "Houria Bouteldja dénonce le rapprochement de Dieudonné avec l'extrême droite," Parti des indigènes de la république, May 20, 2009, www.indigenes-republique .fr; PIR, "Dieudonné, les Juifs et nous," Parti des indigènes de la république, January 12, 2014, www.indigenes-republique.fr. Bouteldja has frequently been accused of anti-Semitism, particularly since the publication of *Whites, Jews, and Us*, which calls for, among other things, a provincialization of the Holocaust—according to her, a European crime, not a universal one. Bouteldja, *Whites, Jews, and Us*, 53–72. For a series of insightful readings that also clarify some of the controversies surrounding Bouteldja's essay, see Mayanthi Fernando and Vincent Lloyd, eds., "Whites, Jews, and Us," Social Science Research Council, *The Immanent Frame: Secularism, Religion, and the Public Sphere*, June 20, 2018, www.ssrc.org.

27. For a representative skit from *L'émancipation*, see InDoCiLe, "Dieudonné: Le tribunal des Lascars 2018," YouTube video, 10:38, July 15, 2020, www.youtube.com. Until recently, the promotional image for *L'émancipation*—Dieudonné coiffed with a

feathered headdress, grinning (or gritting his teeth, it is hard to tell) before a lush, green forest—headlined Dieudonné's YouTube channel, which was shut down by YouTube in June 2020.

28. jeanjackrusso, "Dieudonne Le Championnat de la Victimisation! Foxtrot, 2012 English subtitles," YouTube video, 16:40, June 28, 2015, www.youtube.com.

29. Rothberg, *Multidirectional Memory*, 1–29.

30. Dieudo news—Quenel+, "Dieudonné—Le devoir de mémoire (Dieudonné & les Médias, 2016)," Dailymotion video, 7:57, www.dailymotion.com. I have added an expletive to translate the expression *se démerder*, which evokes the image of extricating oneself from a pile of feces.

31. Stora first tackled the conflicting memories of the Algerian War of Independence and the "archive battles" fought between France and Algeria in his watershed book *La gangrène et l'oubli*, 269–80. For a more recent articulation of memorial conflicts over the legacies of French empire, see Stora, *Le transfert d'une mémoire* and *La guerre des mémoires*. For an overview of the various memory wars plaguing France, from the historiography of the French Revolution to the controversial 2004 law on the memory of France's role overseas, see Blanchard and Veyrat-Masson, *Les guerres de mémoire*.

32. First coined by Henry Rousseau to evoke the "obsession" with France's collaboration with Nazi Germany in public discourse of the 1970s and 1980s, the phrase "un passé qui ne passe pas" is now ubiquitous in discussions surrounding France's colonial past. Rousseau, *The Vichy Syndrome*, 168. See also Conan and Rousseau, *Vichy*.

4. Subjects of Photography

1. Mohamed Rouabhi, in discussion with the author, November 21, 2016. Both the French version of "El menfi" and Sonia Gribaa's translation of the play into Arabic are unpublished. I am grateful to Mohamed Rouabhi for sharing the typescript of the French version of the play along with annex materials from his Palestinian workshops.

2. See Alloula, *The Colonial Harem*; Behdad, *Camera Orientalis*; Sheehi, *The Arab Imago*; Hannoush, "Practices of Photography"; Moser, "Developing Historical Negatives."

3. My analysis of photography as a medium that produces race but is nevertheless subject to subversive remediation is close to Cécile Bishop's readings of photographs from the (post)colonial archive. Bishop argues that photography is not so much evidence of the visibility of race—the photograph of the "Indian" as empirical proof of the continued presence of indigenous Americans—as it is evidence of "the 'visuality' of race: the cultural practices and ideological structures that underpin [race's] visibility." Bishop, "Photography, Race, and Invisibility," 197. See also W. J. T. Mitchell, who contends that "race is not merely a content to be mediated, an object to be represented visually or verbally, or a thing to be depicted in a likeness or image . . . race itself is a medium and an iconic form—not simply something to be seen, but itself a framework for seeing through or (as Wittgenstein would put it) seeing *as*." As such, "the medium of race is always open to *remediation*, to a secondary representation, a double take, a critical reflection." Mitchell, *Seeing through Race*, 13, 89, emphasis in original.

4. Little known outside of militant circles, Rouabhi's plays are usually read as examples of "identitarian theater," when they are discussed at all. Theater critic Olivier Neveux includes one of Rouabhi's few published plays, *Malcolm X*, in his inventory of contemporary militant plays, under the rubric "théâtres identitaires," and qualifies his work as "a new theater of combat." Neveux, *Théâtres en lutte*, 221. Historian of immigration and amateur dramaturge Gérard Noiriel goes further, accusing Rouabhi of

"aggravating the identitarian rifts" that plague French society by attacking the institutions of the Republic—the national school system, the government, the police—and privileging the perspective of "'postcolonial' immigrants" in a nefarious competition for victimhood. Noiriel, *Histoire, théâtre et politique*, 142–54.

5. See in particular Rouabhi's epic play on colonization, migration, and republican racism, "Vive la France," which premiered a year after the urban rebellions of 2005. Rouabhi's father fought in the *contingent colonial* (colonial troops) during World War II and was made prisoner by the Nazis. His mother, a *mujahida* (combatant) for the FLN, was tortured by the French army.

6. For more information on "The Story Kufur Shamma," see Slyomovics, "To Put One's Fingers," 32–33; Slyomovics, *The Object of Memory*, 20–22.

7. Rouabhi, in discussion with the author, July 4, 2018. The play was performed in Modern Standard Arabic. Darija, the colloquial Arabic spoken in North Africa, is shaped by the plural languages of the Maghreb, including Tamazight, French, and Spanish, with wide regional variations.

8. Rouabhi, *Les nouveaux bâtisseurs*, 59.

9. See, for example, Jean-Louis Pinte, "Terrain miné," review of *Les nouveaux bâtisseurs*, by Mohamed Rouabhi, directed by Claire Lasne, Théâtre Paris-Villette, *Figaroscope*, October 8, 1997.

10. Rouabhi, in discussion with the author, March 22, 2017.

11. Ghania Adamo, review of *Les nouveaux bâtisseurs*, by Mohamed Rouabhi, directed by Claire Lasne, Théâtre du Grütli, Geneva, *Le nouveau quotidien*, October 25, 1997.

12. Rouabhi, *Les nouveaux bâtisseurs*, 10–11.

13. My understanding of the theater here is close to that developed by Alain Badiou and Denis Guénoun, who both insist on theater as a medium that makes visible the process of representation itself. "The theater doesn't give explanations, it shows!" Badiou, *In Praise of Theatre*, 69. "The theater (the stands) is the place from which one sees . . . the place where the question of the relation between the visible and the invisible, the sensible and the non-sensible is posed." Guénoun, *L'exhibition des mots*, 25; 37.

14. "Le dramaturge Mohamed Rouabhi dévoile les écorchures des errants d'aujourd'hui," interview by Alexandre Demidoff, *Tribune de Genève*, October 25, 1997.

15. A few years younger than the activists of the 1983 Marche pour l'égalité et contre le racisme, Rouabhi was one of the first to mobilize for the recognition of October 17, thirty years after the massacre of some two hundred unarmed Algerians protesting the racist curfew imposed upon them. In 2001 Nadine Varoutsikos commissioned a play to commemorate the massacre. Rouabhi's "Requiem opus 61," the first theatrical performance to be devoted entirely to this event, is a key intertext for the play that had just premiered in Ramallah and Paris, "El menfi." For a detailed study of "October 17 fiction," see Brozgal, *Absent the Archive*.

16. Rouabhi, *Les nouveaux bâtisseurs*, 9–10; Darwish, "Bitaqat hawiya," 5.

17. As noted in the introduction, Algerians were given citizenship in 1946, but with limited rights, leading Patrick Weil to speak of a "perverted French nationality." Weil, "Le statut des musulmans" (see introduction, n. 49).

18. Rouabhi, in conversation with the author, July 4, 2018.

19. Épinay-sur-Seine is in the Seine-Saint-Denis (93rd) department northeast of Paris, best known as the epicenter of the 2005 urban rebellions that were triggered by the death of Zyed Benna and Bouna Traoré during a police chase in the neighboring commune of Clichy-sous-Bois.

20. Due to the travel restrictions imposed on Palestinians in the Occupied Territories, Rouabhi had to work with three separate interpreters to conduct his workshops in Ramallah and East Jerusalem. Rouabhi, in discussion with the author, November 21, 2016.

21. Mohamed Rouabhi, "Palestine 1999," Les Acharnés, www.lesacharnes.com.

22. Rouabhi, "Ateliers d'écriture," 139. Although Salem's composition is written in a mix of French and English, this is the only passage that is included in both languages, as if she wanted to address a double audience, French and American. I have left all spelling and grammatical errors in place, although they may have been introduced when the typescript was compiled.

23. "Mohamed Rouabhi ou le destin palestinien," interview by Fabienne Arvers, *Les inrockuptibles*, January 23, 2001, www.lesinrocks.com.

24. Rouabhi, "Ateliers d'écriture," 113.

25. Rouabhi, 122.

26. One of Edward Curtis's lesser-known photographs, this cliché bears the title *Lone Tree—Apsaroke* (presumably the name and nation of the photographed subject) and is included in volume 4 of Curtis's photographic encyclopedia *The North American Indian*, published in 1909. Rouabhi discovered Curtis's photographs as a teenager, in a book about "American Indians." Rouabhi, personal communication with the author, December 13, 2020. The scare quotes are Rouabhi's.

27. Rouabhi, "Ateliers d'écriture," 93. Rouabhi provided me with a facsimile of Qawasmi's photo-essay, handwritten below a reproduction of the Curtis photograph. I am grateful to Ramzi Rouighi for helping me decipher the first sentence, which is handwritten in Arabic script in the manuscript.

28. "Photographing the Verge of Catastrophe" is the title of one of the chapters of Azoulay's book *The Civil Contract of Photography*, which analyzes photographs from the Occupied Territories, antebellum America, the Iraq War, and other sites of disaster.

29. Azoulay, *The Civil Contract*, 13.

30. Azoulay's notion of the civil contract of photography is explicitly articulated as a challenge to Roland Barthes's theorization of photography as an irretrievable trace of what has vanished. Against Barthes's nostalgic view of photography, and beyond the humanitarian uses of photography as archive or witness, Azoulay proposes a performative understanding of the medium that implicates the spectator in a political and ethical relationship with the photographed subject. "The civil contract of photography enables citizens and noncitizens alike to produce grievances and claims that otherwise can't be seen and to impose them by means of, through, and on the citizenry of photography." Azoulay, *Civil Contract*, 192. On Barthes, see Azoulay, *The Civil Contract*, 93–94; Barthes, *Camera Lucida*, 76.

31. Rouabhi, "El menfi," 6–10; the first and last elisions are mine.

32. Rouabhi, in conversation with the author, November 21, 2016.

33. Byrd, *The Transit of Empire*, xx.

34. Rouabhi, "El menfi," 35; ellipsis and emphasis are in the original.

35. Noiriel, *The French Melting Pot*, 60–63. For a fuller discussion of the role of anthropometric photography in the genesis of police identification at the end of the nineteenth century, see Morris-Reich, *Race and Photography*, 36–41.

36. Rouabhi, "El menfi," 36.

37. Rouabhi, 24.

38. Rouabhi, 46.

39. Rouabhi, 51.

40. Rouabhi, in discussion with the author, July 4, 2018.

41. Rouabhi, "Par morceaux entiers," 49. In another text published in 2001, Rouabhi makes explicit his disidentification with Arabness when it is used as a naturalized articulation of racial identity. During one of his prison workshops, Rouabhi met a young synagogue arsonist who claimed that he had acted out of solidarity with Arabs. "Pan-arabism has been snuffed out long ago," comments Rouabhi wryly, "and no one thought that one day it would return in the mouth of the 21st century's aspiring activists." Rouabhi, "Le temps de vivre," 69.

42. "Mohamed Rouabhi ou le destin palestinien."

43. Rouabhi, "El menfi," 51–52; the first ellipsis is mine.

44. "I remember that between the moment I finished reading this text," writes Rouabhi, "and the moment I knew that one day I would say it out loud in front of a public, something like a nanosecond passed by." Rouabhi, "Darwish, deux textes," 4. Rouabhi's performance is based on Elias Sanbar's French translation. Darwish, "Discours de l'indien rouge." In this chapter I quote from Fady Joudah's translation of the poem into English. Darwish, *If I Were Another*, 69–77.

45. Darwish's *Une mémoire pour l'oubli* is a key intertext in "El menfi," and a model for Jaber's memoir, which features an encounter with Darwish in the besieged city. Rouabhi, "El menfi," 47; Darwish, *Memory for Forgetfulness.*

46. Darwish's poem also performatively displaces the "cultural erasure" encoded in the transmission of Chief Seattle's speech. As Rebecca Dyer and François Mulot point out, this address was already multiply mediated, from Duwamish to Chinook to English, and from a simultaneously translated speech to Henry A. Smith's transcribed notes, which served as the basis for the text he published three decades later in the *Seattle Sunday Star.* Dyer and Mulot, "Mahmoud Darwish in Film," 80.

47. Darwish, *If I Were Another*, 70.

48. Darwish, "Je ne reviens pas," 56. The promotional materials for "Darwish, deux textes" include excerpts from this interview.

49. Rouabhi, "Darwish, deux textes," 15.

50. Mohamed Rouabhi, "Darwish, deux textes—Chappelle du Verbe Incarné, Avignon—Juillet 2010," Sons & vidéos, www.lesacharnes.com.

51. Rouabhi, "El menfi," 7–8.

52. Godard made an unannounced visit to attend the screening, after Rouabhi had already left the theater. Rouabhi, in conversation with the author, July 4, 2018.

5. Indigeneity at the Borders of Europe

1. Emmelhainz, "From Third Worldism to Empire," 650. One of the French producers of "Jusqu'à la victoire" was Claude Nedjar, the producer of Jean Genet's unrealized film "La nuit venue." De Baecque, *Godard*, 468.

2. De Baecque, *Godard*, 468, 860n80.

3. For a detailed account of the making of "Jusqu'à la victoire," see de Baecque, 466–73.

4. Byrd, *The Transit of Empire*, 6.

5. Sanbar, "Vingt et un ans après," 112.

6. De Baecque, *Godard*, 451.

7. The role of sound is also crucial in *Film socialisme*, where the presence of indigenous Americans and Palestinians is reduced to cryptic "Navajo English" subtitles and a silent reverse shot of the Mediterranean Sea from behind barbed wire. For a compelling reading of the staging of the impossibility of representing Palestine and indigenous America in *Film socialisme*, see Niessen, "Access Denied."

8. Sanbar, *Le bien des absents*, 49.

9. Sanbar, "Vingt et un ans après," 116.

10. Too often attributed to Godard alone, *Ici et ailleurs* is the first film made by Godard and Miéville, equal partners in the production company Sonimage. The absence of Godard's first collaborator, Jean-Pierre Gorin, from the film credits remains a fraught question and something of an irony, given the film's critique of appropriation, although de Baecque claims that Godard invited Gorin to cosign the film and that the latter declined. For a more detailed account of the complicated production history of *Ici et ailleurs*, see de Baecque, *Godard*, 526–33; J. White, *Two Bicycles*, 63–72.

11. Niessen, "Access Denied," 13.

12. J. White, *Two Bicycles*, 69.

13. See Michael Witt, who considers that "the Sonimage work is characterized intellectually by a rejection of the Marxist-Leninist theory that had underpinned the work of the Dziga Vertov Group and the Godard-Gorin collaboration." Witt, "On and under Communication," 319.

14. Emmelhainz, *Jean-Luc Godard's Political Filmmaking*, 74–81, 96–104; Colla, "Sentimentality and Redemption," 355–59.

15. Drabinski, "Separation, Difference, and Time," 155.

16. This is an untranslatable wordplay on *son*, sound, a homonym of *son*, his or her. The sounds and images taken by the filmmakers are, in fact, theirs, even though they are presented as the sounds and images of Palestine. I provide my own transcriptions and translations of the dialogue, voice-over, and title cards in the films discussed in this chapter, unless otherwise indicated.

17. Sanbar, *Le bien des absents*, 46, emphasis in original. This is undoubtedly the same "Dr. Mahjoub" evoked by Jean Genet, who would visit the Fatah bases in Jordan a few short months after the Dziga Vertov group. Genet, *Prisoner of Love*, 28.

18. Dyer and Mulot, "Mahmoud Darwish in Film," 76.

19. Godard, *Des années Mao*, 74.

20. Algerian writer Rachid Boudjedra symptomatically describes *Le petit soldat* as "a film with neofascist tendencies." Boudjedra, *Naissance du cinéma algérien*, 25. French deputy Jean-Marie Le Pen, veteran of the Indochinese and Algerian wars and future leader of the National Front, petitioned for the expulsion of Godard from French territory. Godard also received death threats from the clandestine pro–French Algeria militant group Organisation armée secrète. Brenez, *Jean-Luc Godard*, 400. For a detailed account of the reception of *Le petit soldat*, see de Baecque, *Godard*, 162–68.

21. Brenez, *Jean-Luc Godard*, 403. In the same conversation, Godard contrasts his colonial "education" (*formation*) with Vautier's impeccable anticolonial credentials: "When I was little my grand-parents would make me breakfast, we would eat in plates that had all the generals of the Algerian war on them."

22. Brenez, 138.

23. De Baecque, *Godard*, 467.

24. I borrow the term *implicated subject* from Michael Rothberg, but use it in a sense closer to Byrd's usage when she speaks of "all arrivants and settlers" being *implicated* in U.S. imperialism: "the United States propagates itself as empire transhemispherically and transoceanically, not just through whiteness, but through the continued colonization and settling of indigenous people's lands, histories, identities, and very lives that implicate all arrivants and settlers regardless of their own experiences of race, class, gender, colonial, and imperial oppressions." Byrd, *The Transit of Empire*, 21; Rothberg, *The Implicated Subject*. Where Rothberg explores the ways in which those without direct connection to slavery, for example, can ethically engage

with the descendants of the enslaved, I am interested in Godard's position as some-one who is, in fact, directly implicated in the colonization of Palestine, by virtue of France's role in the colonization of the Levant, the establishment of the state of Israel, and its continued colonization of Palestinians. Though, by virtue of his location in Europe, he is not directly implicated in the continued colonization of indigenous Americans, Godard's deployment of the figure of the Indian does, as I will suggest, implicate him in the production of the colonial cliché.

25. Salaita, *Inter/Nationalism*.

26. Godard, *Les années Cahiers*, 194.

27. Godard, 196, emphasis in original.

28. Godard, 194.

29. Gorin was already Godard's closest collaborator, although the Dziga Vertov group was only formally launched during the summer of 1969, during the filming of *Vent d'est*.

30. Goodwin and Marcus, *Double Feature*, 10, 21.

31. Brenez, *Jean-Luc Godard*, 145.

32. Pennebaker was obliged to fulfill his contract with the Public Broadcasting Laboratory (future PBS), which released *One P.M.* in 1972.

33. De Baecque, *Godard*, 440. The most thorough account of the projected scenario for "One A.M.," by Pennebaker scholar Keith Beattie, includes no mention of the "Indian" in Godard's plans for the film. Beattie, *D. A. Pennebaker*, 68–73. *Vladimir et Rosa*, Godard and Gorin's burlesque satire of the 1968 trial of the "Chicago Eight," filmed in 1970 to raise funds for "Jusqu'à la victoire" ("pour payer les images du film palestinien," according to the voice-over), includes several references to "Indians," among them "Sioux philosophy," in the judge's dismissive remarks, and a shot of a shirt emblazoned with the names of the titular characters (played by Godard and Gorin) placed over a painting of a militant donning a feathered headdress. Echoing the other examples of "redface" performances in Godard's political films, these contemporaneous references make it all the more likely that Rip Torn's Native dress was, in fact, part of Godard's original plans for "One A.M." Godard and Gorin's scenario for *Vladimir et Rosa* is even more explicit about the importance of revolutionary drag in the film: "Vladmir and Rosa are disguised with wigs and slogans written on their forehead, or disguised as Vietcongs (camouflage leaves), as Bolsheviks (a butcher's knife between their teeth, a hammer and sickle drawn on their forehead or as earrings), as Palestinians, as Indians, etc." Brenez, *Jean-Luc Godard*, 160.

34. De Baecque writes that that the interview was interrupted so that Cleaver could get on a plane to Algiers. In reality, Cleaver flew to Cuba first. De Baecque, *Godard*, 439.

35. David Faroult includes "One American Movie" in the filmography of the Dziga Vertov group—even though the group only officially came into existence in summer 1969, during the making of *Vent d'est*—simply noting that Godard and Gorin abandoned the film after watching the rush footage. Brenez, *Jean-Luc Godard*, 132.

36. De Baecque, *Godard*, 455.

37. Corresponding to the ubiquitous figure of the army officer guarding "the last frontier" in Hollywood Westerns (for example, in Anthony Mann's eponymous film), the getup of the "ranger nordiste" in *Vent d'est* might also be read as a sartorial effort to complicate the liberal image of the settler colonial North for a European audience.

38. The expression "leftist spaghetti Western" is Cohn-Bendit's. De Baecque, *Godard*, 451.

39. De Baecque, 455.

40. In a 1996 interview, Godard accuses Pontecorvo of cinematographic and historical "falsification," taking aim at Pontecorvo's romanticization of revolution. Godard, *Jean-Luc Godard*, 382.

41. Sanbar, "Vingt et un ans après," 112, emphasis in original.

42. This vignette is strikingly reminiscent of several passages in Genet's posthumous memoir *Prisoner of Love*, which likewise emphasizes the fedayeen's agency in the construction of their own image. Sanbar, whose wife accompanied Genet and Leila Shahid to the camps of Sabra and Shatila in September 1982, is no doubt paying homage to Genet in this text.

43. In a chapter titled "The Conquest of the East," Sanbar provides ample details concerning the early Zionists' "discovery of America" and their espousal of an "analogous project" which, like the pioneers of North America, masked the "ethnocide" of the indigenous population it supplanted with a discourse of liberation from the metropole (Great Britain, in both cases). The Zionists' "Americanism," for Sanbar, was tantamount to "Indianizing" the Palestinians, that is, "treating the Palestinians like 'Redskins.'" Sanbar, *Palestine 1948*, 79–80, 89–91. It is telling that Sanbar situates his realization that the Palestinians are the "Redskins" of the Israelis in his childhood immersion in Hollywood Westerns. "As far back as I can remember, I was, by instinct, for the Indians and against the cowboys." And yet, according to Sanbar, the now well-documented "link" between indigenous Americans and Palestinians made even his most sympathetic interlocutors smile when he published his book in 1984. Sanbar, *Le bien des absents*, 92–96.

44. On "Palestinians in Native Poetry," see Salaita, *Inter/Nationalism*, 103–32. For an ethnographic account of identification with indigenous Americans in the refugee camp of Shatila, see Salaita, *The Holy Land in Transit*, 169–82. The comparison between U.S. and Zionist/Israeli settler colonialism is well established in the colonial archive, as Salaita amply demonstrates. Solidarity between Palestinians and indigenous Americans is, as he recognizes, a more recent phenomenon.

45. Salaita, *Inter/Nationalism*, 14.

46. In an October 1996 interview with Mohamed Rouabhi, Sanbar claims to have asked Darwish "to imagine a letter, a sort of response" to Chief Seattle's speech. Rouabhi, "Darwish, deux textes," 10. In a recent email exchange, Sanbar confirmed that he had "commissioned" a response to Chief Seattle from Darwish, and that he suggested the inclusion of "Indians" in *Notre musique* (the scare quotes are Sanbar's). Elias Sanbar, in communication with the author, December 18, 2020. On Sanbar's role in the inclusion of indigenous American characters in the film, see Godard, "Juste une conversation," 20.

47. Goytisolo, *State of Siege*, 53.

48. Brenez, *Jean-Luc Godard*, 403–4.

49. When Godard approached Sarah Adler to play the role of a French-Israeli kamikaze, she refused, stating, "That's your opinion, it's not mine." Witt, "The Godard Interview," 30.

50. The interview staged in *Notre musique* is based on Helit Yeshurun's interview with Darwish, which misquotes an Arabic-language interview with Darwish published in *Masharif*. Both interviews are included in *La Palestine comme métaphore*, which becomes, intradiegetically, the text Judith Lerner misquotes in this scene. Darwish, *La Palestine comme métaphore*, 153–54. I base my translation of this scene on the English, French, and Hebrew-Arabic transcript published in the journal

Mediterranéennes, although it inexplicably fails to include Darwish's correction. Darwish and Lerner, "A Dialogue." I am grateful to yasser elhariry for helping me decipher Darwish's correction.

51. "Drowning" (*la noyade*) as a metaphor of expulsion traverses the pages of Sanbar's monographs, and undoubtedly influenced Godard's use of the term. Sanbar, *Figures du Palestinien,* 187.

52. Like most of his statements about Jews, Israel, and Palestine, Godard's commentary on photographs of "Israelites"/"the Jewish people" (Godard's terms) and Palestinians in this scene has come under fire by critics who take issue with what they understand to be Godard's denial of Jewish claims to indigeneity in Palestine. See, for example, Godard's statements about Israel's attachment to the "eternal fiction" of the biblical land of Palestine in Jean Narboni's documentary film, *Morceaux de conversation avec Jean-Luc Godard.* The problematic blurring of the borders between Jewish and Zionist/Israeli identity in Godard's pithy remarks about the relegation of "the Jewish people" to the realm of fiction is exacerbated by the juxtaposition of images that precedes the shot/reverse shot of "Israelites" and Palestinians, an expeditious association Godard has made in other films, including *Ici et ailleurs:* two images of emaciated camp detainees, one bearing the caption "juif," the other "musulman." The fact that camp detainees on the brink of death were dubbed *Musulmänner* (Muslims)—not by Nazi officers or Kapos, as Godard has claimed, but by their fellow concentration (rather than extermination) camp detainees—has been the starting point, in Godard's work, for a sustained reflection on the irony that made the victims of European anti-Semitism perpetrators of ethnic cleansing in Palestine. Maurice Darmon provides the most thorough and careful account of the references to Jews and *Musulmänner,* Israelis, and Palestinians in Godard's films, print publications, and interviews, steering away from the facile equation of anti-Zionism and anti-Semitism without falling into the countervailing trap of hagiography. See in particular his well-documented account of the use of the term *Musulmänner* in Nazi concentration camps, which shows that Godard's associations are on somewhat shaky historical ground. Darmon, *La question juive,* 137–53. Elsewhere, Godard has made the provocative suggestion that, as an "outsider" (*exclu*) of mainstream cinema, "one might say that I am a Jew or a Palestinian of cinema." Godard, "Juste une conversation," 20. For a more polemical approach to Godard's "Jewish question," see Brody, *Everything Is Cinema;* Levy, "Se payer de mots?"

53. Rastegar, *Surviving Images,* 94; Darwish and Lerner, "A Dialogue," 17.

54. Godard, "Juste une conversation," 20, emphasis added.

55. Sanbar, *The Palestinians,* 291.

56. Godard, "Juste une conversation," 20–21.

57. Rancière, *The Intervals of Cinema,* 114.

58. Rancière, 115.

59. Barr, "Shot and Counter-shot," 79, 81. Building on Barr's interpretation of indigenous Americans as "markers of another genocide" in the film, Roberts invokes Deleuze's seminal reflections on the cliché in Godard's cinema—"what is an image which would not be a cliché"—to critique the shot of the "Indians" under the Mostar bridge as "cliché-images of a people denied autonomy over their own representation." Roberts, "Godard in Sarajevo," 347–48; Deleuze, *Cinema 1,* 214.

60. Williams, *Encounters with Godard,* 183.

61. Ravetto-Biagioli, *Mythopoetic Cinema,* 199.

62. Byrd, *The Transit of Empire,* xx.

63. Goytisolo, *State of Siege*, 81. The presence in this scene of Goytisolo, whose novel splices the siege of Sarajevo with anti-immigrant attacks in a working-class neighborhood of Paris, also serves as a reminder of the threat of ethnocidal violence in France. The low-angle shot of a little girl in a red jacket running up the majestic staircase of the ruined library of Sarajevo is a transparent reference to Steven Spielberg's 1993 Holocaust drama *Schindler's List*, which Godard famously called "a falsified document" (he takes aim at the scene where water pours down on deportees in a gas chamber, instead of gas). Godard, *Jean-Luc Godard*, 417.

64. The indigenous Americans' declamation in *Notre musique* is based on Sargon Boulos's translation of Darwish's poem, simply titled "Speech of the Red Indian." Darwish, *The Adam of Two Edens*, 127–45.

65. Darwish, *If I Were Another*, 57–68.

66. Shohat, "Taboo Memories, Diasporic Visions," 209.

67. Darwish, *La Palestine comme métaphore*, 79–80.

68. Raef Zreik makes a similar plea for indigeneity as a site of critique in the settler colonial context of Palestine-Israel. Zreik, "When Does a Settler Become a Native?"

69. Darwish, *La Palestine comme métaphore*, 35.

70. Christophe Kantcheff, "Jean-Luc Godard Elias Sanbar," Association France Palestine Solidarité, January 16, 2006, www.france-palestine.org.

71. Arendt, *The Origins of Totalitarianism*, 276.

72. "All the bodies shown and all the living testimonies to the massacres in Bosnia do not create the bond that was once created, at the time of the Algerian war and the anticolonialist movements, by the bodies, completely hidden from view and from any examination, of the Algerians thrown in the Seine by the French police in October 1961." Rancière, *Disagreement*, 138–39. For Rancière, "the cause of the other"—for the French, "a refusal to identify with a certain self" and "an impossible identification" with the Algerians—is the basis for a political (rather than ethical) relation to the other. Rancière, "The Cause of the Other," 29. Juan Goytisolo is stinging in his indictment of the humanitarian organizations and intellectuals who stood idly by as Serbs massacred Muslim Bosnians with impunity. Goytisolo, *Landscapes of War*, 16, 47.

6. Palestine and the Migrant Question

1. Rosello, *Postcolonial Hospitality*, 3.

2. For examples of the left-liberal plea for "hospitality" toward migrants, see Hobsbawm, *Nations and Nationalism*, 174; Bauman, *Strangers at Our Door*.

3. My use of the term "migrant question" takes up Nicholas De Genova's call to consider migration as one of the main facets of the "European question" today, turning the discourse of crisis on its head to grapple with the problem of European identity. Like the Jewish question and the Negro question before it, the migrant question is a question for Europe. De Genova, "European Question."

4. See Valeria Luiselli's essay on the refugee crisis at the U.S.–Mexico border, the causes of which, she explains, "are deeply embedded in our shared hemispheric history and are therefore not some distant problem in a foreign country that no one can locate on a map." Luiselli, *Tell Me How It Ends*, 85. For a biting critique of the "forgetting" of the colonial history that produced the so-called migrant crisis, see Mbembe, *Politiques de l'inimitié*, 85–86.

5. Stoler, *Duress*, 26–27.

6. Stoler, *Imperial Debris*. On the immobility of the "refugee, migrant, subaltern or stateless," enforced, for instance, by the "mobile" wall in Israel–Palestine, see Fieni,

"Tagging the Spectral Mobility," 351. Kelly Oliver makes a related point about coerced movement by reflecting on migrants' "supposed 'choice' (individual sovereignty) to leave and live or stay and die." Oliver, *Carceral Humanitarianism*, 57.

7. Quotations from the films I discuss in this chapter are based on the English subtitles, although I have made some modifications.

8. Shadi explains that he cannot travel back to the West Bank because the IDF is looking for him, presumably to arrest him for his role in organizing peaceful protests in his village, Wad Rahal.

9. Activists in the struggle for migrant rights, Nambot and Berchache met two months after his arrival in Paris, in April 2011. Before they decided to make a film together, they recorded their conversations as well as conversations with friends and comrades. When they began filming in Super 8 and 16 mm several months later, they did not systematically record synchronous sound, returning instead to the sites where they had filmed to record sound after the fact. In other cases, they filmed images to capture the voices they had recorded previously. The conversation between Maki and Shadi is one of these "reconstituted" scenes. The disjuncture between image and sound is one of the most interesting formal features of *Brûle la mer,* producing an introspective, intimate effect that does not obtain in sync-sound documentary cinema. Nathalie Nambot, in conversation with the author, March 7, 2022.

10. Berchache obtained legal residency during the making of the film. Included in the dossier he submitted to the police prefecture was the film project itself, which received funding from the Centre national de la cinématographie. In one of the most powerful scenes of the film, a long take of hundreds of migrants, including Maki, waiting to file their paperwork for regularization at the town hall of Seine-Saint-Denis, Nambot lists the innumerable papers that that *sans-papiers* must file in an accelerating voice-over as snow falls on the predawn *banlieue*.

11. Maki's estimate is 25,000. According to Maurizio Albahari, 23,500 Tunisians arrived in Lampedusa in January and February 2011 alone. Albahari, *Crimes of Peace,* 163.

12. Pappe, *Ethnic Cleansing,* 8. Speaking of the "ruination" of Palestine, Ariella Azoulay describes the refugee as "that which is left" after the "failure" of ethnic cleansing: "in most cases efforts at complete ethnic cleansing end in failure, manifested in a political language that invents such categories as displaced, dispossessed, and refugees." Azoulay, "When a Demolished House," 203.

13. "Contemporary history has created a new kind of human being—the kind that are put in concentration camps by their foes and in internment camps by their friends." Arendt "We Refugees," 265.

14. "The solution of the Jewish question merely produced a new category of refugees, the Arabs, thereby increasing the number of stateless and rightless by another 700,000 to 800,000 people." Arendt, *The Origins of Totalitarianism,* 290, cited in Said, *The Question of Palestine,* xxxix. Ann Laura Stoler offers a similar analysis of the question of Palestine as exemplary: "This is not to argue that Palestine is the Ur-colonial situation or that Israel is the quintessential colonial state. Instead, it is to see how the dispossession of the Palestinians articulates the so carefully crafted and normalized segregationist policies used to achieve it, providing a window onto forms of duress that are less visible elsewhere, forms that in Palestine are being made acutely resonant and recognizable." Stoler, *Duress,* 54.

15. Said, *After the Last Sky,* 164.

16. Said, *Culture and Imperialism,* 332.

17. These statistics are based on data provided by the United Nations Human

Rights Commission: "Mediterranean Situation," UNHRC, January 30, 2022, https://data2.unhcr.org; "Figures at a Glance," UNHRC, June 18, 2021, www.unhcr.org. On the role of the "spectacle of numbers" in the production of the migrant question as a crisis, see Maurice Stierl, Charles Heller, and Nicholas De Genova, "Numbers (Or, the Spectacle of Statistics in the Production of 'Crisis')," "Europe at a Crossroads," *Zone Books Near Futures Online* 1, www.nearfuturesonline.org.

18. Said, *The Question of Palestine*, xli.

19. On the deterritorialization of Fortress Europe, see Casas-Cortes et al., "New Keywords," 73–77; Garelli and Tazzioli, *Tunisia as a Revolutionized Space*, 89–91.

20. Slama, "Chasse aux migrants à Mayotte," 3.

21. Cottias, *La question noire*.

22. The migrant crisis in the Indian Ocean gives historical acuity to the metaphor of migration as a new Middle Passage. In her landmark book, Christina Sharpe excavates "the semiotics of the slave ship . . . from the forced movements of the enslaved to the forced movements of the migrant and the refugee." Sharpe, *In the Wake*, 21. See also Patrick Chamoiseau's poetic treatise *Frères migrants*, which places the history of slavery—and the Palestinian question—within the purview of the migrant question. Chamoiseau, *Migrant Brothers*, 11, 14–15.

23. Appanah, *Tropic of Violence*, 94–96, translation modified; Appanah, *Tropique de la violence*, 112–13.

24. Appanah, *Tropic of Violence*, 41.

25. I borrow the phrase "Gaza as metaphor" from a recent volume that works against the global resonances of Gaza as a metaphor for, among other things, the global refugee crisis. Tawil-Souri and Matar, *Gaza as Metaphor*. See also John Collins, who explores "the globalization of Palestine and the Palestinization of the globe," and Eyal Weizman, for whom "Gaza—where the system of humanitarian government is now most brutally exercised—is the proper noun for the horror of our humanitarian present." Collins, *Global Palestine*, 2; Weizman, *The Least of All Possible Evils*, 6. To my knowledge, Mahmoud Darwish was the first to speak of "Palestine as metaphor." Darwish, *La Palestine comme métaphore*.

26. The critique of humanitarianism is a feature of both Palestine and migrant studies. On the "military-humanitarian continuum" in the context of contemporary mass displacements, see Albahari, *Crimes of Peace*, 20; and Oliver, *Carceral Humanitarianism*, 14. For a critique of "the humanitarian present" that connects the migrant and Palestinian questions, see Weizman, *The Least of All Possible Evils*, 3–4.

27. Appanah, *Tropic of Violence*, 55.

28. Appanah, 38.

29. Appanah, *Tropique de la violence*, 51.

30. Genet, *Un captif amoureux*, 25–26. My translation. Barbara Bray's version, while easier to read, omits several key elements that are essential to my reading of Genet: "ils ont fait des petits," an expression reserved for animal husbandry that surreptitiously evokes racist clichés about immigrants, and the Orientalist lexicon that produces the "fantastic" image of the nomad encampment. Although I do not follow Genet's rogue syntax to the letter (or punctuation mark), Bray's strict adherence to the laws of English grammar have a domesticating effect on the text. I retain Bray's happy translation of "nations 'assises'" as "'settled' nations," which is both etymologically sound and politically fortuitous (in French, a settlement is *une colonie*). For the Bray translation, see Genet, *Prisoner of Love*, 15.

31. The structure of the camp provides yet another point to track the intersection of the Jewish, Palestinian, and migrant questions. Giorgio Agamben notes, with

respect to the Spanish camps in Cuba and the English camps in South Africa, that "in both cases one is dealing with the extension to an entire civilian population of a state of exception linked to a colonial war," before discussing the examples of migrant camps in Italy, airport holding zones in France, the French *banlieue,* and the American ghetto. Agamben, "What Is a Camp?," 38, 42. On the colonial genealogy of migrant camps, see Le Cour Grandmaison, "Les origines coloniales"; and Mbembe, *Politiques de l'inimitié,* 98–107.

32. Didi-Huberman, "Hauteurs de vue." Marxiano Melotti also takes Ai Weiwei to task for his provocative installations based on the migrant crisis, and his "use of the refugee tragedy in an art creation [as] a form of commodification." Melotti, "The Mediterranean Refugee Crisis," 6. Didi-Huberman's and Melotti's critiques are partly based on the artist's presence in the film, and his performance in several of the installations. For a countervailing argument on the ways in which *Human Flow* stages "the production of crisis" by including Ai Weiwei and his crew in the frame, see Eszter Zimanyi, "The Production of Crisis: Ai Weiwei's Human Flow," *Docalogue,* 2018, www.docalogue .com.

33. "Ai Weiwei on the Refugee Crisis: 'People Have Been Forced into a State of Movement,'" interview by John Weiner, *Nation,* October 13, 2017, www.thenation.com.

34. Without citing Genet's *Un captif amoureux,* Didi-Huberman claims that in Ai Weiwei's film the drone's-eye view reproduces *"visual clichés . . . in the manner of the glossy paper of so-called geography magazines, which are in fact more like tourist brochures than anything else."* Didi-Huberman, "Hauteurs de vue," 68, emphasis in original.

35. Dana Regev, "Chinese Artist Ai Weiwei Visits Gaza and the West Bank," *Deutsche Welle,* May 14, 2016, www.dw.com.

36. On destruction as a feature of the "inner grammar" of Israeli sovereignty in the Occupied Territories and Gaza, see Azoulay, "(In)Human Spatial Condition," 159. On the difficulties of distinguishing between the "layers of rubble" that have been piling up since 1947, and the ruins of Palestine as a "book of destruction," see Weizman, who characterizes the camp itself as a marker of destruction: "the camp is not a home, it is a temporary arrangement, and its destruction is but the last iteration in an ongoing process of destruction." Weizman, *The Least of All Possible Evils,* 144–45.

37. I have not been able to find a source that separately lists the number of Palestinians (refugees or occupied Palestinians) who have come to Europe since 2011. UNRWA, which keeps track of Palestinian refugees in the Middle East, has estimates for Palestinian refugees displaced within and outside of Syria. "Syria@10," United Nations Relief and Works Agency for Palestine Refugees in the Near East, www.unrwa .org. On Palestinian refugees leaving Lebanon for Europe, see "Palestinians Desperate to Flee Lebanon Refugee Camp," *Al Jazeera,* April 5, 2015, www.aljazeera.com.

38. Kanafani, *Adab al-muqawama.*

39. Harlow, "Resistance Literature Revisited," 10, 15; Genet, *Prisoner of Love,* 15, translation modified, Genet, *Un captif amoureux,* 25.

40. In revisiting Kanafani in the era of the war on terror, Harlow is invested in recuperating a political notion of resistance that is erased in the category of the migrant: "discounted as refugees, not yet, by any means, 'enemy combatants,' nor even yet resistance fighters, but the proverbial 'economic migrants.'" Harlow, "Resistance Literature Revisited," 15. My reading is closer to David Fieni's, which also links the Palestinian and migrant questions via *Men in the Sun.* Fieni, "Tagging the Spectral Mobility," 362.

41. Kanafani, *Men in the Sun,* 25–26.

42. Several of the archival images used in Salih's montage on the camps, including the one reproduced here, can be viewed on UNRWA's website. "RL-Nahr El-Bared-1," UNRWA photo and film archive for Palestinian Refugees, www.unrwa.org.

43. Said, *The Question of Palestine*, xli.

44. Didi-Huberman and Giannari, *Passer, quoiqu'il en coûte,* 31, emphasis in original.

Epilogue

1. Founded in 2012, Génération identitaire was dissolved by the French government on March 3, 2021, after a number of spectacular actions to repel migrants at the borders of France. The group has chapters in Italy, Austria, Germany, and the UK and has connections to other anti-immigrant groups in France and Europe.

2. On the recent transatlantic fortunes of Raspail's novel, see Alduy, "What a 1973 French Novel Tells Us." For an early example of the thesis that Europe risks being "submerged" by migrants from the Global South, see French demographer Alfred Sauvy's 1987 book *L'Europe submergée.*

3. Raspail, *Le camp des saints,* 11–12.

4. Benoist, *Vu de droite,* 263.

5. "Racisme et violences policières: À Paris, la manifestation a rassemblé 15,000 personnes," *Le Parisien,* June 13, 2020, www.leparisien.fr.

6. Yazid Bouziar's Twitter feed, June 13, 2020, www.twitter.com.

7. In his book on "the new Judeophobia," Pierre-André Taguieff cites Samuel Huntington to characterize the "re-Islamization" of the Third World as a form of "re-indigenization." Taguieff, *La nouvelle judéophobie,* 158–59. Symptomatic of the anachronistic nature of sociological studies of Islam, Taguieff's use of colonial terminology to speak of Islamic traditionalism—itself an inherently modern phenomenon, as Talal Asad and other have shown—also reveals, albeit inadvertently, the colonial roots of scientific studies of Islam in France. Asad, *Genealogies of Religion.* For an example of a noncritical use of *indigénisme* as a synonym for "traditionalism" in the field of anthropology, see Amselle, *L'Occident décroché,* 37.

8. In January 2021, Houria Bouteldja and Youssef Boussoumah, cofounders of the movement, published a statement detailing the circumstances that led to their resignation from the PIR, the failures of "indigenous autonomy," and the "missed encounters" between the PIR and, among other antiracist groups, the Comité Adama. Houria Bouteldja and Youssef Boussoumah, "Splendeurs et misères de l'autonomie indigène. 2005/2020: Le PIR, ou l'histoire courte d'une réussite politique et de sa conjuration," QG Décolonial, January 18, 2021, www.qgdecolonial.fr, translated by David Fernbach as "The Parti des Indigènes de la République—A Political Success and the Conspiracy against It (2005 to 2020)," Verso Press blog, October 6, 2021 www.versobooks.com.

9. Ayla Aglan et al., "Sur l'islamisme, ce qui nous menace, c'est la persistence du déni," *Le Monde,* October 31, 2020, www.lemonde.fr.

10. Vidal initially expressed reservations about her colleague's tirade against Islamo-leftism. Frédérique Vidal, "L'université n'est pas un lieu d'encouragement ou d'expression du fanatisme," *L'opinion,* October 26, 2020, www.lopinion.fr. Excerpts of Vidal's statements on CNews and at the Assemblée nationale are available on YouTube. Le Huffington Post, "La proposition de Vidal sur l'islamo-gauchisme a fait bondir ces universitaires," YouTube video, 3:19, February 16, 2021, www.youtube.com. The CNRS posted a sharp response to her invitation on its website, as did the usually circumspect Conference of University Presidents. "L''islamogauchisme' n'est pas une réalité scientifique," Centre national de la recherche scientifique, February 17, 2021,

www.cnrs.fr; "'Islamo-gauchisme': Stopper la confusion et les polémiques stériles," Conférence des présidents d'universités, February 16, 2021, www.cpu.fr.

11. "L'Observatoire du décolonialisme et des idéologies identitaires," *Le Point,* https://www.lepoint.fr/dossiers/societe/decolonialisme-separatisme/, last accessed February 8, 2022.

12. L'Observatoire du décolonialisme et des idéologies identitaires, www .decolonialisme.fr, last accessed February 8, 2022. The Observatoire was launched under the aegis of the Laboratoire d'analyse des idéologies contemporaines (LAIC, an acronym that also means "secular"), founded in 2016 as a counter to deconstructive theory in the university. "Notre association," Laboratoire d'analyse des idéologies contemporaines, www.association-laic.org, last accessed February 8, 2022.

13. Pierre-André Taguieff, "Aux sources de l'"islamo-gauchisme,'" *Libération,* October 26, 2020, www.liberation.fr. For a more detailed genealogy of Taguieff's use of the term and its subsequent adoption by "conspiracy theorists," see Taguieff, *Liaisons dangereuses,* 72–77.

14. Taguieff, *Rising from the Muck,* 106–8, 45.

15. "What Is Antisemitism? Non–Legally Binding Working Definition of Antisemitism," International Holocaust Remembrance Alliance, https://www .holocaustremembrance.com/resources/working-definitions-charters/working -definition-antisemitism, last accessed February 8, 2022.

16. In France as in other European countries, legal attempts to curb pro-Palestinian support have focused on civil society campaigns in support of the Boycott, Divestment, and Sanctions (BDS) movement. In 2015, France's highest court upheld the criminal conviction of eleven BDS activists from the Palestine 68 Collective, charged in 2013 by the Colmar Court of Appeal with "incitement to discrimination" for distributing BDS leaflets in a supermarket in Illzach, Alsace, in 2009 and 2010. On June 11, 2020, the European Court of Human Rights ruled that the conviction violated the principle of freedom of expression. "Affaire Balsassi et autres c. France," European Court of Human Rights, June 11, 2020, www.hudoc.echr.coe.int.

17. Bouteldja, *Whites, Jews, and Us,* 29–30, translation modified, emphasis in original; Bouteldja, *Les Blancs, les Juifs, et nous,* 25.

18. Bouteldja, *Whites, Jews, and Us,* 27. Bouteldja's use of a juridical vocabulary to speak of "white guilt" (including her own) parodies, and subverts, the discourse on "colonial repentance" in France, in a provocative reactualization of the Sartrean notions of responsibility and commitment. White guilt, of course, is a bogeyman of the republican right. For a classic example, see Bruckner, *The Tears of the White Man.*

19. Bouteldja, *Whites, Jews, and Us,* 119, translation modified; Bouteldja, *Les Blancs, les Juifs et nous,* 117.

BIBLIOGRAPHY

Abdallah, Mogniss H., and the Réseau No Pasaran. *J'y suis, j'y reste! Les luttes de l'immigration en France depuis les années soixante*. Paris: Reflex, 2000.

Agamben, Giorgio. "What Is a Camp?" In *Means without End: Notes on Politics*, translated by Vincenzo Binetti and Cesare Casarino, 37–45. Minneapolis: University of Minnesota Press, 2000.

Ahmed. *Une vie d'Algérien, est-ce que ça fait un livre que les gens vont lire?* Paris: Seuil, 1973.

Aissaoui, Rabah. *Immigration and National Identity: North African Political Movements in Colonial and Postcolonial France*. London: Tauris, 2009.

Albahari, Maurizio. *Crimes of Peace: Mediterranean Migration at the World's Deadliest Border*. Philadelphia: University of Pennsylvania Press, 2015.

Albertini, Dominique, and David Doucet. *La fachosphère: Comment l'extrême droite a remporté la bataille d'internet*. Paris: Flammarion, 2016.

Alduy, Cécile. "What a 1973 French Novel Tells Us about Marine Le Pen, Steve Bannon, and the Rise of the Populist Right." *Politico*, April 23, 2017. www.politico.com.

Allen, Chadwick. *Trans-Indigenous: Methodologies for Global Native Literary Studies*. Minneapolis: University of Minnesota Press, 2012.

Alloula, Malek. *The Colonial Harem*. Translated by Myrna Godzich and Wlad Godzich. Minneapolis: University of Minnesota Press, 1986.

Alloula, Malek. *Le harem colonial: Images d'un sous-érotisme*. Paris: Garance, 1981.

Alsultany, Evelyn. *Arabs and Muslims in the Media: Race and Representation after 9/11*. New York: New York University Press, 2012.

Amselle, Jean-Loup. *L'ethnicisation de la France*. Paris: Lignes, 2011.

Amselle, Jean-Loup. *Les nouveaux rouges-bruns: Le racisme qui vient*. Paris: Lignes, 2014.

Amselle, Jean-Loup. *L'Occident décroché: Enquête sur les postcolonialismes*. Paris: Stock, 2008.

Anziska, Seth. *Preventing Palestine: A Political History from Camp David to Oslo*. Princeton: Princeton University Press, 2018.

Appanah, Nathacha. *Tropic of Violence*. Translated by Geoffrey Strachan. Minneapolis: Graywolf Press, 2020.

Appanah, Nathacha. *Tropique de la violence*. Paris: Gallimard, 2016.

Arendt, Hannah. *The Origins of Totalitarianism*. London: Harcourt, 1968.

Arendt, Hannah. "We Refugees." In *The Jewish Writings*, edited by Jerome Kohn and Ron H. Feldman, 264–74. New York: Schocken Books, 2007.

Asad, Talal. *Genealogies of Religion: Discipline and Reasons of Power in Christianity and Islam*. Baltimore: Johns Hopkins University Press, 1993.

Azoulay, Ariella. *The Civil Contract of Photography*. Translated by Rela Mazali and Ruvik Danieli. New York: Zone Books, 2008.

Azoulay, Ariella. "The (In)Human Spatial Condition: A Visual Essay." Translated by Tal Haran. In *The Power of Inclusive Exclusion: Anatomy of Israeli Rule in the Occupied Palestinian Territories*, edited by Adi Ophir, Michal Givoni, and Sari Hanafi, 153–77. New York: Zone Books, 2009.

Azoulay, Ariella. "When a Demolished House Becomes a Public Square." In *Imperial Debris: On Ruins and Ruination*, edited by Ann Laura Stoler, 194–224. Durham, N.C.: Duke University Press, 2013.

Badiou, Alain. *In Praise of Theatre*. Translated by Andrew Bielski. Cambridge, UK: Polity Press, 2015.

Barr, Burlin. "Shot and Counter-shot: Presence, Obscurity, and the Breakdown of Discourse in Godard's *Notre musique*." *Journal of French and Francophone Philosophy* 18, no. 2 (2010): 65–85.

Barthes, Roland. *Camera Lucida: Reflections on Photography*. Translated by Richard Howard. New York: Vintage Press, 2000.

Bauman, Zygmunt. *Strangers at Our Door*. Cambridge, UK: Polity, 2016.

Beattie, Keith. *D. A. Pennebaker*. Urbana: University of Illinois Press, 2011.

Begag, Azouz. *Le gone du Chaâba*. Paris: Seuil, 1986. Translated by Naïma Wolf and Alec G. Hargreaves as *Shantytown Kid* (Lincoln: University of Nebraska Press, 2007).

Behdad, Ali. *Camera Orientalis: Reflection on Photography of the Middle East*. Chicago: University of Chicago Press, 2016.

Belghoul, Farida. *Georgette!* Paris: Barrault, 1986. Reprinted as *Georgette! ou La petite fille qui n'avait pas de nom*. Paris: Kontre Kulture, 2013.

Bellity Peskine, Lynda, and Albert Dichy, eds. *La bataille des "Paravents": Théâtre de l'Odéon, 1966*. Paris: IMEC Éditions, 1991.

Ben Jelloun, Tahar. *French Hospitality: Racism and North African Immigrants*. Translated by Barbara Bray. New York: Columbia University Press, 1999.

Ben Jelloun, Tahar. *Hospitalité française: Racisme et immigration maghrébine*. Paris: Seuil, 1984.

Ben Jelloun, Tahar. *Jean Genet, menteur sublime*. Paris: Gallimard, 2010.

Ben Jelloun, Tahar. *La plus haute des solitudes: Misère sexuelle d'immigrés nord-africains*. Paris: Seuil, 1977.

Ben Jelloun, Tahar. *La réclusion solitaire*. Paris: Denoël, 1976.

Benoist, Alain de. *Europe, Tiers Monde, même combat*. Paris: Robert Laffont, 1986.

Benoist, Alain de. *Salan devant l'opinion*. Paris: Éditions Saint-Just, 1963.

Benoist, Alain de. *View from the Right: A Critical Anthology of Contemporary Ideas*. Translated by Robert A. Lindgren and Roger Adwan. 3 vols. London: Arktos, 2017–19.

Benoist, Alain de. *Vu de droite: Anthologie critique des idées contemporaines*. Paris: Labyrinthe, 2001.

Benoist, Alain de, and Gilles Fournier. *Vérité pour l'Afrique du Sud*. Paris: Éditions Saint-Just, 1965.

Benoist, Alain de, and François d'Orcival. *Le courage est leur patrie*. Paris: Éditions Saint-Just, 1965.

Bernard, Anna. "'They Are in the Right Because I Love Them': Literature and Palestine Solidarity in the 1980s." In *The Edinburgh Companion to the Postcolonial Middle East*, edited by Anna Ball and Karim Mattar, 275–92. Edinburgh: Edinburgh University Press, 2018.

Bishop, Cécile. "Photography, Race, and Invisibility: The Liberation of Paris, in Black and White." *Photographies* 11, nos. 2–3 (2018): 192–213.

Blanchard, Pascal, and Isabelle Veyrat-Masson, eds. *Les guerres de mémoires: La*

France et son histoire; Enjeux politiques, controverses historiques, stratégies média-tiques. Paris: La Découverte, 2008.

Bodichon, Eugène. *Études sur l'Algérie et l'Afrique.* Algiers: Eugène Bodichon, 1847.

Bouamama, Saïd. *Dix ans de Marche des Beurs: Chronique d'un mouvement avorté.* Paris: Desclée de Brouwer, 1994.

Boudjedra, Rachid. *Naissance du cinéma algérien.* Paris: François Maspero, 1971.

Boudjedra, Rachid. *Topographie idéale pour une agression caractérisée.* Paris: Denoël, 1975.

Boukhedenna, Sakinna. *Journal "Nationalité: Immigré(c)."* Paris: L'Harmattan, 1987.

Bouteldja, Houria. *Les Blancs, les Juifs, et nous: Vers une politique de l'amour révolu-tionnaire.* Paris: La Fabrique, 2016.

Bouteldja, Houria. *Whites, Jews, and Us: Toward a Politics of Revolutionary Love.* Translated by Rachel Valinsky. South Pasadena: Sémiotext(e), 2017.

Brenez, Nicole, ed. *Jean-Luc Godard, documents.* Paris: Centre Pompidou, 2006.

Brody, Richard. *Everything Is Cinema: The Working Life of Jean-Luc Godard.* New York: Holt, 2008.

Brozgal, Lia. *Absent the Archive: Cultural Traces of a Massacre in Paris, 17 October 1961.* Liverpool: Liverpool University Press, 2020.

Bruckner, Pascal. *Le sanglot de l'homme blanc: Tiers Monde, culpabilité, haine de soi.* Paris: Seuil, 1983.

Bruckner, Pascal. *The Tears of the White Man: Compassion as Contempt.* Translated by William R. Beer. New York: Free Press, 1986.

Byrd, Jodi A. *The Transit of Empire: Indigenous Critiques of Colonialism.* Minneapolis: University of Minnesota Press, 2011.

Byrd, Jodi A., and Michael Rothberg. "Introduction: Between Subalternity and Indi-geneity." *Interventions* 13, no. 1 (2011): 1–12.

Camus, Albert. *L'étranger.* Paris: Gallimard, 1942. Translated by Sandra Smith as *The Outsider* (London: Penguin, 2012).

Camus, Renaud. *Le grand remplacement.* Plieux: Renaud Camus, 2015.

Camus, Renaud. *You Will Not Replace Us!* Plieux: Renaud Camus, 2018.

Casas-Cortes, Maribel, Sebastian Cobarrubias, Nicholas De Genova, Glenda Garelli, Giorgio Grappi, Charles Heller, Sabine Hess, Bernd Kasparek, Sandro Mezzadra, Brett Nielson, Irene Peano, Lorenzo Pezzani, John Pickles, Federico Rahola, Lisa Riedner, Stephan Scheel, and Martina Tazziolo. "New Keywords: Migrations and Borders." *Cultural Studies* 29, no. 1 (2015): 55–87.

Chakrabarty, Dipesh. *Provincializing Europe: Postcolonial Thought and Historical Dif-ference.* Princeton: Princeton University Press, 2008.

Chamoiseau, Patrick. *Frères migrants.* Paris: Seuil, 2017.

Chamoiseau, Patrick. *Migrant Brothers: A Poet's Declaration of Human Dignity.* Translated by Matthew Amos and Fredrik Rönnbäck. New Haven: Yale University Press, 2018.

Charef, Mehdi. *Le thé au harem d'Archi Ahmed.* Paris: Mercure de France, 1983. Trans-lated by Ed Emery as *Tea in the Harem* (London: Serpent's Tail, 1989).

Charrieras, Damien. "Racisme(s)? Retour sur la polémique du 'racisme anti-Blancs' en France." In *De quelle couleur sont les Blancs? Des "petits Blancs" au "racisme anti-Blancs,"* edited by Sylvie Laurent and Thierry Leclère, 244–252. Paris: La Découverte, 2013.

Cixous, Hélène. *Entretien de la blessure: Sur Jean Genet.* Paris: Galilée, 2011.

Clancy, Geneviève, and Philippe Tancelin. *Les tiers idées: Pour une esthétique de combat.* Paris: L'Harmattan, 2019.

Colla, Elliott. "Sentimentality and Redemption: The Rhetoric of Egyptian Pop Culture Intifada Solidarity." In *Palestine, Israel, and the Politics of Popular Culture,* edited by Rebecca L. Stein and Ted Swedenburg, 338–64. Durham, N.C.: Duke University Press, 2005.

Collins, John. *Global Palestine.* New York: Columbia University Press, 2011.

Comtat, Emmanuelle. "From *Indigènes* to Immigrant Workers: *Pied-Noir* Perceptions of Algerians and People of Algerian Origin in Postcolonial France." *Settler Colonial Studies* 8, no. 2 (2018): 262–82.

Conan, Eric, and Henry Rousseau. *Vichy: Un passé qui ne passe pas.* Paris: Fayard, 1994.

Cottias, Myriam. *La question noire: Histoire d'une construction coloniale.* Paris: Bayard, 2007.

Coulthard, Glenn Sean. *Red Skin, White Masks: Rejecting the Colonial Politics of Recognition.* Minneapolis: University of Minnesota Press, 2014.

Curtis, Edward. *The North American Indian: The Complete Portfolios.* Cologne: Täschen, 1997.

Daoud, Kamel. *Meursault, contre-enquête.* Algiers: Barzakh, 2013. Translated by John Cullen as *The Meursault Investigation* (New York: Other Press, 2016).

Darmon, Maurice. *La question juive de Jean-Luc Godard: Filmer après Auschwitz.* Cognac: Temps qu'il fait, 2011.

Darwish, Mahmoud. *The Adam of Two Edens.* Edited by Munir Akash and Daniel Moore. Syracuse: Syracuse University Press, 2000.

Darwish, Mahmoud. *Ahada 'ashara kawkaban.* Beirut: Dar Al-Jadid, 1992.

Darwish, Mahmoud. "Bitaqat hawiya." In *Awraq al-zaytun,* 5–10. Haifa: Matba'at Al-Itihad Al-Ta'awuniya, 1964.

Darwish, Mahmoud. "Discours de l'indien rouge." Translated by Elias Sanbar. *Revue d'études palestiniennes* 46 (1993): 3–10.

Darwish, Mahmoud. *If I Were Another.* Translated by Fady Joudah. New York: Farrar, Straus and Giroux, 2009.

Darwish, Mahmoud. "Je ne reviens pas, je viens." Interview with Mahmoud Darwish. By Helit Yeshurun. Translated by Simone Bitton. *Revue d'études palestiniennes,* n.s., 9 (1996): 53–80.

Darwish, Mahmoud. *Une mémoire pour l'oubli.* Translated by Yves Gonzales-Quijano and Farouk Mardam-Bey. Arles: Actes Sud, 1994.

Darwish, Mahmoud. *Memory for Forgetfulness: August, Beirut, 1982.* Translated by Ibrahim Muhawi. Berkeley: University of California Press, 2013.

Darwish, Mahmoud. *La Palestine comme métaphore: Entretiens.* Translated by Elias Sanbar and Simone Bitton. Arles: Actes Sud, 1997.

Darwish, Mahmoud, and Judith Lerner. "A Dialogue." *Méditerranéennes* 14 (2010): 17–21.

de Baecque, Antoine. *Godard: Biographie.* Paris: Grasset, 2010.

Debrauwere-Miller, Nathalie, ed. *Israeli-Palestinian Conflict in the Francophone World.* New York: Routledge, 2010.

De Genova, Nicholas. "The European Question: Migration, Race, and Postcoloniality in Europe." *Social Text* 34, no. 3 (2016): 75–102.

Deleuze, Gilles. *Cinema 1: The Movement-Image.* Translated by Hugh Tomlinson and Barbara Habberjam. Minneapolis: University of Minnesota Press, 1986.

Deloria, Vine, Jr. *Custer Died for Your Sins: An Indian Manifesto.* New York: Macmillan, 1969.

Di-Capua, Yoav. "Palestine Comes to Paris: The Global Sixties and the Making of a Universal Cause." *Journal of Palestine Studies* 50, no. 1 (2021): 19–50.

Didi-Huberman, Georges. "Hauteurs de vue." *Esprit* 446 (2018): 65–78.

Didi-Huberman, Georges, and Niki Giannari. *Passer, quoiqu'il en coûte*. Paris: Minuit, 2017.

Drabinski, John. "Separation, Difference, and Time in Godard's *Ici et ailleurs*." *SubStance* 37, no. 1 (2008): 148–58.

Durham, Scott. "The Deaths of Jean Genet." *Yale French Studies* 91 (1997): 159–84.

Dyer, Rebecca, and François Mulot. "Mahmoud Darwish in Film: Politics, Representation, and Translation in Jean-Luc Godard's *Ici et ailleurs* and *Notre musique*." *Cultural Politics* 10, no. 1 (2014): 70–91.

El Maleh, Edmond Amran. *Jean Genet: Le captif amoureux et autres essais*. Grenoble: La Pensée Sauvage, 1988.

El Yazami, Driss. "France's Ethnic Minority Press." Translated by Alec G. Hargreaves and Marc McKinney. In *Post-colonial Cultures in France*, edited by Hargreaves and McKinney, 115–30. London: Routledge, 1997.

Emmelhainz, Irmgard. "From Third Worldism to Empire: Jean-Luc Godard and the Palestinian Question." *Third Text* 23, no. 5 (2009): 649–56.

Emmelhainz, Irmgard. *Jean-Luc Godard's Political Filmmaking*. Cham: Palgrave Macmillan, 2019.

Fanon, Frantz. *Les damnés de la terre*. Paris: La Découverte, 2002.

Fanon, Frantz. *The Wretched of the Earth*. Translated by Richard Philcox. New York: Grove Press, 2004.

Feldman, Keith P. *A Shadow over Palestine: The Imperial Life of Race in America*. Minneapolis: Minnesota of University Press, 2015.

Fieni, David. "Tagging the Spectral Mobility of the Stateless Body: Deleuze, Stasis, and Graffiti." *Journal for Cultural Research* 20, no. 4 (2016): 350–65.

Finkielkraut, Alain. *Au nom de l'autre: Réflexions sur l'antisémitisme qui vient*. Paris: Gallimard, 2003.

Fonds Jean Genet. Institut des mémoires de l'édition contemporaine. Abbaye d'Ardenne, Caen.

Fonds Saïd Bouziri. La contemporaine. Université Paris Nanterre.

Garelli, Glenda, and Martina Tazzioli. *Tunisia as a Revolutionized Space of Migration*. New York: Palgrave Macmillan, 2017.

Genet, Jean. *Un captif amoureux*. Paris: Gallimard, 1986.

Genet, Jean. *The Declared Enemy: Texts and Interviews*. Translated by Jeff Fort. Stanford: Stanford University Press, 2004.

Genet, Jean. *L'ennemi déclaré: Textes et entretiens*. Edited by Albert Dichy. Paris: Gallimard, 1991.

Genet, Jean. "Four Hours in Shatila." Translated by Daniel R. Dupêcher and Martha Perrigaud. *Journal of Palestine Studies* 12, no. 3 (1983): 3–22.

Genet, Jean. *Lettres à Ibis*. Paris: Gallimard, 2010.

Genet, Jean. "The Palestinians." *Journal of Palestine Studies* 3, no. 1 (1973): 3–34.

Genet, Jean. *Les paravents*. Paris: Gallimard, 1961.

Genet, Jean. *Prisoner of Love*. Translated by Barbara Bray. New York: New York Review of Books, 2003.

Genet, Jean. "Quatre heures à Chatila." *Revue d'études palestiniennes* 6 (1983): 3–19.

Genet, Jean. *The Screens*. Translated by Bernard Frechtman. New York: Grove Press, 1962.

Gèze, François. "Les 'indigènes' au secours de la république?" *Mouvements* 42 (2005): 124–26.

Giudice, Fausto. *Arabicides: Une chronique française, 1970–1991*. Paris: La Découverte, 1992.

Gobineau, Arthur de. "Essai sur l'inégalité des races humaines." In *Oeuvres I*, 133–1174. Paris: Gallimard, 1983. Translated by Adrian Collins as *The Inequality of Human Races* (London: William Heinemann, 1915).

Godard, Jean-Luc. *Godard par Godard: Les années Cahiers (1950 à 1959)*. Paris: Flammarion, 1989.

Godard, Jean-Luc. *Godard par Godard: Des années Mao aux années 80*. Paris: Flammarion, 1991.

Godard, Jean-Luc. *Jean-Luc Godard par Jean-Luc Godard, tome 2 (1984–1998)*. Paris: Cahiers du Cinéma, 1998.

Godard, Jean-Luc. "Juste une conversation." Interview by Jean-Michel Frodon. *Cahiers du cinéma* 590 (2004): 20–22.

Goodwin, Michael, and Greil Marcus. *Double Feature: Movies and Politics*. New York: Outerbridge & Lazard, 1972.

Gordon, Daniel A. *Immigrants and Intellectuals: May '68 and the Rise of Anti-racism in France*. Pontypool: Merlin Press, 2012.

Gourgouris, Stathis. *Does Literature Think? Literature as Theory for an Antimythical Era*. Stanford: Stanford University Press, 2003.

Goytisolo, Juan. *Forbidden Territory and Realms of Strife: The Memoirs of Juan Goytisolo*. Translated by Peter Bush. London: Verso, 2003.

Goytisolo, Juan. *Landscapes of War: From Sarajevo to Chechnya*. Translated by Peter R. Bush. San Francisco: City Lights Books, 2000.

Goytisolo, Juan. "Le poète enterré à Larache." Translated by Aline Schulman. *Revue d'études palestiniennes* 45 (1992): 101–5.

Goytisolo, Juan. *State of Siege*. Translated by Helen R. Lane. San Francisco: City Lights Books, 2002.

Guattari, Félix. "Genet retrouvé." *Revue d'études palestiniennes* 21 (1986): 28–42.

Guène, Faïza. *La discrétion*. Paris: Plon, 2020.

Guénoun, Denis. *L'exhibition des mots et autres idées du théâtre et de la philosophie*. Paris: Circé, 1998.

Guha, Ranajit. "Not at Home in Empire." *Critical Inquiry* 23, no. 3 (1997): 482–93.

Hajjat, Abdellali. "Alliances inattendues à la Goutte d'Or." In *68: Une histoire collective, 1962–1981*, edited by Philippe Artières and Michelle Zancarini-Fournel, 525–31. Paris: La Découverte, 2008.

Hajjat, Abdellali. "Comités Palestine (1970–72): On the Origins of Solidarity with the Palestinian Cause in France." Translated by Rayya Badran. In *Transnational Solidarity: Anticolonialism in the Global Sixties*, edited by Zeina Maasri, Cathy Bergin, and Francesca Burke, 54–76. Manchester: Manchester University Press, 2022.

Hajjat, Abdellali. "Les comités Palestine (1970–1972): Aux origines du soutien de la cause palestinienne en France." *Revue d'études palestiniennes* 98 (2006): 74–92. https://halshs.archives-ouvertes.fr/halshs-00370072/document.

Hajjat, Abdellali. "Éléments pour une sociologie historique du Mouvement des Travailleurs Arabes (1972–1976)." MA thesis, École des Hautes Études en Sciences Sociales/École Normale Supérieure, 2005.

Hajjat, Abdellali. *Les frontières de l'"identité nationale": L'injonction à l'assimilation en France métropolitaine et coloniale*. Paris: La Découverte, 2012.

Hajjat, Abdellali. "The Movement for Arab Workers and the Assifa Theater Company."

Translated by Katherine Petit and Paul Buck. In *The Tempest Society,* by Bouchra Khalili, 58–67. London: Book Works, 2018.

Hajjat, Abdellali. "Révolte des quartiers populaires, crise du militantisme, et post-colonialisme." In *Histoire politique des immigrations (post)coloniales: France, 1920–2008,* edited by Ahmed Boubeker and Hajjat, 249–64. Paris: Amsterdam, 2008.

Hajjat, Abdellali. *The Wretched of France: The 1983 March for Equality and against Racism.* Translated by Andrew Brown. Bloomington: Indiana University Press, 2022.

Hannoush, Michèle. "Practices of Photography: Circulation and Mobility in the Nineteenth-Century Mediterranean." *History of Photography* 40, no. 1 (2016): 3–27.

Hargreaves, Alec. *Voices from the North African Immigrant Community in France.* New York: Berg, 1991.

Harlow, Barbara. "Resistance Literature Revisited: From Basra to Guantanamo." *Alif* 32 (2012): 10–29.

Harrison, Olivia C. *Transcolonial Maghreb: Imagining Palestine in the Era of Decolonization.* Stanford: Stanford University Press, 2016.

Hecker, Marc. "Un demi-siècle de militantisme pro-palestinien en France: Évolution, bilan, et perspectives." *Confluences Méditerrannée* 86 (2013): 197–208.

Hecker, Marc. *Intifada française: De l'importation du conflit israélo-palestinien.* Paris: Ellipses, 2012.

Hennebelle, Guy. *Guide des films anti-impérialistes.* Paris: Éditions du Centenaire, 1975.

Hobsbawm, Eric. *Nations and Nationalism since 1870: Programmes, Myth, Reality.* Cambridge, UK: Cambridge University Press, 1990.

Hochberg, Gil Z. "The 'Problem of Immigration' from a Child's Point of View: The Poetics of Abjection in Albert Swissa's *Aqud* and Farida Belghoul's *Georgette!*" *Comparative Literature* 57, no. 2 (2005): 158–77.

Houari, Leïla. *Zeida de nulle part.* Paris: L'Harmattan, 1985.

Hugonnet, Ferdinand. *Souvenirs d'un chef de bureau arabe.* Paris: Michel Lévy Frères, 1858.

Jablonka, Ivan. *Les vérités inavouables de Jean Genet.* Paris: Seuil, 2004.

Kanafani, Ghassan. *Adab al-muqawama fi filastin al-muhtala: 1948–1966.* Beirut: Dar al-Adab, 1970.

Kanafani, Ghassan. *Men in the Sun and Other Palestinian Stories.* Translated by Hilary Kilpatrick. Boulder, Colo.: Lynne Rienner, 1999.

Kassir, Samir, and Farouk Mardam-Bey. *Itinéraires de Paris à Jérusalem: La France et le conflit israélo-arabe.* 2 vols. Washington, D.C.: Institut des Études Palestiniennes, 1993.

Kateb, Yacine. "Mohamed prends ta valise." In *Boucherie de l'espérance: Oeuvres théâtrales,* edited by Zebeida Chergui, 205–370. Paris: Seuil, 1999.

Katz, Ethan. *The Burdens of Brotherhood: Jews and Muslims from North Africa to France.* Cambridge, Mass.: Harvard University Press, 2015.

Kauffmann, Alexandre, Bouchra Khalili, and Philippe Tancelin. "On Bearing Witness: Conversation between Bouchra Khalili, Phillipe Tancelin and Alexandre Kauffmann." In *The Tempest Society,* by Khalili, 78–88. London: Book Works, 2018.

Kettane, Nacer. *Droit de réponse à la démocratie française.* Paris: La Découverte, 1986.

Kettane, Nacer. *Le sourire de Brahim.* Paris: Denoël, 1985.

Khalidi, Rashid. *Under Siege: PLO Decisionmaking during the 1982 War.* New York: Columbia University Press, 2014.

Khalili, Bouchra. *Foreign Office.* Mixed media installation. 2015.

Khalili, Bouchra. *The Mapping Journey Project*. Video installation. 2008–2011.

Khalili, Bouchra. "The Radical Ally." Artist's publication for the solo exhibition "Bouchra Khalili: Poets & Witnesses," Museum of Fine Arts, Boston, 2019. Offset newsprint. 36 pages. Coedited by Bouchra Khalili, Xavier Nueno, and León Muñoz Santini. Published by Gato Negro Ediciones and instituto de investigaciones independientes. PDF file. Courtesy of Bouchra Khalili.

Khalili, Bouchra. *Speeches—Chapter 1: Mother Tongue*. Video installation. 2012.

Khalili, Bouchra. *The Tempest Society*. London: Book Works, 2018.

Khatibi, Abdelkebir. *Figures de l'étranger dans la littérature française*. Paris: Denoël, 1987.

Kleppinger, Kathryn. *Branding the "Beur" Author: Minority Writing and the Media in France, 1983–2013*. Liverpool: Liverpool University Press, 2015.

Lambert, Léopold. *États d'urgence: Une histoire spatiale du continuum colonial français*. Toulouse: Premiers Matins de Novembre Éditions, 2021.

Laroche, Hadrien. *Le dernier Genet*. Paris: Seuil, 1997.

Le Cour Grandmaison, Olivier. *Coloniser, exterminer: Sur la guerre et l'état colonial*. Paris: Fayard, 2005.

Le Cour Grandmaison, Olivier. *De l'indigénat: Anatomie d'un monstre juridique*. Paris: Zones, 2010.

Le Cour Grandmaison, Olivier. "Les origines coloniales: Extension et banalisation d'une mesure d'exception." In *Le retour des camps: Sangatte, Lampedusa, Guantanamo*, edited by Le Cour Grandmaison, Gilles Lhuilier, and Jérôme Valluy, 31–41. Paris: Autrement, 2007.

Lefeuvre, Daniel. *Pour en finir avec la repentance coloniale*. Paris: Flammarion, 2006.

Levy, Ophir. "Se payer de mots? Godard, l'histoire, les 'camps.'" *Critique* 814 (2015): 164–77.

Limbrick, Peter. *Arab Modernism as World Cinema: The Films of Moumen Smihi*. Oakland: University of California Press, 2020.

Lionnet, Françoise, and Shu-mei Shih. "Thinking Through the Minor, Transnationally." Introduction to *Minor Transnationalism*, edited by Lionnet and Shih, 1–23. Durham, N.C.: Duke University Press, 2005.

Luiselli, Valeria. *Tell Me How It Ends: An Essay in Forty Questions*. Minneapolis: Coffee House Press, 2017.

Maatouk, Frédéric. "Le théâtre des travailleurs immigrés en France." PhD diss., Université François Rabelais, Tours, 1979.

MacBride, Seán. *Israel in Lebanon: The Report of the International Commission to Enquire into Reported Violations of International Law by Israel during Its Invasion of the Lebanon*. London: Ithaca Press, 1983.

Malik, Serge. *Histoire secrète de SOS-racisme*. Paris: Albin Michel, 1990.

Mamarbachi, Alexandre. "Émergence, construction, et transformations d'une 'cause': Sociologie historique des dévouements en faveur de la 'cause' des Palestiniens: 1960–2010; Recherche historique et enquête ethnographique." PhD diss., Université Paris Nanterre, 2020.

Mamdani, Mahmood. *Good Muslim, Bad Muslim: America, the Cold War, and the Roots of Terror*. New York: Doubleday, 2004.

Mamdani, Mahmood. *Neither Settler nor Native: The Making and Unmaking of Permanent Minorities*. Cambridge, Mass.: Harvard University Press, 2020.

Mamdani, Mahmood. *When Victims Become Killers: Colonialism, Nativism, and the Genocide in Rwanda*. Princeton: Princeton University Press, 2001.

Mandel, Maud. *Muslims and Jews in France: A History of Conflict.* Princeton: Princeton University Press, 2014.

Martin, Thomas. "Anti-racism, Republicanism, and the Sarkozy Years: SOS Racisme and the Mouvement des Indigènes de la République." In *France's Colonial Legacies: Memory, Identity, and Narrative,* edited by Fiona Barclay, 188–206. Cardiff: University of Wales Press, 2013.

Marty, Éric. *Bref séjour à Jérusalem.* Paris: Gallimard, 2003.

Mauriac, Claude. *Et comme l'espérance est violente.* Paris: Grasset, 1976.

Mbembe, Achille. *Critique of Black Reason.* Translated by Laurent Dubois. Durham, N.C.: Duke University Press, 2017.

Mbembe, Achille. *Politiques de l'inimitié.* Paris: La Découverte, 2016.

McAuley, James. "How Gay Icon Renaud Camus Became the Ideologue of White Supremacy." *Nation,* June 17, 2019. www.thenation.com.

Melotti, Marxiano. "The Mediterranean Refugee Crisis: Heritage, Tourism, and Migration." *New England Journal of Public Policy* 30, no. 2 (2018): 1–26.

Mitchell, W. J. T. *Seeing through Race.* Cambridge, Mass.: Harvard University Press, 2012.

Morris-Reich, Amos. *Race and Photography: Racial Photography as Scientific Evidence, 1876–1980.* Chicago: University of Chicago Press, 2016.

Moser, Gabrielle. "Developing Historical Negatives: The Colonial Photographic Archive as Optical Unconscious." In *Photography and the Optical Unconscious,* edited by Shawn Michelle Smith and Sharon Sliwinski, 229–63. Durham, N.C.: Duke University Press, 2017.

Ndiaye, Pap. 2008. *La condition noire: Essai sur une minorité française.* Paris: Calmann-Lévy.

Neveux, Olivier. "Apparition d'une scène politique: Le théâtre révolutionnaire de l'immigration." In *Une histoire du spectacle militant: Théâtre et cinéma militants, 1966–1981,* edited by Christian Biet and Olivier Neveux, 324–43. Vic la Gardiole: L'Entretemps, 2007.

Neveux, Olivier. *Théâtres en lutte: Le théâtre militant des années 1960 à aujourd'hui.* Paris: La Découverte, 2007.

Niessen, Niels. "Access Denied: Godard Palestine Representation." *Cinema Journal* 52, no. 2 (2013): 1–22.

Noiriel, Gérard. *The French Melting Pot: Immigration, Citizenship, and National Identity.* Translated by Geoffroy de Laforcade. Minneapolis: University of Minnesota Press, 1996.

Noiriel, Gérard. *Histoire, théâtre, et politique.* Marseille: Agone, 2009.

Noiriel, Gérard. *Immigration, antisémitisme, et racisme en France, XIXe–XXe siècle: Discours publics, humiliations privées.* Paris: Pluriel, 2007.

Oliver, Kelly. *Carceral Humanitarianism: Logics of Refugee Detention.* Minneapolis: University of Minnesota Press, 2017.

Pappe, Ilan. *The Ethnic Cleansing of Palestine.* London: Oneworld Publications, 2006.

Perreau, Bruno. *Queer Theory: The French Response.* Stanford: Stanford University Press, 2016.

Pervillé, Guy. "Comment appeler les habitants de l'Algérie avant la définition légale d'une nationalité algérienne?" *Cahiers de la Méditerrannée* 54, no. 1 (1997): 55–60.

Rahmani, Zahia. *France, récit d'une enfance.* Paris: Sabine Wespieser, 2006. Translated by Lara Vergnaud as *France, Story of a Childhood* (New Haven: Yale University Press, 2016).

Rancière, Jacques. "The Cause of the Other." Translated by David Macey. *Parallax* 4, no. 2 (1998): 25–33.

Rancière, Jacques. *Disagreement: Politics and Philosophy.* Translated by Julie Rose. Minneapolis: University of Minnesota Press, 1999.

Rancière, Jacques. *The Intervals of Cinema.* Translated by John Howe. London: Verso, 2014.

Raspail, Jean. *Le camp des saints.* Paris: Laffont, 1985.

Raspail, Jean. *The Camp of the Saints.* Translated by Norman Shapiro. New York: Scribner, 1975.

Rastegar, Kamran. *Surviving Images: Cinema, War, and Cultural Memory in the Middle East.* Oxford: Oxford University Press, 2015.

Ravetto-Biagioli, Kriss. *Mythopoetic Cinema: On the Ruins of European Identity.* New York: Columbia University Press, 2018.

Reeck, Laura. *Writerly Identities in Beur Fiction and Beyond.* Lanham: Lexington Books, 2011.

Roberts, Phillip. "Godard in Sarajevo: Media Control in Deleuze and Virilio." *Cultural Politics* 10, no. 3 (2014): 333–53.

Robine, Jérémy. "Les 'indigènes de la république': Nation et question postcoloniale; Territoires des enfants de l'immigration et rivalité de pouvoir." *Hérodote* 120 (2006): 118–48.

Rocé. *Par les damné.e.s de la terre.* Hors Cadres. 2018. Compact disc.

Rosello, Mireille. "The 'Beur Nation': Toward a Theory of 'Départenance.'" Translated by Richard Bjornson. *Research in African Literatures* 24, no. 3 (1993): 13–24.

Rosello, Mireille. *Declining the Stereotype: Ethnicity and Representation in French Cultures.* Hanover, N.H.: University Press of New England, 1998.

Rosello, Mireille. "*Georgette!* de Farida Belghoul: Télévision et départenance." *L'esprit créateur* 33, no. 2 (1993): 35–46.

Rosello, Mireille. *Postcolonial Hospitality: The Immigrant as Guest.* Stanford: Stanford University Press, 2001.

Rothberg, Michael. *The Implicated Subject: Beyond Victims and Perpetrators.* Stanford: Stanford University Press, 2020.

Rothberg, Michael. *Multidirectional Memory: Remembering the Holocaust in the Age of Decolonization.* Stanford: Stanford University Press, 2009.

Rouabhi, Mohamed. "Ateliers d'écriture." Unpublished manuscript, May/June 1999. PDF file.

Rouabhi, Mohamed. "Darwish, deux textes." Press release, 2009. PDF file.

Rouabhi, Mohamed. *Malcolm X.* Arles: Actes Sud, 2000.

Rouabhi, Mohamed. "El menfi (L'exilé)." Unpublished manuscript, 2000. PDF file.

Rouabhi, Mohamed. *Les nouveaux bâtisseurs suivi de Ma petite vie de rien du tout.* Arles: Actes Sud, 1997.

Rouabhi, Mohamed. "Par morceaux entiers." *Vacarme* 9 (1999): 48–50.

Rouabhi, Mohamed. "Requiem opus 61, une prière pour les morts." Unpublished manuscript, 2001. PDF file.

Rouabhi, Mohamed. "Le temps de vivre et le temps d'oublier." *Vacarme* 15 (2001): 68–69.

Rouabhi, Mohamed. "Vive la France." Unpublished manuscript, 2006. Microsoft Word file.

Rousseau, Henry. *The Vichy Syndrome: History and Memory in France since 1944.* Translated by Arthur Goldhammer. Cambridge, Mass.: Harvard University Press, 1991.

Said, Edward W. *After the Last Sky.* New York: Pantheon Books, 1986.

Said, Edward W. *Culture and Imperialism.* New York: Knopf, 1993.

Said, Edward W. *On Late Style: Music and Literature against the Grain.* New York: Vintage, 2006.

Said, Edward W. *The Question of Palestine.* New York: Vintage, 1992.

Salaita, Steven. *The Holy Land in Transit: Colonialism and the Quest for Canaan.* Syracuse: Syracuse University Press, 2006.

Salaita, Steven. *Inter/Nationalism: Decolonizing Native America and Palestine.* Minneapolis: University of Minnesota Press, 2016.

Sanbar, Elias. *Le bien des absents.* Arles: Actes Sud, 2001.

Sanbar, Elias. *Figures du Palestinien: Identité des origines, identité de devenir.* Paris: Gallimard, 2004.

Sanbar, Elias. *Palestine 1948: L'expulsion.* Paris: Institut des Études Palestiniennes, 1984.

Sanbar, Elias. *The Palestinians: Photographs of a Land and Its People from 1839 to the Present Day.* Paris: Hazan, 2014.

Sanbar, Elias. "Vingt et un ans après." *Trafic* 1, no. 1 (1992): 109–19.

Sansal, Boualem. *2084: La fin du monde.* Paris: Gallimard, 2015.

Sartre, Jean-Paul. *Saint Genet, Actor and Martyr.* Translated by Bernard Frechtman. Minneapolis: University of Minnesota Press, 2012.

Sartre, Jean-Paul. *Saint Genet, comédien et martyr: Oeuvres completes de Jean Genet.* Vol. 1. Paris: Gallimard, 1952.

Sauvy, Alfred. *L'Europe submergée: Sud–Nord dans 30 ans.* Paris: Dunod, 1987.

Sayad, Abdelmalek. *The Suffering of the Immigrant.* Translated by David Macey. Cambridge, UK: Polity, 2004.

Sebbar, Leïla. *Shérazade, 17 ans, brune, frisée, les yeux verts.* Paris: Stock, 1982. Translated by Dorothy S. Blair as *Sherazade* (Northampton, Mass.: Interlink, 2014).

Sharpe, Christina. *In the Wake: On Blackness and Being.* Durham, N.C.: Duke University Press, 2016.

Sheehi, Stephen. *The Arab Imago: A Social History of Portrait Photography, 1860–1910.* Princeton: Princeton University Press, 2016.

Shepard, Todd. *The Invention of Decolonization: The Algerian War and the Remaking of France.* Ithaca: Cornell University Press, 2006.

Shohat, Ella. "Taboo Memories, Diasporic Visions: Columbus, Palestine, and Arab-Jews." In *Taboo Memories, Diasporic Voices,* by Shohat, 201–32. Durham, N.C.: Duke University Press, 2006.

Sieffert, Denis. *Israël–Palestine, une passion française: La France dans le miroir du conflit israélo–palestinien.* Paris: La Découverte, 2004.

Slama, Serge. "Chasse aux migrants à Mayotte: Le symptôme d'un archipel colonial en voie de désintégration." *La revue des droits de l'homme* 10 (2016): 1–5.

Slyomovics, Susan. *The Object of Memory: Arab and Jew Narrate the Palestinian Village.* Philadelphia: University of Pennsylvania Press, 1998.

Slyomovics, Susan. "'To Put One's Fingers in the Bleeding Wound': Palestinian Theatre under Israeli Censorship." *Drama Review* 35, no. 2 (1991): 18–38.

Sopo, Dominique. *S.O.S. antiracisme.* Paris: Denoël, 2005.

Stoler, Ann Laura. *Along the Archival Grain: Epistemic Anxieties and Colonial Common Sense.* Princeton: Princeton University Press, 2009.

Stoler, Ann Laura. *Duress: Imperial Durabilities in Our Times.* Durham, N.C.: Duke University Press, 2016.

Stoler, Ann Laura, ed. *Imperial Debris: On Ruins and Ruination.* Durham, N.C.: Duke University Press, 2013.

Spitz, Chantal. "Traversées océaniennes." *Multitudes* 30 (2007): 29–36.

Stora, Benjamin. *La gangrène et l'oubli: La mémoire de la guerre d'Algérie.* Paris: La Découverte, 1991.

Stora, Benjamin. *La guerre des mémoires: La France face à son passé colonial. Entretiens avec Thierry Leclère.* Paris: L'Aube, 2011.

Stora, Benjamin. *Le transfert d'une mémoire: De "l'Algérie française" au racisme anti-arabe.* Paris: La Découverte, 1999.

Taguieff, Pierre-André. *The Force of Prejudice: On Racism and Its Doubles.* Translated and edited by Hassan Melehy. Minneapolis: University of Minnesota Press, 2001.

Taguieff, Pierre-André. *L'imposture décoloniale: Science imaginaire et pseudo-antiracisme.* Paris: Éditions de l'Observatoire, 2020.

Taguieff, Pierre-André. *Liaisons dangereuses: Islamo-nazisme, islamo-gauchisme.* Paris: Hermann, 2021.

Taguieff, Pierre-André. *La nouvelle judéophobie.* Paris: Mille et une nuits, 2002.

Taguieff, Pierre-André. *Rising from the Muck: The New Anti-Semitism in Europe.* Translated by Patrick Camiller. Chicago: Ivan R. Dee, 2004.

Taïa, Abdallah, ed. *Jean Genet, un saint marocain.* Tangier: Éditions LDC, 2010.

Tancelin, Philippe. *L'ivre traversée de clair et d'ombre, suivie de Les camps oubliés.* Paris: L'Harmattan, 2011.

Tawil-Souri, Helga, and Dina Matar, eds. *Gaza as Metaphor.* London: Hurst & Co, 2016.

Tocqueville, Alexis de. *Democracy in America and Two Essays on America.* London: Penguin, 2003.

Tocqueville, Alexis de. *Sur l'Algérie.* Edited by Seloua Luste Boulbina. Paris: Garnier Flammarion, 2003.

Tocqueville, Alexis de. *Writings on Empire and Slavery.* Edited and translated by Jennifer Pitts. Baltimore: Johns Hopkins University Press, 2001.

Tuck, Eve, and K. Wayne Yang. "Decolonization Is Not a Metaphor." *Decolonization: Indigeneity, Education & Society* 1, no. 1 (2012): 1–40.

von Bülow, Catherine, and Fazia Ben Ali. *La Goutte d'Or ou Le mal des racines.* Paris: Stock, 1979.

Weil, Patrick. "Le statut des musulmans en Algérie coloniale: Une nationalité française dénaturée." *Histoire de la Justice* 16 (2005): 93–109.

Weiss, Peter. "The Material and the Models: Notes towards a Definition of Documentary Theatre." Translated by Heinz Bernard. *Theatre Quarterly* 1, no. 1 (1971): 41–43.

Weizman, Eyal. *The Least of All Possible Evils: A Short History of Humanitarian Violence.* London: Verso, 2017.

White, Edmund. *Genet: A Biography.* New York: Vintage, 1993.

White, Jerry. *Two Bicycles: The Work of Jean-Luc Godard and Anne-Marie Miéville.* Waterloo, Ontario: Wilfrid Laurier Univerity Press, 2013.

Williams, James S. *Encounters with Godard: Ethics, Aesthetics, Politics.* Albany: State University of New York Press, 2016.

Witt, Michael. "The Godard Interview: I, a Man of the Image." *Sight and Sound* 15, no. 6 (2005): 28–30.

Witt, Michael. "On and under Communication." In *A Companion to Jean-Luc Godard,* edited by Tom Conley and T. Jefferson Kline, 318–50. Oxford: Wiley, 2014.

Wolfe, Patrick. *Traces of History: Elementary Structures of Race.* London: Verso, 2016.

Yaqub, Nadia. *Palestinian Cinema in the Days of Revolution.* Austin: University of Texas Press, 2018.

Youssef, Magdi. "France's Théâtre d'Al-Assifa: An Arab-Based Alternative Theater Model." *Arab Stages* 1, no. 2 (2015): n. pag. https://arabstages.org.

Zedong, Mao. *Quotations from Chairman Mao Tsetung*. Peking: Foreign Language Press, 1972.

Zobel, Clemens. "The 'Indigènes de la République' and Political Mobilization Strategies in Postcolonial France." *e-cadernos CES* (2010). https://doi.org/10.4000/eces.390.

Zreik, Raef. "When Does a Settler Become a Native? (With Apologies to Mamdani)." *Constellations* 23, no. 3 (2016): 351–64.

FILMOGRAPHY

La bataille d'Alger. Directed by Gillo Pontecorvo. Casbah Films/Igor Film, 1965.

Biladi. Directed by Francis Reusser. Francis Reusser, 1971.

À bout de souffle. Directed by Jean-Luc Godard. Société Nouvelle de Cinématographie/ Productions Georges de Beauregard, 1960.

Brûle la mer. Directed by Maki Berchache and Nathalie Nambot. Les Films du Bilboquet, 2014.

Les camps oubliés. Directed by Philippe Tancelin. CICEP Edition, 2012.

La chinoise. Directed by Jean-Luc Godard. Anouchka Films/Les Productions de la Guéville/Athos Films/Parc Films/Simar Films, 1967.

Compter sur ses propres forces. Directed by Yannis Tritsibidas. Groupe Cinéma de Vincennes, 1973.

Entre la foule et le désert. Directed by Anne Quesemand, Didier Loiseau, and Christian Guillon. Les Films de l'Homme Terminus/Films Sans Coeur/INA, 1979.

Festival Panafricain d'Alger. Directed by William Klein. Office national pour le commerce et l'industrie cinématographiques/Centre national de la cinématographie et de l'audiovisuel, 1970.

Film socialisme. Directed by Jean-Luc Godard. Vega Film/Wild Bunch/Canal+, 2010.

Fort Apache. Directed by John Ford. Argosy Pictures, 1948.

Genet à Chatila. Directed by Richard Dindo. Lea Produktion/Les Films d'Ici, 1999.

Human Flow. Directed by Ai Weiwei. Participant Media/AC Films/Amazon Studios, 2017.

Ici et ailleurs. Directed by Jean-Luc Godard and Anne-Marie Miéville. Sonimage/INA/ Gaumont, 1974.

"Jusqu'à la victoire" ("Méthodes de pensée et de travail de la révolution palestinienne"). Directed by Jean-Luc Godard and Jean-Pierre Gorin. Groupe Dziga Vertov, 1970. Unrealized film.

The Last Frontier. Directed by Anthony Mann. Columbia Pictures, 1956.

Al-Makhdu'un (The Duped). Directed by Tawfiq Salih. Damascus: Mu'assisat al-'Amat li al-Sinama, 1972.

Man of the West. Directed by Anthony Mann. Ashton Productions, 1958.

Morceaux de conversation avec Jean-Luc Godard: sept rendez-vous avec Jean-Luc Godard. Directed by Jean Narboni. Editions Montparnasse, 2010.

Notre musique. Directed by Jean-Luc Godard. Avventura Films/Périphéria/Canal Plus/Arte/Vega Film/TSR/France 3, 2004.

"La nuit venue" ("Le bleu de l'oeil"). Directed by Jean Genet. Claude Nedjar, 1976. Unrealized film.

Off Frame AKA Revolution Until Victory. Directed by Mohanad Yaqubi. Torch Films, 2015.

L'olivier. Directed by Ali Akika, Guy Chapoullie, Danièle Dubroux, Serge Le Péron, Jean Narboni, and Dominique Villain. Groupe Cinéma de Vincennes, 1976.

"One American Movie" ("One A.M."). Directed by Jean-Luc Godard, Richard Leacock, and D. A. Pennebaker. Leacock-Pennebaker Inc., 1968. Unrealized film.

One P.M. Directed by D. A. Pennebaker. Leacock-Pennebaker Inc., 1972.

Palestine vaincra. Directed by Jean-Pierre Olivier. Cinéastes Révolutionnaires Prolétariens, 1969.

Le petit soldat. Directed by Jean-Luc Godard. Productions Georges de Beauregard/Société Nouvelle de Cinématographie/Rome-Paris Films, 1960.

Schindler's List. Directed by Steven Spielberg. Amblin Entertainment, 1993.

Si Moh, pas de chance. Directed by Moumen Smihi. Groupes de Recherches et d'Essais Cinématographiques, 1971.

Stagecoach. Directed by John Ford. Walter Wanger Productions, 1939.

The Tempest Society. Directed by Bouchra Khalili. Bouchra Khalili and Alexandre Kauffman, 2017.

Twenty-Two Hours. Directed by Bouchra Khalili. Bouchra Khalili and Alexandre Kauffman, 2018.

Vent d'est. Directed by Jean-Luc Godard and Jean-Pierre Gorin. CCC-Poli Film/Kunst-Film/Anouchka Films, 1969.

Vladimir et Rosa. Directed by Jean-Luc Godard and Jean-Pierre Gorin. Munich Tele-Pool/Grove Press Evergreen Films, 1970.

Week-end. Directed by Jean-Luc Godard. Films Copernic/Ascot Cineraïd/Comacico/Lira Films, 1967.

INDEX

Page numbers in italics refer to figures.

OLIVIA C. HARRISON is associate professor of French and comparative literature at the University of Southern California. She is the author of *Transcolonial Maghreb: Imagining Palestine in the Era of Decolonization* and coeditor of *Souffles-Anfas: A Critical Anthology from the Moroccan Journal of Culture and Politics.*